D0952118

Little Bubble Gum Trooper

To Katelynn

God Bless

Make-A-Wish

A Mother's true story of how the
Make-A-Wish Foundation® began.

Linda Bergendahl Pauling

Dedicated to

All the children worldwide who have dreams of
I want to be . . . I want see . . . I want to meet . . .
I want to have . . . "Thank you" to everyone worldwide
who has helped make those cherished dreams come
true.

A Special "Thank You" To The Arizona Department of
Public Safety, Arizona Highway Patrol, To All The
Officers Who Rose Above and Beyond The Call Of
Duty To Make A Little Boy's Dream Come True.

Christopher James Greicius
August 8, 1972 – May 3, 1980
Arizona Trooper

"Every time another one of our officers dies, in a
quiet moment, I ask Chris to greet them, and show
them the ropes."

Ron Cox
Department of Public Safety,
Arizona Highway Patrol, (Ret.)

Published by Red Rose Press LLC
P.O. Box 250
Scottsdale, Arizona 85252-0250

Library of Congress Cataloging-in-Publication
00-190975

Linda Joy Bergendahl-Pauling
Little Bubble Gum Trooper
Is an original work of the author and not a publication of the
Make-A-Wish Foundation® of America. The facts and
recollections contained in the book are those of the author.
Make-A-Wish is a registered trademark of the
Make-A-Wish Foundation.®

ISBN 0-9701534-0-6

Edited by Gwen Henson
Book design by Graphisphere
Heidi and Bob Whitney
Printed by United Graphics Inc., Mattoon, Illinois
Printed and bound in the United States of America

First Edition

Contents

Contents

Contents

Inspired Memories is devoted to the people you
will read about. Each has written or told his or her
own story and memories in his or her own way.

Inspired Memories

Foreword

Paula Van Ness

President and CEO
Make-A-Wish Foundation of America

The Make-A-Wish Foundation is thrilled that the poignant and inspiring story of Christopher James Greicius and the legacy he left behind can now be shared with people across the world. Twenty years and eighty-thousands wishes after this brave young boy inspired a group of benevolent volunteers to establish the Make-A-Wish Foundation, the organization is still driven by its vision that people everywhere will share the power of a wish. Linda Bergendahl-Pauling is truly an inspiration to us all.

Foreword

Karla Blomberg

President Make-A-Wish Foundation of Minnesota
Past President, Make-A-Wish Foundation of America
Past President, Make-A-Wish Foundation International

It was in the spring when the Make-A-Wish
Foundation executive director called me, on behalf of the
Foundation and said a message had been received from
Linda, Chris's mom. She wanted to speak to the president,
my role at the time. I was thrilled! The only information I
had regarding Linda was that she had chosen not to have
contact with the organization because of the pain in
associating with her loss.

I returned the call immediately, and we made plans to
meet when I arrived in Phoenix for a scheduled meeting
only weeks away. Our meeting lasted a couple of hours,
and the time flew by. As a mother, I wept as she described
her courageous son's battle with cancer, and I marveled at
the sequence of events that led to our Foundation. She
shared with me the names of the Founding board
members and encouraged me to contact them
individually, which I did.

One by one they unfolded the story of a well loved
little boy, a chance meeting with a DEA agent, a wish
come true, and a friendship of only a few days, which
forever bound the individuals after the death of the boy

that brought them together. They filled in the pieces of how they tackled the formation of a not-for-profit organization, and they also said how happy they were to receive my call. They were a collective group of individuals who had gone on with their lives in different directions but they never stopped loving the flowers that grew from the seeds they had planted.

It was obvious that chapter members everywhere would embrace meeting these people and plans were made to have these original volunteers join members at the upcoming October conference. As they say, the rest is history.

From the smallest chapter to the largest international affiliate, audiences have had the pleasure to meet three of the original five founders special. Linda Bergendahl-Pauling, Scott Stahl, and Frank Shankwitz have remained active and have since embraced Make-A-Wish of America and Make-A-Wish International with support and pride.

That spring meeting was in 1992, and Linda's book was a work in progress. I am very happy to have that work be finalized and shared with the world in the pages that follow.

Preface

My desire for more than twenty years was to write this story because of my personal, endless search, in 1979, for non-existing support groups and books on library shelves. I hoped that somewhere, someone might have shared his or her emotions, feelings of guilt, and unanswered questions of "why my child?"

My New Year's resolution for 1990, was to write Christopher's story. For about an hour I sat staring at an empty computer screen. The unopened journal that I had started writing thirteen years ago, when Christopher was diagnosed, was lying on the kitchen table.

Opening the book I read the first paragraph. Within seconds, every emotion, every sense of touch and smell from those years reemerged. As, I reached for tissue after tissue. I began my first sentence, continuing to type for twelve to fourteen hour a day and ending five months later with several hundred pages.

On April 29, 1997, seventeen years after Christopher had his dream come true, I finished the story. Then I placed it in a box on the top shelf of my closet for the next three years. In January 2000, my New Year's resolution was to get it published, so everyone could share Chris's story.

Through his dream, today over eighty thousand children around the world have also experience their dream come true through the Make-A-Wish Foundation because of the "The Little Bubble Gum Trooper."

Linda J. Bergendahl-Pauling

Acknowledgments

Thank you to all the officers and people involved on April 29, and May 1, 1980, that rose above and beyond the call of duty to make a little boy's dream come true.

Thank you to all the dedicated staff, volunteers, donors, and sponsors of the Make-A-Wish family around the world for helping to make wishes come true for these very special children.

Thank you, Heidi and Bob Whitney of Graphisphere, Scottsdale, Arizona for designing the cover.

Thank you, April Byran, for your enthusiasm for the story that gave me the encouragement and motivation that I needed.

A special "thank you" to Fred and Jean, in 1990, for the spiritual encouragement to start writing this book, and to all my family and friends for their love, support and encouragement to "make this book happen."

Thank you to Keven Pauling, of Keven's Landscaping, for his encouragement and support for this story.

Thank you to my wonderful husband, Eugene M. Pauling, for his love and support. Hugs and kisses forever and always.

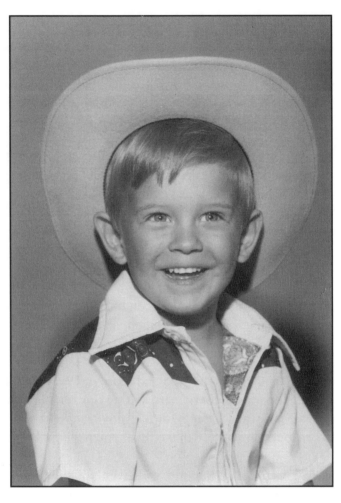

Christopher James Greicius
Happy Birthday   August 8, 1976
Four Years Old

Introduction

The Power of a Wish

It has been almost twenty years since leukemia claimed the life of my seven-and-one-half-year-old son, Chris. His simple wish to one day serve as a police officer became the inspiration for the birth of the Make-A-Wish Foundation.

His eight-by-ten-inch portrait brightens the lobby of the Make-A-Wish national office in Phoenix. You'll find me there, too, stopping in to offer my time and meeting with various departments for foundation briefings and updates. Making rounds has never been so exciting. As we head toward the foundation's twentieth birthday, stardust sweeps the halls of every chapter house and affiliate. I sense the exhilaration across the United States and around the world as I take in the sight of his portrait.

Twenty years of memories rush in all at once, taking me back to a time when the boy in the frame laughed and played. I can hear his voice and feel his hand in mine. I see the bloody nose and the hospital. I see images that no child should ever have to see. But among the somber visions, I am reminded of Chris's wish. It was through his wish that the Make-A-Wish Foundation came to be.

I am still in awe as I think of how the foundation has grown to encompass the world with eighty-one chapters in the United States and twenty international affiliates with multiple chapters within each country. By the end of the year 2000, the foundation will have granted its eighty-thousandth wish.

Today, excitement surges throughout the foundation worldwide as the twentieth birthday party approaches. Department heads present the founders with an exhaustive list of corporate donors, futures projections, milestones, and several outstanding individuals' efforts. A detailed timeline representing the foundation's history and milestones is complete. Testimonials from wish children, celebrities, parents, medical professionals, volunteers, and friends of the foundation are in the final stages. Advertising companies have donated millions of dollars to help us radiate the national campaign slogan, "Share the Power of a Wish."

The foundation has come a long way since the founders sprawled out on the floor with our hands in our pockets, digging out $37.76 to start The Chris Greicius Make-A-Wish Memorial. Cheering and exchanging high-fives, the five of us pledged our commitment that day, developing an unbreakable bond. Frank Shankwitz, Scott Stahl, Kathy McMorris, Allan Schmidt, and I made a promise to make a difference in the world by making Make-A-Wish not just another charity.

Twenty years later, I'm proud to admit that we are still alive, and the five of us continue to serve as volunteers. You'll find us stuffing envelopes, joking around at fund-raising events, and delivering inspirational

messages through public speaking engagements. We
continue to provide the foundation with our time and
enthusiasm, whether we are granting wishes, visiting
various chapters, or pitching in to help tidy up the office.

In addition to my involvement with a rainbow of
Make-A-Wish events throughout the year, I've been
occupied with numerous local, national, and international
committees, making plans for the perfect twentieth
birthday party.

I am honored that after two decades of hard work and
a lot of tears, I have the privilege of being part of such a
wonderful organization. I've made friendships around the
world and been blessed with a joyful tear each time I've
heard that yet another child has seen a wish come true. I
can't speak for the other four founders, but for me it is
very simple: The gifts from the foundation are twofold.
First, I wanted the foundation to serve as a vessel for
anyone who wanted to volunteer his time, talent, and
services helping to enrich someone else's life—an
atmosphere where anyone could walk through the doors
and feel welcome instantly. She would be greeted with a
smile and open arms. More than just a corporation, Make-
A-Wish is a family, and everyone is invited to participate.

My second greatest gift is the ability to give back to
other kids and their families, the love, happiness, and
memories of a special day—a day where the children can
live the fulfillment of their dreams and the parents can
cherish it forever. I wanted to give them a day where
hospitals, wheelchairs, doctors, and pain are forced into
the background, if only for a brief moment, as the child

and family enjoy a day of special excitement that will last a lifetime.

All children have dreams of growing up and becoming a jet fighter pilot, fireman, policeman, teacher, or ballerina. But for children who will never get the chance to accomplish those dreams on their own, I pray that the foundation will always be able to give them a day that nothing can claim but its own enchantment. Fulfilling requests like I want to be . . . I want to see . . . I want to meet . . . I want to have . . .

Today thousands of individuals donate their talents and time to various chapters across the nation and around the world. Wish parents and wish kids who have beat their illness return with loving arms, all working together to grant a wish to a child.

You will find the same loving concept in the true story taken from a journal I kept during Christopher's illness. It portrays how we chose to "live our lives to the fullest," Chris's dream of becoming a policeman, and the birth of the Make-A-Wish Foundation.

1

The First Day

It was February 4, 1977. I stood beside my pale, frightened four-and-one-half-year-old son, Christopher, wiping the blood oozing from his nose, as he sat on the edge of the doctor's examination table. I heard the gray-haired, beardless Santa Claus-type man speaking softly. He calmly spoke to Chris while pricking his finger for a blood sample.

Trying to hide my own fear from Chris, I leaned on the table, placing my arm around his waist, reassuring him that soon we would be back home at Grandma's house, and he could watch his cartoons.

Glancing around the small, dark-paneled room with shiny, stainless steel medical equipment, I noticed a couple of pictures reflecting the Southwest culture. Even the building, what little I had seen of it, suggested Spanish architecture. They reminded me even more that my little blue-eyed, blond-headed boy and I were in another world.

My guts told me the two of us weren't going back home to Illinois for a *long* time . . . if ever.

I wondered why I had let Mom talk me into going to the doctor's office that morning. This was our first day in Phoenix: beautiful palm trees, warm sunshine, and no snow. I just wanted to sit by Mom's pool and soak up the rays. Deep down, though, I knew something was wrong because of Mom's expression the week before when she saw Christopher for the first time in six months, at my brother Gary's home in Moline, Illinois.

I kept telling myself that this whole ordeal was a mistake. Chris had only a small nosebleed that would take care of itself in due time. I rationalized that he was upset because he couldn't figure out where Grandpa Wally, his buddy, was.

Neither could he understand why Mom and Grandma Vie had flown back to Illinois to visit us, or why Uncle Gary was driving Grandpa's car to Phoenix and Grandpa wasn't there. On the three-day trip across the country, Chris sat in my lap staring out the window, occasionally turning to me with sad little eyes only to repeat his same question again.

"Where is Grandpa Wally, Mommie? We have to go back and get him." I hurt every time I looked into those teary eyes of confusion and bewilderment.

Waiting in the small exam room for the doctor to return, Chris scooted himself around on the table to face me. Reaching out, he placed his hands on my shoulders, wanting me to pick him up and hold him.

Chris laid his head on my shoulder, and I held the towel under his nose. Gently rubbing his back, I fluttered soft kisses across his forehead. I tried to reassure him that he was safe and that everything would be all right.

When the doctor returned, he closed the door behind him. The look on his face sent terror through my entire body.

"Why don't you sit down on the table with Chris; I have the result back from the blood test. Maybe Chris would like to wait outside in the waiting room with your mother and brother for a few minutes?"

"No," I sharply answered in a snappy, frightened voice. "He's staying with me. We're in this together," turning to Chris, "whatever it is, aren't we little buddy?"

Chris felt feverish to me as he clung to my neck. His voice was weak as he mumbled, "Mommie, I'm cold. Can I lie down and stay in here with you, please?"

The doctor quickly got a blanket to cover him. I laid Chris down on the table and began tucking the blanket in around him the way he liked it.

I stood there looking at my son as he lay on his side. His eyes were closed as he snuggled up in the blanket. The doctor took a deep breath, scratched his graying temple, and steadied himself against the door.

"This is never easy to tell a parent. It's the worst part of being a doctor." He cleared his throat, glued his rolling eyes to the ceiling, in search for words. I couldn't stand the suspense any longer. I had to know what was happening to Chris. The knot in the pit of my stomach was intensely throbbing, growing tighter, harder, and larger with each passing second.

"Doctor, what does Chris have, and how can it be fixed? Do we have to go to the hospital? Can you give him some medicine or a shot?" I wanted answers.

The doctor drew a deep breath and began. "Chris has leukemia," he explained. "His blood count is very low, accounting for the nosebleeds and fatigue." His eyes moved over the piece of scratch paper in his hand.

"I've phoned Phoenix Memorial and made arrangements for you to meet with a doctor there. Chris is going to need medical attention right away. It's urgent that you get to the hospital immediately, Linda—no stops by the house for pajamas or toys or lunch—just get to the hospital now." The blanket was exchanged for written doctor's orders as I lifted Chris up into my arms.

The doctor's footsteps echoed mine as we headed for the receptionist's desk. As he phoned to notify the hospital that we were on our way, I stiffened my upper lip and prepared to face my family. Out in the waiting room, my support system sat anticipating the delivery of good news. Mom and Gary held high hopes that all Chris needed was a simple shot or an over-the-counter cold remedy. The reality of having to disappoint them blended with my ignorance of the disease. Fear filled my body, consuming every fiber, every emotion. The wheels began to turn, and the questions came in mighty waves. What was happening to my Christopher?

As the doctor followed me into the waiting room, Mom and Gary gazed at us with wide-eyed wonder. It wasn't every day the doctor followed the patient out into the lobby. I fumbled as I tried to hand Mom the instructions while holding Chris and blotting his bloody nose with a towel. Their expressions began to change as they focused on the doctor. Mom and Gary gave their undivided attention as Dr. Sam repeated the instructions, making sure that there were no questions as to where we were headed and whom we would be seeing. He must have known that I was in no shape to drive.

The doctor's somber words laid a crease in my mother's brow, and as her face blanched a winter white, she shifted her eyes to me. The terror building in my mother's gaze opened deeper floodgates of fear. It was becoming clear that something horrifying was happening.

I clenched Chris to my chest. He seemed almost lifeless as I carried him to Mom's car. She handed the keys to Gary while opening the back door for me. I halfway heard them discussing which streets to take to travel to the hospital in the shortest time.

I sat in the back seat of Mom's gold '76 Cadillac holding my motionless son. The sun hit the back of my neck, as I weaved in and out of the conversation between Gary and Mom. Everything was happening too quickly.

Only days before, my little boy had been at home playing with his toys, and now with each second that passed, Chris seem to become less and less conscious. I grazed his colorless face hoping to rouse him enough to get a peek at those marvelous baby blues. Instead, I was gifted with a faint, trusting smile as I brushed the blond locks from his feverish forehead. And then my good boy whispered, "I love you, Mommie."

A glance out the window found the streets filled with mid-morning traffic and cherry-red lights that seemed to be waiting for us at every intersection. It was the longest twenty-minute drive of our lives.

"I've been expecting you," the gray-haired receptionist called out, rising to meet us as we rushed into Phoenix Memorial at last. We crowded the information desk as she put in an immediate call to the doctor.

I took a seat not far from the desk, holding Chris in my arms. Mom unzipped her purse and took out her checkbook, ready to write any amount necessary to get Chris admitted for immediate help. Gary stood nearby, one hand propping his slim body against the wall and the other making a home in his blue jeans's pocket. He hadn't planned to stay for a visit. He had driven Mom's car to Phoenix and was flying back home to Illinois about 1:00 p.m. the next day. Watching Gary's solemn face, I remembered happy times when his little boy, Jeff, and Chris were playing in the front yard of the farm. I released a small sigh; I wished we were back on the farm.

The lobby was fairly busy with doctors, nurses, and visitors moving about. It wasn't long before a nurse dressed in a crisp white uniform appeared with the name of another doctor and instructions to another hospital.

"I'm sorry, but the doctor here at Phoenix Memorial treats only adults with leukemia. He has called St. Joe's, and Dr. Paul Baranko is waiting in the emergency room for you right now. Do you know how to get there?"

Mom nodded "yes" and put her wallet away.

Gary took my arm to help me up from the chair. I can't really remember leaving the hospital and getting back into the car, but in a matter of minutes, Gary pulled up to the emergency entrance of St. Joseph's Hospital.

Standing before the sliding double glass doors with a sick little boy in my arms, I felt the massive, seven-story, stucco building represented life and death. The reality that Chris might not leave the hospital overpowered me.

A middle-aged man with dark hair and an olive complexion stood surrounded by several nurses. The clean, white coat and immediate eye contact let me know that I'd found Dr. Baranko. We walked towards each other, and without speaking, I placed Chris in his arms. The medical team quickly disappeared through a set of double doors.

My arms, body, and soul were tired from the exhaustion and confusion of the entire morning. I felt, for the first time, the physical separation from Chris. I stood there staring for what seemed an eternity at the word "EMERGENCY" in big red letters above the door. I felt empty inside and had doubts that I would ever see Chris again.

I wanted to sit down in the middle of the floor right there and lose it. I wanted to scream, cry, pound on the walls and doors, and kick the furniture, but I fought to remain in control. Hearing footsteps behind me, I turned to see Gary and Mom standing a few feet from me.

Gary placed his hand on my shoulder, not really knowing what to do or say. Mom stood before me, fighting her own fear and attempting to dam the tears at the same time. She kept wiping her eyes and trying to jot down her phone number. Once she had collected herself, she handed me the number with a twenty-dollar bill.

"Do you want me to stay and wait with you? I can come back after taking Gary home."

"No, that's OK. I'll be all right." I replied. "There isn't much we can do, I guess."

I explained to Mom that Grandma Vie and Grandma and Grandpa Pete needed her at home. I told them that there was no sense in the both of us sitting around.

"I'll be all right, you guys; everything is going to be fine." I faintly smiled at her and Gary. She tearfully returned my smile as she turned to Gary looking for support. "Gary, take Mom home, and I'll call you when I know something."

"Well, OK then, but if you need something or the doctor tells you anything, just call." Mom replied

"I will. I promise, Mom. I promise."

To this day, I have very little recollection of what took place from the point when Mom and Gary left until later that evening. The few bits and pieces of memory that have since surfaced appear as a tangled web of strange smells and interim sounds blending numbers with weird abbreviations of words.

I remember sitting in a waiting room outside the double door, watching for signs of Chris to come running out at any minute, but it seemed that people only went in; no one came out.

I wandered endlessly that day. I remember walking down a hall, seeing and hearing everything, but nothing seemed real! I felt that I was the only one in this nightmare who was alive. Everyone else was in some sort of other world, and they couldn't hear or see me for some reason.

The cruel time-warped dimension that Chris and I had entered had become soundless and motionless, except for the echoing in my mind of Chris's voice calling me, begging to be held in my arms. I could see him in my mind's eye, lying on a table while doctors and nurses worked on him. I wanted only to hold him and tell him how much I loved him.

The veil lifted from time to time forcing me to deal with the reality of what Chris and I were facing. I found myself sitting in a little room on the second floor near pediatrics. I'm not sure how I got there, but I was drinking coffee and smoking cigarettes like there was no tomorrow.

It was an odd-shaped, triangular room with three chairs ranging from dark brown to green—none of which matched—and a small, very worn cushioned sofa. A couple of old end tables cluttered with a variety of worn magazines rested next to the old cream-colored walls and speckled tile.

I wondered how many others had sat there before me, praying and waiting for answers, waiting for doctors to tell them whether their loved one would live or die. The many prayers said and tears cried included mine, which now took their place inside the walls of this little room.

I leaned against the wall and looked up at the ceiling, wanting to cry out to someone, while trying to be strong inside. Fighting the fear of the unknown, the anger of ignorance, and the lack of confidence that I could handle this, I turned to the only source I knew to turn to—God.

"Please, dear Lord, forgive me for not being able to cry right now. The tears just don't want to come, but please, don't let my prayers go unanswered!"

Then a phrase I had heard entered my mind:

The Lord will never give you any more than what you can handle.

"Well, Lord, this is a lot to handle, but I know you will see us through, so just stick close to me, OK?"

The passing hour brought no word about my son. I walked toward the nurses station, trying to remain calm and in control of the emotions that seemed to pulsate from every part of my body. Standing in front of the nurses' brightly decorated but efficient desk, cartoon characters covering the walls and the front of the desk, I heard the sounds of kids crying and laughing. As I continued to roam the hallways, I thought, *I wish I could wake up from this terrible nightmare.*

As I approached the desk again, my eyes fell upon a young mother, her little girl, and a cherry-red wagon. They made merry playing a game of stop and go, filling the nurses station with laughter. I wondered if I would ever laugh like that again.

I stood leaning on the counter glancing around at the various activities behind the desk and in the hallways. A nurse approached me carrying a clipboard. I started to drift back into the time-warped dimension when I heard a voice.

Another mother wheeled her child down the hall into a room filled with toys. I imagined Chris and I headed there to play—building giant block houses and making music on plastic guitars. As they turned into the play area, I wondered if I would ever have the chance to take Chris to the toy room.

But just as quickly as my hopes had risen, so did my doubts. Questions lit with panic began to blaze within me. What ifs crackled and snapped like newspaper in flame. What if hopes of red wagons and plastic guitars were pointless now? What if I were only fooling myself? *Maybe they can't save Chris, and they can't find me to tell me. Maybe it's already too late.* The doubts were strong, but my faith proved stronger.

"NO! I refuse to give in; I refuse! Chris is alive, and everything is going to be all right."

I directed my declaration to the Heavens. "Do you hear me, Lord? Everything!"

The stainless steel medical chart snapped shut. "Can I help you?"

"Yes, please. Do you have any information about my son?" I stammered, speaking with my heart in my throat. "I brought him in here several hours ago, and I haven't heard anything about his condition." Arms firmly resting on the counter, I gripped its edge as if I were clinging to my son's life. "I don't have any idea what's happened since we were in emergency."

The nurse reached for my hand. Attempting to calm me with a gentle touch, she asked my son's name. She turned and flipped through charts but found no Christopher. Before I could ask another question, a man in a plain business suit approached the desk and asked for me. I spun around and announced, "I'm Chris's mother." My voice took on a stern tone, as I demanded details. "Do you know where he is? Is he all right?"

He was calm, evaluating my sense of desperation. "I don't have any information on his condition, but the doctor is with him, and I'm sure he is going to be fine. I need to get some information from you, if I can. The hospital wants to know what type of medical insurance you or your husband has and whom it is through—the name, address, and policy number, if you know it."

We headed back to my little triangular room to tackle a heap of paperwork. I felt like telling him to get lost, but I knew the man was only doing his job.

Once he left the little room that had become my security zone, I poured another cup of coffee. Drawing in the taste of a freshly lit cigarette, I sat in solitude knowing nothing more than I had when I had given Chris to Dr. Baranko in emergency.

Three cups of coffee and two cigarettes later, I headed to the cafeteria for a change in scenery. Wandering the noisy, lemon-tinted hallways, I sensed that slow-motion time warp returning. I fought to preserve my senses, but my vision blurred and passersby spun me as they crowded the noisy halls. The pungent odor of disinfectant blended with old wood consumed my sense of smell. The floors were so shiny they looked like waves as the overhead lights reflected off the tile.

The hallways continuously filled with people. Some visited friends or family. Doctors walked busily through the halls. Men and women in green clothes and wearing paper shoes seemed to be gathered in groups throughout the halls.

The names of people paged over the intercom system mixed with the rumble of the conversations of people standing in the halls. Television noise emanated from various patients' rooms.

As I walked, that feeling of moving in another time came over me once again, and only the space within a few feet of me was in focus. Everything else was a blur. I fought to keep the rest of my senses fully alert to the surroundings, but I just couldn't break out of the slow-motion, time-warped dimension.

I meandered in and out of elevators and around corners further crowded with blurred faces and intermittent chatter, ultimately losing myself in the maze of corridors and floors. I had only worn myself out, and by this time, I was no longer hungry. I simply longed to return to my safe little room. Funny, but I found it fairly easily. I was probably never that far from it in the first place.

"No more wandering around the halls of St. Joe's, I'm staying in my little room," I thought.

Safely tucked away in my sanctuary, I let my mind drift back to two weeks earlier, when my father had come to Illinois to visit Gary and me for a few days. Chris and I had been planning to drive back to Phoenix with Dad for a vacation.

I had wanted to get away from all the snow and ice for a couple of weeks. I also wanted to do some thinking about my marriage, which had been slowly going downhill the past couple of years.

I had been missing both Mom and Dad, plus my grandparents, who were also living in Phoenix. It seemed they had been nearby my whole life, and when I would drive by the old farm, it was empty—gone forever. Another family had bought it, but it wasn't the same.

The family road trip never materialized. Nothing could have prepared me for the phone call I received just days before the scheduled departure.

The previous week, on January 25, 1977, at about 9:00 p.m., I had checked on Chris in his bed to make sure he hadn't kicked off his covers when my sister-in-law called me in a panic-stricken voice.

"Linda! Linda, don't panic," she began, her agitated tone instantly riveting my attention. "A doctor just called here looking for Gary. I guess your dad must have given our number in case of an emergency." Her next words would change my life forever. "He said that your father was DOA at the hospital."

My husband, Tony, sensing something terrible had happened, came into the room to find me sitting at the kitchen table holding the phone in shock. I did not respond to his inquiry about what was wrong. It was all I could do at that point to listen. My sister-in-law continued.

"I called the plant and left word for Gary to go to the hospital. He should be there in a few minutes. I hope Gary calls me. If he does, I'll call you back and let you know what is happening. This is unreal. I can't believe it—I just can't."

I lived about sixty miles away, and that evening a huge snowstorm was raging outside. I knew there was no hope of even trying to drive down the hill by our house let alone making it to the hospital in Moline. Within breathless seconds, I was on the line to the hospital, filled with questions, prepared to give them the name of Dad's heart doctor. The receptionist rustled through some papers then returned to the phone.

"Miss."

"Yes, I've got the name of my father's cardiologist right here."

"There is no need for that." the woman interrupted. "He's dead."

No words came as my mind reeled and my heart raced. I didn't know what to say next. I steadied myself against the kitchen table, listening to the winter wind whipping the snow against the windows of the house that Dad had helped Tony and I to build.

The receptionist paused to attend to a walk-in. He was asking the same questions I had. The receptionist's voice was muffled as she covered the phone with her hand.

"I think I have your sister on the phone," I heard her say. "Do you want to talk to her?"

Gary picked up the phone, his voice cracking as he fumbled for words.

"Hi, kid." A long pause followed, amplifying the sounds of the ER staff bustling like rush hour traffic in the background. I drew a shaky breath and broke the silence.

"Gary, I already know. . . . He's dead."

He let out a mighty sigh, relief mixed with the fear of telling Mom.

"I can't believe this, but I guess I'm glad you know, because I sure didn't know how to tell you."

"I'll call Mom in Phoenix and the rest of the family. I can't believe this either, Gary. I really can't. Man, Grandma Vie (Dad's mother) is really going to take this hard."

"Yeah, I know. Mom will be all right. She's gone through enough heart attacks with him; that's for sure."

"Gary, do you know where to tell the doctors to have the body sent?"

"Yeah. Are you OK, kid?"

"Yeah, I'm OK, Gary. There isn't much we can do for Dad now except try to make this as easy as possible for Mom and Grandma Vie when they fly here."

"Let me call you later. I think the doctor is here and wants to talk to me," Gary said. "I'll call you when I get home. OK?"

"I will be waiting all night, if need be, so call anytime."

One week later, I sat in my little safe room wondering if I was going to bury my son, as well. The door of the room opened suddenly, and in walked the doctor, a nun, and a priest. I felt my heart stop, in fear of the words I was about to hear. If they were going to tell me that Chris was dead, then I would just as soon my heart didn't start beating again.

My mind braced itself for the words my heart wouldn't accept. I stared at the three solemn faces, studied the sadness projected through their eyes. I just knew what the doctor was going to say—it was within their pained expressions. I resigned myself to the bad news; I waited for the doctor to tell me that I had lost my baby boy.

Both the sister and the doctor sat down beside me on the sofa. The priest took one of the chairs near the sister.

"Chris is going to live, but he does have leukemia."

I hung my head, and tears of relief poured from the depths of my soul. I reached for tissues on the table to wipe my eyes, which by now looked like a raccoon's.

Every part of my being was alive and wanting just to hold my son in my arms again.

The doctor continued, "I will help to arrange for a second opinion, if you want me to. I know of several excellent doctors that I will call and set up something for you, if you like, but we have to start him on treatment immediately to get some of his strength back."

Dr. Baranko leaned towards me; the sister gently rubbed my back and softly placed her hand over mine. "Listen to me carefully. I don't care if I ever get paid for my services. I don't care if this hospital gets paid. I don't care if you don't have a pot to piss in. I will stand on my head in the corner of this room if you want me to. Please let me treat your son."

I cracked a little smile behind my tear-washed red eyes. Glancing over at the sister, I caught her smile of sympathy. Looking back at the doctor, I nodded my head. I closed my eyes for a second to thank God, then told the doctor, "Yes," as I breathed a huge sigh of relief.

"I would like to list him as my private patient. That way you can call the hospital anytime, and they will take care of everything for you. You don't have to worry about anything. Just let me try to help your son . . ."

I sat there a minute beholding the total sincerity shining in the doctor's eyes. The sister took my hand, and the priest bowed his head in prayer. I bowed my head and wiped my eyes. Following the prayer, I raised my head, and looked the doctor straight in the eyes.

"There's no need for another opinion, because I have confidence that you will do everything possible for him."

"I will, that's a promise. And thank you for your trust. Chris is resting in his room now. He has an IV in his arm, and it's tied down so he can't touch it or try and pull it out. The medical research in this area is—"

Apologizing for interrupting the doctor in the middle of his sentence, I asked him to give it to me straight.

"What are the treatments, and how long will they last? Please, just give me the bottom-line truth. When will Chris be all right? In layman's terms, please. Doctor? What exactly are you trying to tell me?"

He glanced over at the sister, then the priest, collecting his thoughts, perhaps trying to find the right words to tell me what the next three years would entail for Chris and me. No doubt he was searching for the words to say that there probably wouldn't be a fourth year.

I sat listening intensely to every word that came out of his mouth, trying to freeze every gesture his body made as he talked calmly about treatments for Chris.

"There is no cure for leukemia at this time, Linda. Your son will have to undergo a series of bone marrow tests, spinal taps, injections, and radiation treatments to move him towards remission."

"Doctor, what is remission?" I asked. "I feel stupid saying this, but I have never heard the word leukemia, let alone know what a remission is."

Dr. Baranko was extremely sympathetic at this point; he moved a little closer and smiled. "Leukemia is a cancer of the blood. His body is producing abnormal cells. Remission is when Chris can maintain a level of normalcy with simple medication. His blood will produce normal cells on its own. Once in remission, various medications will be used to try to keep him there. Hopefully, through research, in three years there will be a cure."

"How long do these remissions last?" I asked him. "And what happens when you can't get him back into one?"

"Each child and case of leukemia is different. Typically, the second remission lasts about half the length of the first remission, the third usually half the length of the second and rarely does a patient have another remission."

Understanding that he was telling me that there was not another remission—just death—my mind grasped the reality of the conversation, but my heart rejected it— totally. It felt as though Chris and I had been cruelly plunged into a nightmare that was somewhere between heaven and hell.

"It's kind of like a ball game, if you want to put it that way. Three strikes and you're out."

Leaning back, resting my head against the sofa, I took a deep breath, almost gasping for air. Dr. Baranko released a deep sigh, then continued. "I'll do by best to keep him in this first remission as long as possible. Please believe me. I will do everything possible to do just that!"

After an hour of conversation, I was still sitting there trying to absorb everything the doctor had said. Chris's first remission! Nothing seemed real, not the words the doctor spoke, the hospital room, the sister, or the priest. I felt I had been placed in a movie where I waited for the director to say, "Cut! That's a wrap!" A tear slowly trickled down my cheek; I quickly wiped it away. My mind changed gears at that point. The doctor was going to do whatever possible to keep Chris in his first remission, and I was going to do everything possible to live a lifetime with Chris—in whatever time we had left.

"Do you have any other questions you'd like to ask me? Maybe I didn't explain something clearly enough?"

There was only one question that kept repeating itself like a digital time and temperature display on the bank back home. I didn't want to ask it, but knew I had to.

Part of me knew the answer already from everything the doctor had said. Part of me had to hear him say it in order for it to become reality. The motherly part of me rejected everything the doctor told me, fighting for Chris's survival with every ounce of strength I had inside of me.

I sat for a second remembering giving birth to him. The doctor and nurses had tried to warn me that he might not live because he was only four pounds, seven ounces. I had fought with everything I had then, and I was ready and willing to do the same now. I had to know the truth.

"Doctor, since there is no cure for leukemia, how long does he have to live?" My voice broke a little, as I lit another cigarette.

The doctor took a deep breath and glanced over at the priest and the sister once again. It was with deep sadness and extreme regret in his voice that he regarded me as he prepared to serve me my son's death sentence.

"Pending a cure, *about three years*, if we don't find a cure before that. Hopefully, through research, we will be able to extend those years and find a cure." My heart stopped for a second time. I could not speak, and I felt no hope, no future.

2

The Longest Night

The doctor reached for my hand. "Chris will be able to go home tomorrow. I will set up a series of appointments for him and meet with you in the morning."

I got up from the sofa slowly, trembling with weak knees, shook hands with the doctor and the priest, and thanked them for their honesty and their help. The priest left with the doctor. Sister Madonna Maria was going to accompany me to Chris's room. We sat talking for a short time, about what, I don't remember. Shortly, it was time to walk down the hallway to his room.

"Let's go. I'm eager to meet Chris, and I'm sure he can't wait to see his Mommie."

We joined hands and headed for Chris's room.

The halls were quiet as we paused outside the light oak door. Drawing a deep breath, I straightened my shirt and tried to collect myself. Squeezing the sister's hand, I put a smile on my face and silently prayed.

"Thank you, Lord, for giving us three years to live a lifetime and for not taking him home with you tonight. Help me to be the best mother that I can be and make his life happy, please . . ."

It was starting to get dark. Outside, I could see the city lights coming through the bay window in the toy room at the end of the hall. The entire hospital had a peaceful presence about it. We stood there a minute outside the door just looking at each other. I took a deep breath, smiling at the sister as she smiled back, embracing me with strength by the soft touch of her hand.

I knew that this was one time I had to be strong, be cheerful, show no worry. The easy part was showing Christopher that I loved him. The hard part would be suppressing my own fears and doubts. I knew I had to leave my fear outside the door. I had to step out of my time warp and into Chris's brave new world.

"Are you ready to go in?" Sister asked. "Chris is a very special little boy that loves his Mommie very much. The nurse said he has been asking for you ever since she put him in bed."

I squeezed her hand again and nodded. "Yes, I'm ready."

Chris was lying in the bed close to the door. He was drowsy from the medication. Pausing for a second, I smiled down at him. Brushing his blond hair from his forehead, I noticed a needle mark on his neck. Starting to weaken in the knees again, fighting back emotions of what my little guy must have gone through, I just wanted to hold him, love him, kiss him, and never let him go.

Chris looked up and smiled, "Please, Mommie, don't touch my IV."

"I promise I won't touch it," I whispered, straightening out his blanket. "I love you. How are you feeling, sweetheart?"

"The doctor told me why I had to have my arms tied down like this. It's because he thought I might try to scratch myself or accidentally pull the IV out."

Brushing his hair from his forehead with my fingers, I gave him a kiss.

Sister Madonna Maria said her good-byes and told us that she would see us in the morning. She gave us both a thumbs up accompanied by a grand smile. I returned the favor with a thumbs up to her and a grand, "Thank you."

Once the heavy oak door closed, the tiny night-light above Chris's bed dimly lit the room.

"Mommie, are you staying here all night?" his sleepy little voice asked. "I don't want you to leave."

Still fiddling with his hair, I kissed him again, reassuring him.

"Now, just where else would you expect me to be but in that chair beside your bed all night long? We're buddies, aren't we?"

"Yes."

"Well then, you just try to get rid of me, little man. Mommie is staying right here all night."

His smile told me all I needed to know. Soon, he drifted off to sleep feeling safe and secure.

I phoned Mom from the room and quietly filled her in on what had happened, requesting that she bring a couple of things to the hospital for me. I sat by Chris until Mom came about an hour later. She carried in the suitcase that I hadn't unpacked.

I could see that she was having a hard time with the situation. We took our discussion out into the hall. As she headed home, I told her I would call in the morning when Chris was released.

The night was quiet and dark. The nurses came in and checked on us from time to time. They introduced me to their personal coffee room, and I made good use of that.

Chris would wake up, usually when I was getting a refill, and I would hear his faint voice call me. It never failed; I'd sit there for hours and the split second I left the room, he would wake up mumbling.

"Mommie, Mommie where are you?"

It was about three in the morning when I found myself standing in front of the window overlooking the bright lights of Phoenix, Arizona.

I reached out and gripped each side of the bars that covered the window, leaning my head against the center bar. I knew in my heart that Chris and I weren't going back to Illinois in two weeks. Arizona would be our home for the next three years, hopefully for Chris, even longer. Things like this just didn't happen to small-town, barefoot, 110-pound, five-and-one-half-foot brunette, Midwestern farm kids. Things like this happened to people you read about in the newspaper.

Gazing out at the big city lights that seemed to go on forever, I knew I had to find a job, and a place to live and face whatever the next three years had in store for us.

Many things went through my mind that night as I sat in the chair beside his bed watching Chris sleep. I remembered the night I had given birth to him. The nurse had placed him in my arms and then told me not to get too attached, that he was too small in weight—only four pounds, seven ounces—and might not live. I couldn't believe what I was hearing! I just lay there for a moment then, with what little strength I had left, angrily blurted out at the top of my lungs, *he will live!!!*

I recalled the day I brought him home from the hospital. I had dressed him in an adorable little blue outfit that Mom had bought and wrapped him in a cute, little, creamy white receiving blanket, decorated with cartoon characters that I received at a shower my friends had given me.

"Hi, little guy. I'm your Mommie, and I love you very much." With all the love any mother could give, I held him in my arms, adoring his little wrinkled red face.

Chris had been a happy little boy who loved to play with my pots and pans, as well as unload the food from the lazy Susan or crawl in corners, semi-hiding, and call out, "Mommie, come find me." He played around the house in his shorts, socks, and tee shirts, riding the vacuum cleaner like a wild pony as I cleaned.

These heart-warming memories were thrust in the dark as, still gripping the bars, I turned my head to watch him sleep. I heard a hateful inner voice unleash its despair.

"Lots of luck, stupid. You don't have any job skills that anyone wants. Who is going to hire someone like you? You're even uglier than you are stupid!"

Still clutching the bars with my hands, I looked up towards the sky. The lights of the city skyline dimmed the stars. Another voice calmly eased my mind.

"I will never leave you or forsake you, my child. I love you and will never give you more than you can handle. Trust in me, and I will see you through. For I have loved you since before you were born."

I leaned my head against the bars again and started to cry.

"I have to trust you, Lord, and I do because you're the only one who can help me now. I can't do this alone. I just can't. Please help me, Lord. Please . . ."

The city lights flicked endlessly as I gripped the bars even tighter, twisting my hands against them. I became consumed with guilt for not realizing that something had been wrong.

"Why didn't I know he was ill? Why couldn't I see it? Maybe I could have prevented this horrible moment for him."

What was left of the night found me in the chair beside Chris's bed, waiting for morning to come. It was 9:00 a.m. when the nurse came in to give Chris some pills and remove the IV. It took a good thirty minutes to get the pills down the littler squirt, and that was with the help of chocolate ice cream and thirty cents. The bitter pills were so bad even the nurse scowled.

In the other bed was a little blond girl, about two years old, that had gotten in a bottle of bleach and rubbed it in her eyes. She was sleeping peacefully in cartoon-character PJs with her favorite blanket. The father of the little girl offered a dime for every pill Chris got down. He was a tall, slim young man with a big cowboy hat, blue jeans, and weathered boots. He appeared to be a man who had worked hard all his life.

His technique proved successful, and I figured I would have to lay in a supply of dimes and ice cream so Chris would take the pills when I took him home to Mom's house.

It was nearly twenty-four hours between our arrival at the emergency room to being released by the doctor. I called Mom to pick us up. The doctor met with us for further instructions and handed me the schedule of appointments. At last we were released to go home.

Sister Madonna Maria came to say good-bye and asked how things had gone during the night. She and Chris got along great. He asked her if he could see her the next time he came to the hospital.

"You better call me when you're here, or I'm going to be very hurt that I missed you. You're my special friend, aren't you?" Chris beamed with happiness as the sister bent down to kiss him good-bye.

"Yes, and my Mommie will let you know when we are here. OK?"

I don't know who got the biggest kick out of the spunk that this little kid had, the sister or me. Sister Madonna Maria wheeled Chris down to the bright, sunny lobby. As she bent down to talk with Chris, I beheld the beautiful reception area with its pale pink walls, healthy green plants, and glass-like floor. I smiled to myself, wishing I'd found such an oasis during the lonely hours.

Standing before the double doors that would lead us into a brand new world and brand new place in our lives, I looked up to find consolation and inspiration in a five-foot statue mounted over the door. The magnificent statue was of Jesus. As I stood there filled with grace, I thanked him with an unspoken prayer. "Thank you. In all things, you said to give thanks, and I do."

When Mom arrived at the entrance a few minutes later, Sister Madonna Maria wheeled Chris to the curb. I picked him up in my arms, and as Mom opened the car door, I laid him down in the back seat. Sister poked her head in the back window and said she would see us later. Chris hugged her good-bye, and I thanked her for all she had done.

I walked back to the hospital entrance pushing the wheelchair with the sister. I thanked her again as she embraced me with love and friendship. When I returned to the car, climbing into the front seat, I leaned over and asked Chris if he was "OK, back there."

He smiled, happy to be in familiar surroundings again, as Mom started the car. Checking the traffic, she pulled away from the curb. I looked over at her; while leaning against the headrest, I closed my eyes.

The world as Chris and I knew it, was now gone forever. Twenty-four hours ago a doctor was taking a blood test, telling me that my son had leukemia. The initial shock of our "New World" was over now. The doctors and hospital staff had gone to work, fighting the battle against death. Now the guilt of not having known or realized that something was wrong started to consume me.

Smiling at Mom as she pulled out into the street heading home I could only think of one thing—Chris.

Everything else blanked out of my mind. I only wanted to get Chris settled comfortably in bed at Mom's and take it from there.

As I put my sunglasses on, I glanced back at Chris peacefully resting, then over to Mom. Breaking the tension with an old phrase that I had used on more than one occasion growing up, I requested, "Home, James."

3

Our New World

As Mom pulled into the driveway of the house that she and Dad had bought seven months ago, I awakened from my nap. I caught my first glimpse of where I had slept our first night in Phoenix. As Mom had written, it was spacious enough to accommodate her and Dad, her parents, and Grandma Vie.

Chris, too, had fallen asleep, but opened his eyes as I lifted him towards my chest. His little arms reached out and hugged my neck as Mom closed the car door.

The grandparents stood in the doorway that led to the kitchen as I carried Chris in the house. The expressions on their faces almost made me cry as they quietly sat down at the kitchen table, trying to stay out of the way and hold their questions until I got Chris settled.

"I want you and Chris to have the master bedroom. The bed is bigger, and you'll have your own bath," Mom said.

"Mom, that's OK. We'll be fine in one of the other rooms, and that brown leather sofa is really comfortable, you know."

"No, you two are going to stay in my room, and I will sleep in the spare bedroom. Besides, you can go outside when you want without going through the whole house."

I carried Chris into the bedroom and gently laid him down on the bed. It occurred to me that Mom might have needed an excuse to sleep in the guestroom. Maybe with Dad gone, the memories were too much.

"OK, you sold me, Mom. Where do I sign in? By the way, where is Gary?"

"I took him to the airport this morning before I picked you up, remember?" Her expression was that of concern. Possibly the lack of sleep mixed with the stress of all that was happening with Chris was affecting me. "I think you need some rest. Why don't you take a nap, too? I'll call you when lunch is ready."

"Yeah, I think I would like to relax for a while. Lunch sounds good, Mom. I don't think I've had anything except coffee in paper cups for a day or two."

I cuddled up on the pillow next to Chris. I longed for slumber, but my mind was darting in too many directions. I couldn't keep my eyes closed but for a few seconds at a time.

I smiled at Chris with a sigh of relief to have him safely home. I moved Billy "cop" Bear so they both could sleep a little more comfortably. Chris opened his eyes.

"Mommie."

I leaned over him and kissed his forehead. "Shh, Mommie is right here with you. Close your eyes, sweetheart, and go back to sleep. Mommie isn't going anywhere. I'll be right here; I promise." Hugging his Billy Bear, he fell into a peaceful sleep.

I figured I might as well unpack. I couldn't help wondering what I would have done if Mom hadn't been there or hadn't been living in Arizona, for that matter. What would have happened?

If Dad hadn't come to visit, I probably would have found Chris dead in his bed one morning. Horrible thought, but true. At least he was alive for now, I thought, and had medical help.

I opened my suitcase and shook out my wrinkled clothing. The closet was like another room. My few tops, blue jeans and dirty sneakers somehow didn't fit into the decor, but the room would have to accept them for now. Dad's big mahogany and leather desk sat against one wall with a television on the other.

The bath, about as big as the closet, had a door that led outside to the swimming pool. With plush carpet, two sinks, and a wall-to-wall mirror reflecting lush hand towels and beautiful fresh cut flowers in a vase, this place looked like a model home—something out of a magazine. I wandered outside for a few minutes to have a cigarette and stretch my legs.

The grandparents were all sitting out on the back porch enjoying the midmorning sun. I sat for a few minutes, and we chatted about nothing. I knew they wanted to ask questions, but I felt they understood that I wasn't ready. I finished my cigarette and excused myself to check on Chris again.

During lunch around the kitchen table, I filled them in on what the doctor had told me. They sat listening quietly, sipping their coffee, and gazing out the window.

I knew they didn't want to believe it. The expressions on my grandparents' faces were grief stricken, helpless, and broken-hearted.

Grandma Vie just sat with her fist clenched about as tight as her lower jaw. Although Grandma had sustained Dad's death fairly well, Chris's illness seemed too much to accept. Grandma Pete, sitting next to Vie, kept shaking her head back and forth, unable to accept the harsh reality.

Grandpa Pete had taken over the role as the man of the house, and although he believed every word, he knew he couldn't help in any way. Mom was clearing the lunch dishes, and although I knew she was listening, she made no comments.

After lunch, Mom and I sat having a cup of coffee at the kitchen table while the grandparents, my "oldies but goodies," took a nap.

After we finished our coffee, I went to check on Chris. He was still sleeping, and I was getting tired, nearly exhausted. Lying down beside him, I kept thinking of the past two weeks and the twisted turn of events.

When Mom and Grandma Vie flew to Illinois for Dad's funeral, I never in my wildest dreams expected that Chris and I would be living here. I had been planning to come to Phoenix for a few weeks to visit and help Mom.

I had never expected that Dad would die, but there we were driving his gold Caddie across the country. Grandma

Vie, Chris, and I sat in the back seat, while Mom sat in the front, with Gary driving.

Somewhere in the middle of Texas, I got a terrifying feeling that something was wrong with Chris. We had checked into a motel for the evening. Chris was fresh from a warm bath, sitting on the bed in his PJs. I noticed a bit of blood in his nostrils, and as I reached with a tissue to wipe it, a long blood clot emerged.

My stomach tightened in fear, knowing that this was not right. I rationalized that Chris was upset because he couldn't figure out where Grandpa Wally was. His only question on the trip so far had been, "Mommie, where is Grandpa Wally? Why are we driving his car and he isn't here? We have to go back and get him."

"Chris, Grandpa Wally is in heaven." I kept trying to explain to him. "We have to take his car to Phoenix because that's where Grandma and all the other grandmas and Grandpa Pete live now. Uncle Gary is driving us so we all get there safe and sound. Okey-dokey, alligator?"

Grandma Vie was trying to humor Chris. "You know when your mom was a little girl, we used play the same game of okey-dokey, alligator, and after while, crocodile." But Chris was angry with all of us for "leaving" his Grandpa Wally behind. He was having a hard time understanding and clung to my chest with his arms wrapped around my neck.

The next morning on the road, I rubbed his back to comfort him and wiped his bloody nose as I stared out the window, watching his reflection as miles of fence posts, pasture, and endless flatlands passed by. I seriously wondered whether, if Dad and I had made the trip as planned, Dad or Chris, or either, would have made it at all.

"Jesus, what if something had happened to both of them? I swear I would have lost it all at that point. Just locked the car and walked down the freeway until someone stopped me . . . and they would have to be big, because it would have taken a lot to stop me at that point . . . believe me, Lord . . ."

Still not able to sleep, I reached for my cigarettes and made good use of the private back door that led to the pool. I sat for a while wondering how to tell my husband, Tony, that our son had leukemia.

Chris was sleeping in the bed, so I stretched the telephone cord into the bathroom, closing the adjoining door, in hopes that Chris couldn't hear me if he woke up. I lit up a cigarette while dialing the phone and waited for Tony to answer.

The conversation began like any other; we talked about the weather. I searched my mind and heart for a gentle, delicate way to tell Tony our son was dying. Finally, I just blurted it out. "Tony, I've got something important to tell you. Chris and I can't come back home; he has leukemia."

The long pause of silence from us both seemed like a re-gathering of thoughts.

"What do you mean leukemia? What are you saying?"

I tried not to cry because Chris was asleep, and I didn't want him to wake up. Besides, by that time, I didn't think I had any tears left inside me to cry.

"Tony, listen to me, and I'll try to explain it as the doctor explained it to me. Chris has acute lymphoblastic leukemia," I began. "The white blood cells have multiplied without restraint, overpowering the bone marrow, spleen, and liver. This prevents the normal red blood cells from producing normally.

"The doctor is going to start him on a program to try to get his leukemia into remission. We have to go three times a week for two months for a series of shots, spinal taps, and bone marrow tests. I have medication to give him at home along with what the doctor gives him." I paused, hoping Tony would say something, then continued.

"He said the first remission will probably be his longest, and the second is usually about half as long as the first remission. The third," my voice cracked trying to swallow the lump in my throat. "Well, there usually isn't any third remission.

"Chris has about three years to live. Hopefully, through research, they can extend it a little longer. The doctor said he would explain it to you when you get here."

"I guess you pretty well covered everything," Tony replied. "I'll come out as soon as I can, but it will be a month or so. We have spring planting starting, you know, and my mom and dad need me here until it's finished." I really didn't want to hear about planting fields at that time.

I sat there on the floor, holding the phone between my shoulder and ear, staring up at the ceiling. I held back my frustration and answered with a shaky voice, ending softly.

"Fine. When you do come out, please bring my things and Chris's, also. You shouldn't have any problem getting the stuff in the truck. Tony, I also need to get the insurance company's name, the policy number, and the address for the hospital."

I wished that he had promised to be on the next flight out and had asked how I was holding up, or something. But that didn't happen. At least I could keep Chris happy.

"I will go and wake Chris up so you can talk to him. He's been asking about his daddy. Hold on."

I dragged the phone cord over to the bed. Chris woke up as I placed the receiver to his ear.

"Chris, Daddy's on the phone. Can you say hi?"

He pressed the receiver to his ear with both hands, all smiles as he lay in bed looking up at me.

"Hi, Daddy. I miss you." Chris's excitement was contagious. "I have my own doctor out here, and he's going to help me to get better so we can come home. He's nice, and I like him."

Chris smiled and listened intently to his Daddy's words during his silent moments. "Daddy, when you come out, Grandma Alice has a swimming pool in her back yard that we can swim in. A big one!"

Chris was silent as he listened, reaching for his Billy Bear. "Daddy, I miss you and love you, and when are you coming out with my toys?"

Chris's grin lit up the room until he relinquished the receiver. Then Tony and I talked a little longer. That night Chris went to sleep a very happy little boy. He knew his daddy would be with him soon, and he would bring all his toys.

Realizing that I would have to find a job to survive in this city, I planned on hitting the newspaper classified ads after breakfast. The paper looked like an encyclopedia compared with the one back home. I managed to mark an X over ninety-five percent of the employment ads, designing a truly off balance game of tic-tac-toe. At least the general labor section offered me some hope.

I made a few phone calls, but all my enthusiasm drained very quickly. As the voices on the phone advised me to come down and fill out an application form, I began counting out my wardrobe on one hand. I had neither transportation nor the slightest idea how to get around the city.

Chris was taking a nap, so I wandered out to sit by the pool and think. I decided it might be best to wait for Tony to come out with my truck and the rest of my things.

Chris and I spent the next couple of days by the pool. We had fun taking little walks around the yard and picking flowers for Grandma. Chris was always sure to give his other Grandma and even Grandpa a flower, too.

Tucked away in our room at night, I'd turn on the television and snuggle in beside Chris. We'd watch his favorite programs until he fell asleep. Most of the time I was thinking about our future.

During that time, I became determined to go back to school. The Phoenix job market was decidedly different from that of Kewanee, Illinois. I couldn't just walk down to the local hardware store and get hired that day. Of course, I worried from sun up to sun down over my age—twenty-six years old. Was I too old? The idea of juggling school books, a career, and a sick little boy spun me around. The thought of going to college captured my mind throughout the night.

Several days passed, and Chris was walking very well and wanting to play. It was a special time for both of us. Chris had his Mommie all to himself all day long, as well as the attention of the grandparents. I had my little buddy and best friend alive and feeling better.

We played hide-and-seek in the house, which usually only lasted a few rounds before he grew tired and wanted to rest. Watching him play, I realized how fast a precious little life can go with no warning.

Later that night, I got up, reached for my cigarettes and headed out to the patio. Sitting there watching the moon and stars I told myself. "Tomorrow morning Mom is driving us to the doctor's office for our first visit. I really don't know what to expect. Maybe I'm better off not knowing; maybe ignorance is bliss at this point."

That morning Mom was busily finishing up breakfast for the grandmas and Grandpa Pete. Chris and I were munching on a piece of toast while getting dressed. Mom, more nervous than I was, asked, "Do you have the instructions to the doctor's office?"

"Yes, Mom, I have them in my purse. Are you almost ready?" In a matter of minutes, we were off, looking for street signs again and the landmarks the doctor had described.

"There it is, Mom. That's the building across from the hospital."

"Mommie, is this where my doctor lives?"

"No, Chris, this is where his office is. Remember that big building over there across the street?"

"Maybe."

"Well, that's where you spent the night in the hospital three days ago, and Mommie sat in the room with you all night."

I turned to my mother. "Mom, do you want to come up with us and see what this is all about?"

"I guess I should. You never know, I might need to bring him here by myself someday. At least I'll know where I'm going."

Chris attempted to walk on his own as Mom opened the door to the doctor's office. His eyes lit up when he spied the candy counter as we passed through the pharmacy. As our eyes met, I knew exactly what was on his mind. I saved him the trouble of asking. "Yes, Chris, we can stop here on our way out!" This became a tradition upon every visit.

Watching for the elevator, Chris stretched out his arms towards me. Picking him up, I could sense that he was somewhat frightened. I kissed him, trying to comfort him from any fear by rubbing his back.

"Mommie, can I have two pieces of candy?"

I agreed with a hearty laugh. "You sure can, but only if I get two pieces, too."

Mom and Chris had a seat while I introduced myself to the receptionist and signed Chris in on the roster.

Taking in the landscape of faces filling the room, it was hard to believe that such a mix of children shared the same disease. Some of them looked so healthy, playing with the zest for life that was typical of any kid. Some kids were just sitting on their parent's lap. A few of the kids were bald.

At this point, I felt like Chris and I were the newest entry on some statistical data form. We had joined the ranks of the hopeful, waiting for a cure. There was no way, I was determined, that we were going to live as some helpless pieces of paper bound together by fasteners and false hopes. Chris and I were prepared to live life to the fullest. God willing, we were going to live an entire lifetime in three years, or whatever time we had.

It seemed only a few minutes had passed when the nurse called our name. Everything became real. It was our turn to walk through the door and down the hall. Turning back to look at my mother's worried face, I caught her half smile, her attempt to be strong.

"Hi, Chris," the nurse said. "Dr. Baranko is waiting for you in room three. Do you and your Mommie want to follow me? Your grandma can come, too, if she wants." The nurse threw her a smile.

"I'll wait here; you and Chris go ahead." Mom reached for a magazine and sent us off with a sweet wink.

We followed the nurse to room three where she helped Chris onto the examination table. She took his temperature, blood pressure, and pulse.

"What's your name?" he asked.

"It's Terri, and your name is Chris. Right?"

"Right, and that's my Mommie."

Terri nodded her head and smiled as she charted his vitals. She talked with Chris then gave him a wave as she prepared to leave.

"I hope I'm here every time you come to see Dr. Baranko, and if I'm not you'd better leave me a hello and a kiss at the front desk. OK?"

"OK, I will," Chris beamed. "Good-bye, Terri."

The door opened gently, and Dr. Baranko walked in with a big smile on his face and a warm "hello" for both of us.

"How are you feeling today, Chris? Have you been eating OK?" He leaned on the table, giving me a glance.

Chris, who never knew a stranger, began telling Dr. Baranko, "My Grandma Alice fixes me anything I want, and Mommie does, too. My other grandmas and Grandpa Pete have a basket of fruit in their room, so I go and visit with them when I get hungry for that stuff. My other Grandma Vie keeps candy in her room and gives me a piece when I visit her."

"You are one lucky little boy to have all those grandmas and a grandpa around."

I explained the living arrangement to Dr. Baranko. "Somehow we all get along and help each other," I paused to count my blessings. "That's just the way our family is."

There was no denying the hypodermic needle that lay on a tray on the table. The doctor stepped to the tray and began to prepare Chris for what we came to know as a "pokie."

"Chris, I'm sorry, but this might hurt a little," he began, "I'll try and get it over with as soon as possible. OK, Sport?"

"What are you going to do?" Chris asked, his courage shining through.

"I'm going to inject this needle in the vein in your hand."

Taking Chris's hand, the doctor showed him just where the needle was going to go. Chris listened with fascination as Dr. Baranko explained the medication's importance and benefits in great detail.

"OK, I'm ready now, Dr. Baranko. You can do it . . . *Ouch!*"

"There, it's all over Chris. That wasn't so bad, was it?"

"No, I guess not," Chris responded, toughing it out and smiling at Dr. Baranko.

The doctor finished the exam, and soon we were on our way to the pharmacy in search of candy.

Driving away from the medical building, I realized that several things had taken place on our first visit to the doctor.

A trusting friendship had begun between Chris, Dr. Baranko, and myself. Mom, being in a denial frame of mind about the whole thing, somehow partially accepted the truth about Chris. I think she knew it was real but just didn't want to believe it was happening to her grandson.

I knew deep within my spirit that I had three years to make the most of it. I didn't dare waste a precious moment, regardless of what anyone said or thought about how we spent it. It was now three years or bust!

Mom stopped on our way home for some groceries she needed, so Chris and I decided to walk to the little bookstore in the shopping center. I found a book that would help improve reading skills and teach speed-reading. Chris also found a book he wanted about dinosaurs. On the way home, I *had* to start reading it to him.

Later that afternoon while Chris was taking his nap, I sat by the pool reading my book. In no time, the thunderclouds of doubt rolled in, raining on my parade and insisting that I was foolish to consider college. "How do I register?" I wondered out loud, "What classes do I take?"

The book was closed, and a steady stream of negativity found its way out of my mouth as I sat there doubting myself.

"I'm going to look like a fool sitting in the classroom with a group of young kids. What's a person like me even thinking about going to college for? I've got enough on my hands with Chris, trying to make a life for us somehow. Besides college is only for certain people who are smart enough to go."

My mind drifted back eight years to when I had been a senior in high school. I'd wanted to go to college so badly. I'd talked with my aunt and uncle in Phoenix about living with them and attending a junior college because it was cheaper. I had planned on getting a part-time job, so my parents wouldn't have to send money.

I presented my case to my parents. Dad just sat there listening—his mind already made up—and Mom had mixed feelings. I saw in her eyes that, rather than college, she wanted me to live on my own for a while before I decided to get married.

My closing statement that evening was more a plea for their support and encouragement. I explained that I wanted there to be far more to my life than to just grow up, get married, and have a family. My declaration was not met with understanding.

"You're a girl and don't need an education like that," Dad said. "Plus, we don't want you that far away from home. So marry Tony and raise a family. It will be better in the long run. I wish Gary had your desire to get an education; he could go far."

Nearly eight years later, I was in Phoenix, with a dying son who would live about three years. My marriage was in shambles, I was trying to register for college, and I was living with my mother and three grandparents.

I gave Chris his medication, tucked him in, and snuggled against him. Once he'd fallen off to sleep, I strolled outside to sit by the pool and do some thinking. The night was very warm. The sky was beautiful, filled with brightly shining stars. All the glory of the cosmos couldn't stop the tears that came as I faced the truth that I was just plain scared as hell about the future.

"What's going to happen when he dies?" I cried to the moonlit heavens. "How am I going to handle it? What's it going to be like without Chris? No one to call me Mommie, no little voice hollering. 'Mommie, I can't find my socks.' nor 'Will you make me my favorite dinner?' I don't have the strength to go through this."

Echoing memories haunted me that night as I sat in the dark listening to the traffic passing by and hearing Chris's voice from days gone by. I prayed that there would be time to make many more memories.

I remembered times when Chris would dress himself in the craziest things: little cowboy boots, a pair of pull-on shorts, and his favorite sweatshirt in the dead of winter. I asked, why the shorts? He told me he wanted to see his new cowboy boots. So that day everyone saw his brand new cowboy boots.

The past four-and-one-half years had been the happiest I had ever known. For so long, I had wanted a baby boy to love and hold. The love I had received from Chris was more than I had ever experienced in my life. He was more than my son. He was my strength and my reason for living.

As I walked back into the bedroom, the entire house was dark and silent. With everyone asleep, I crawled into bed next to Chris and kissed him, pulling the sheet up to his chest.

I lay there just watching him sleep, with funny expressions on his face from dreams that were going through his mind. Smiles, frowns, and excitement changed his facial expression faster than he could click the television through its channels.

Turning over and resting on my back, I had a little talk with the Lord. Towards the end of the conversation, I came to the conclusion that if Chris could endure this for the next three years, I could get an education and give him a good life while he was alive.

4

Accepting a New Life

After breakfast the next morning, I called Scottsdale Community College. A couple of days later, a catalogue and admissions forms arrived in the mail. The pages of that book brought the excitement of making a positive step forward, along with the renewal of a shattered dream from eight years ago.

Chris would be my number one priority, with school following second. And maybe, just maybe, things would turn out for the best.

As I sat at the kitchen table filling out the form, Chris came up to me.

"Mommie, what are you doing? Can I write, too?"

"Sure you can. Come here, sweetheart."

Picking him up and setting him on my lap, I reached over and tore off a piece of notebook paper. I gave him an ink pen, and soon he was scribbling all over the paper.

Reaching over to tear off another piece of paper, I started to write a letter requesting my high school transcript. More and more I felt from within that things were going to be OK.

Once I had addressed the envelope, I walked outside and placed it in the mailbox. After closing its little black door, I felt happy about myself.

I knew that I would have to wait to hear whether I would be accepted or not, but I was smiling the whole time as I walked up the driveway. I knew I had made the right decision. It just felt right.

I picked Chris up and set him back down in my lap.

"Let's draw our numbers and letters! We like to do that, don't we? Remember how to write your numbers one through ten?"

He sat there with a puzzled smile. I wrote the numbers across the top of the page for him. He seemed baffled. I was baffled, too. This was a boy who could count to fifty and write his ABCs.

"Chris, can you write these numbers for Mommie?"

He sat there for a while. As he made an attempt to count from one to ten, I could see he was having serious trouble. I could also see that he was aware that he had once known his numbers, but he'd left them behind somehow.

I played the game of telling him the answers and then praising him for repeating them to me. As we sat at the table playing school, I recalled other questions that he had asked, "How do you spell dog? What is this called, Mommie?" pointing to a picture of a horse. "What is that thing called where Grandma keeps the food cold, Mommie?" At the time they didn't make sense, but they were beginning to now.

When I asked the doctor about it, he wasn't unnecessarily concerned, but he offered an explanation and some advice. It was apparent that during that first day in the hospital when his oxygen level was so low, it had done something to his memory cells.

"Chris is young and will relearn those things that he has forgotten very easily. The little fellow has been through a lot. Let him take his time in re-learning his ABCs."

"I'm not pushing him, by any means, Dr. Baranko. I just wondered what had happened, because of all the questions he asks. When he couldn't count to ten for me, I thought at first he was playacting again."

"Everything will be all right. Just give him time—and yourself, too."

Chris and I spent the next couple of weeks in the pool. He had just learned to swim and longed to spend every waking hour in the water. The grandmas and Grandpa Pete would entertain themselves for the afternoon by sitting on the patio watching us splash and play.

We spent our evening playing a game that consisted of crawling on the floor in the bedroom like a one-year-old. I had purchased a book on child development, which stated that crawling stimulates the motor response in a child's brain, so, that's what we did. He would get a turn to ask a question, then it was my turn to crawl and point to something, and he would have to name it.

I had bought various learning aids for the age bracket of two to four years old. Sometimes I'd play dumb, and Chris would spout out the answer, giggling as I made a funny face. Sometimes he made faces at me, and I'd lean backwards laying flat on the floor. He would crawl up on top of me, kissing and tickling me as much as he could. It was fun for both of us, and I knew that Chris would learn everything in due time. I wanted him to have self-confidence. It was tough for him when he couldn't remember things.

With the help of a trusty city road map, I learned my way around the city. I studied at night in the bedroom after Chris fell asleep. I looked up addresses of places that we wanted to go, then looked them up on the map to calculate driving time.

Chris and I found a little zoo just a couple of blocks from the house. Several afternoons we walked there, spending the afternoon feeding the monkeys, watching the birds, and naming other animals. Generally, I ended up carrying him back home in my arms and putting him to bed for a nap, because he tired so easily.

Finally getting some smarts, I accepted the loan of a wheelchair from the hospital, so I didn't have to carry him. I just pushed him.

In the evenings, Mom and I sometimes took a long walk through the neighborhood, taking turns pushing Chris in the chair. He didn't need it all the time, only after the spinal taps and bone marrow tests. By that time, the appointments were three times a week.

The shots, tests, and pills continued for nine weeks. His legs were weak, and his back became stiff from the treatments.

Chris just seemed to accept it all as if it were a part of life. Even the doctor was amazed at Chris's great attitude towards everything.

My little trooper just kept trooping onward.

Two weeks had passed, and it was "Happy twenty-sixth birthday, Mommie." I spent most of the day sitting in bed next to Chris watching television. He'd had a spinal tap the day before, and his back hurt so badly that he couldn't walk. I carried him to the living room and bathroom.

Happy Birthday, Mommie, March 7, 1977

Chris was on Prednisone, a drug that made him want to eat everything in sight. His little face looked like a chipmunk's. He'd become such a little "porker," that even his clothes became too small. The only things that fit him were his pajamas. Mom bought him some little shorts and shirts so when I took him out in public, people wouldn't wonder why the kid was still in his PJs in the middle of the afternoon.

My little porker, eating every hour on the hour.

A few weeks later, Tony arrived in Phoenix with my truck packed with all our clothes and all of Chris's toys. Chris was so happy to see his Daddy and play with his toys. Tony heard firsthand about Dr. Baranko, his nurse, Terri, and Sister Madonna Maria. I tried to stay out of the way that evening and rest. After dinner was over and Chris went to sleep, Tony and I talked.

Sitting by the pool as a cool March evening breeze gently stirred the sent of orange blossoms, Tony asked me how Chris was. I told him everything the doctor had told me in the beginning and continued to bring him up to date. He didn't have too much to say, which was easy to understand. His world was being turned upside down also.

"There isn't anything either of us can do to stop our son from dying. I wish there were, but there just isn't. Look, why don't you come to the doctor's office with us and maybe he can answer any question that I couldn't."

I thought that if he heard it from the doctor, it might make it easier to accept.

"When is your next appointment?"

"Two days from now, so think about if you want to go with us. If so, I will call the doctor and let him know that you're coming, so he can schedule extra time for us."

"I want to go, I really do, but I'm just afraid."

"Well, the decision is yours. You can't be any more terrified than I was, Tony. Quite honestly, I feel you need to be a part of this and hear the facts for yourself instead of just from me. So plan on going."

"OK, I guess you're right."

The doctor confirmed everything I had told Tony about Chris's condition. The hour-long consultation ended with the doctor asking, "Do you two want more children?"

"No, I do not. I had a miscarriage before Chris, and I can't handle the thought of going through another pregnancy again and perhaps leukemia again."

"Well, I just wanted to say that if you did want more children, your next child might not have leukemia."

"But what are the odds that it might?"

Tony sat there silently listening to the conversation bounce back and forth across the doctor's desk.

"There is a fifty-fifty chance that the next baby may develop leukemia."

"There is no way I'm even going to entertain the thought. My answer is a definite, NO! I will not have another child. End of conversation," I declared.

After leaving the doctor's office, Chris made it very clear that he wanted to have lunch at his favorite restaurant, as we always did after our appointments. It was plain to see that he was happy having his Mommie and Daddy with him. I also knew it was going to be hard for him to understand why his Daddy wasn't going to stay. I wasn't sure how to tell him, but I had a couple of weeks to think about it. At least Chris could enjoy the next two weeks as a normal little boy with his Mommie and Daddy together again.

Our days were filled with going to the zoo, doctor's appointments, and visiting Chris's favorite mall, Chris Town. He called it his mall, because it shared his name. The evenings rapidly filled with discussing Chris and our marriage. Both of us knew that the marriage had died several years before, but, as many people do, we had stayed together for the sake of our son.

Chris was asleep in the bed, so Tony and I kissed him good night before we continued our nightly conversation. We sat on the bathroom floor, because I wanted to be close to Chris in case he woke up. I started the conversation knowing that I had to put all the cards on the table.

"Tony, I'm going to go to school, but you already know that. What I want to know is are you planning on coming back out here to visit or to live?"

Staring at the floor he said, "I don't know. I'll be back, but I don't know when."

I lit another cigarette while looking out the door towards the patio then turned back towards him.

"This is just as hard for me as it is for you. Chris and I can't go home. He will die back there. At least out here he has a few years to live. There are no doctors in our hometown that know how to treat this. The nearest is Chicago or Tennessee. Both are at least four hundred miles away.

"I'm going to find a job, a place to live, and try to live a lifetime in the next three years. If you want to live here with us, we will be a family until the end. The only thing that counts now is that child's happiness. We will have our lives after his is over, then you can go your way, and I'll go mine."

Tony looked up from the floor and straight into my eyes. With confusion, hurt, and distress he asked, "You want a divorce, don't you?"

I knew that he didn't want to hear what I was about to say. My stomach tied in one big knot; my throat tightened up, but the truth had to be voiced.

"Yes, I want a divorce. We can wait, if you want, till everything is over. You can find a job out here, and we will stay together for Chris's sake, or if you want to help us from back in Illinois and just visit, that's OK, too."

He was having a hard time with all I had said. There were so many things I wanted to say to him, but the time wasn't right. There probably never would be a right time. I figured what was past was past; just let it alone.

Both of us sat in silence. My mind flashed back to when we had moved into our new home, furnished in second-hand furniture. We were happy and proud of what we had accomplished.

I was particularly proud of my kitchen with a brand new avocado refrigerator, stove, and dishwasher, all matching. I had picked them out months ago when we first had decided to build. Every Friday I would spend my lunch hour walking to the appliance store to make my $25 payment and look at them.

If seemed that throughout our seven years of marriage we had had our problems as well as our happy times, but we grew apart more than we grew together.

"I don't have a smile on my face anymore, Tony. I can't pretend everything is all right with our marriage. I'm facing the fact that it is never going to be right. For right now, I'm devoting all my time and energy to Chris."

Tony, understanding, looked up at me with tears in his eyes. "I'll sell the house, and the profit will help you get started here. I'll send money every week, and extra if I can. Just send the medical insurance papers to me, and I'll take care of them."

"When you come and visit us you will always have a place to stay. We have to agree that we are going to be the happy little family whenever we're together. OK?"

"OK." He happily smiled.

A day or two later, I took Tony to the airport in our pickup truck. He carried Chris in his arms every minute. The two were inseparable. We told Chris that Daddy would be back later, but that he had to return to work for a while in Illinois.

Chris took it very well, as he did everything. The sad smiles mixed with tearful light laughter as we all hugged good-byes, until that someday came to pick Daddy up at the airport again.

I knew it was a blessing that Chris was too young to fully understand what was happening—why Daddy was going home to Illinois and why we couldn't all live together like we used to. Tony and I tried to explain to Chris that for now it was the way it had to be. Daddy could help us the most by living and working in Illinois, rather than being here in Phoenix. Chris seemed to accept that explanation as long as Daddy promised to come back soon.

5

One Step at a Time

Treatments for Chris continued three times a week for several weeks, including a series of injections and different medications. Dr. Baranko talked to me about chemotherapy and the additional bone marrow and spinal taps that would soon become necessary.

For the time being, Chris seemed to be improving. He was happy, walking, and wanting to play more. His memory made a comeback, as we practiced our ABCs, worked with numbers, and played our crawling game in the bedroom.

Things seemed to settle down into a somewhat normal routine. When I received hospital bills, I forwarded them to Tony. Every couple of weeks, he would send extra money to keep us going. I knew that there was just so much one paycheck could handle; I was grateful for what he was able to contribute.

It was the end of May, and we had been with Mom about four months. Summer school would be starting soon, and my decision to attend would mean either moving closer to the college or driving the distance. Chris and I talked it over one evening while sitting in our bedroom. He wanted to have his own bedroom again, and he was eager to play with the rest of his toys. I felt that it was time for us to get our own apartment and start building a life again.

With Chris and I in agreement, I told Mom that we were going to look for a place to live in Scottsdale. It would be nothing fancy, but I knew it would be better if we were on our own.

Mom really didn't want us to leave, but she understood my reasons. I reminded her that she already had a house full of people for whom to care, and with Dad's estate settled, I explained that I would feel better in a place of my own. All things considered, I felt that moving was the best choice.

I had no idea where to start looking, so Mom called her real estate woman who led me to a Realtor named Jay.

Mom insisted on watching Chris, bribing him with going shopping. This freed me to drive with Jay all over the city looking for a rental apartment within my budget, something that was "as cheap as possible."

We discussed everything under the sun. Jay imparted a wealth of information concerning schools, educational opportunities, good day care centers for Chris, places that we might enjoy visiting, and a couple of places we shouldn't visit on our own. The next four days we drove, talked, laughed, and became good friends.

We would stop and have lunch at a posh restaurant, with discussions that always led to Chris's condition and to what prognosis the doctor had given me. It was exciting to talk to someone who asked me questions and encouraged me to think on a different wavelength.

We talked about my desire for an education, a place to live, and a job to sustain Chris and me over the course of the next three years. She gave me food for thought, not just for the next three years, but for my life afterwards. Most of all, it was wonderful to be able to express my concerns about Chris and not just explain what the doctor had said or done on our visit.

When Jay asked me about my job skills, I wanted to tell her that I had worked as a nurse or dental assistant, but my career path had turned down a different road. I had worked as a maid and front desk clerk for a local hotel. After I married, I went to work in the housewares department of the local hardware store. Although I balanced the checkbook, budgeted household expenses, had no problem in asking questions, and always read the fine print before signing a contract, I simply considered that to be common sense. Jay's smile gave me encouragement, somehow, as if she approved of my job skills. Looking back on those days with Jay, she probably had my job skills in mind, while finding us a place to live.

One afternoon Jay called and said she had the perfect place for us. "It's close to the college, and there are several hotels on Scottsdale Road where you can apply for a part-time job."

"Is there a school close by for Chris?"

"Several schools, Linda, and I'll be glad to show you which ones would be best for him. Meet me at the apartment in about an hour." She gave me the address.

"We're on our way! See you in an hour, Jay, and thanks again."

Chris clapped his hands and jumped up and down on the bed with excitement.

"Mommie, are we going to see our new apartment?" His eyes were wide with excitement.

"Yes, so get your shoes on so we can go, and then Jay will meet us over there."

He scrambled to the closet to find his tennis shoes as I reached for a clean T-shirt. He could hardly sit still as I struggled to pull the shirt over his head. He kept trying to tie his shoes at the same time. As I reached for my purse, Chris took a flying leap off the bed and into my arms. I caught the flying four-and-one-half-year-old boy, and out the door we went.

During our sixty-minute drive through palm-studded Phoenix, Chris asked more questions than I could keep up with.

"Mommie, is there a school for me to go to?"

"Jay is going to show us where the best one is so you can have lots of little friends to play with. How's that for you?"

"This is going to be fun, Mommie, and I can have all my toys in my room." My favorite music group played softly on the eight-track, as Chris talked away. "I hope there are other kids in the apartments by us."

"I'm sure there will be, honey. It will just take a little time to get to know them, that's all. But I'm sure that you will have lots of kids to play with, before you know it."

"Can we go to the parks and play, like that one that has the little train in it?"

"Scottsdale Railroad Park. Well, maybe not today, but I'm sure we can plan a picnic very soon. Maybe we will have a park close by our new apartment."

I made a silly face, and Chris giggled as he sat in the seat beside me clasping his hands and wiggling his feet.

Chris had a big fascination with police officers. When we would pass one on the road, he would almost wear his arm out waving to him. He had a knack for spotting a police car sitting alongside the road, which was nice for me.

He loved to give me tickets. Every time I went through a yellow light, out came his little book, and he scribbled me out a ticket. He would also insist that we wear our seat belts at all times. By the time we arrived at the new apartment, I had several "tickets" issued and stuffed in my purse.

Jay was waiting for us with open arms. Chris greeted her with a big hug complete with a kiss and a plea for her to hurry up and open the door so we could see our new apartment.

I think Jay knew she had a deal. There was no way Chris was going to let me get away without writing a check that day for the deposit. I had saved a little money, and although I didn't have a job yet, I'd come up with the necessary funds from somewhere.

Chris and I celebrated our new home by treating ourselves to a hamburger, fries, and malt at the nearby fast food restaurant. His shiny little face was beaming with excitement at the thought of swimming in the pool, playing with the other kids, and having all his toys again.

I arranged to meet with Jay later to sign the papers for the apartment. That afternoon, she showed me where the nursery schools were so Chris would be cared for while I went to school.

Jay and her husband spent time talking with me and helping me to start thinking about a career job so Chris and I could have a better life again. Jay and I had became good friends in a very short time

. Chris and I moved into our first apartment at the end of May 1977. It was a four-plex, with each unit having its own back gate and patio area. Ours had a plain cement slab with an old, weathered, board fence around it. There was an outside storage area with a washer and dryer hook-up that I hoped I would get to be use someday.

A fresh coat of white paint on the walls and deep rust color carpets added to the excitement of our first apartment together. The kitchen had the standard apartment-style dark, laminated cupboards, but the little pantry off the side was a welcome bonus.

I liked the see-through bar between the kitchen and the living room and the breakfast area with its window looking out to the patio. The stairway was partly open, with two bedrooms and a bath upstairs.

Each bedroom had a large window, although Chris's window overlooked the storage room rooftop, which wasn't much of a view.

I later learned that most of the kids in the complex shared the same rooftop view and used their windows as escape hatches to leap onto the storage roof then to the grass or patio below. I had a little talk with my son, and he assured me he would do no climbing or jumping out of windows.

I called Tony to give him our new phone number and address so that he could ship the furniture and the rest of our things.

Chris was excited about moving, mostly because there were other kids his age to play with—something he had never had living on the farm.

A week later, a huge moving van pulled up to our back gate. Our things had arrived at last! I kept busy unpacking boxes, hanging up clothes, and getting the place in order. Chris was busy making new friends, showing them all his toys, and of course looking at their toys.

The first night in our new apartment was filled with laughter as we played hide-and-seek in the boxes until they no longer resembled boxes. Chris explored his room and placed all his toys just where he wanted them. Our hamburgers and french fries sure tasted good that night. After a while, Chris climbed into my lap and settled back for the evening watching his favorite television program. It wasn't long before he was fast asleep.

Watching him sleep in my arms, I tried to guess what he was dreaming about by the expressions on his face. A good guess was he was catching bad guys and putting them in jail. Chris loved to play policeman. He wanted to be a cop when he grew up, and believe me, I hoped he would make it.

During breakfast the next morning, I would hear all about the fast police car chase and how he finally got them stopped. Then he had to arrest them and "put all these guys in jail." Occasionally he would have to rescue a poor girl and then she would fall in love with him and want to marry him.

By this time, I had gone through a couple of cups of coffee and his breakfast was cold, with little resemblance to what it started out as. I never forced him to eat. If he were hungry he would eat. Chris usually got most of it down, so I didn't worry too much.

Most of the next week we spent together getting the apartment in order, grocery shopping (which Mom insisted on springing for), and finding the right nursery school for Chris. After crossing out several discouraging attempts, we finally found the right one. It looked perfect from the outside, and when we walked inside, the receptionist offered a warm greeting. She gave us the grand tour and explained the rules to Chris. We thanked her for all the help, and I explained that my son and I needed a few minutes to discuss it and think it over.

Chris and I walked outside so we could sit in the truck and talk about the school. We always talked everything over and each had an equal say in any situation. We had to agree before making any decision that concerned our lives.

It worked best that way for us. Chris felt a sense of importance and maturity, knowing that he could be totally honest about his feelings and that I would respect them.

"Mommie, I like it here. Can I go to school here?"

Before I could answer, he had jumped up from the seat of the truck and was pointing.

"Look, Mommie. There is a big swing in the playground. I don't want to look anymore. I vote for this

school, OK?" He could hardly contain himself as he
pressed his hands to the window. Turning his head, he
looked at me with wide-eyed excitement, hoping that I'd
say "yes."

"It's OK by me. I just want you to be happy, Chris,
because you're going to have to be here when Mommie is
at her school. Okey-dokey?"

"I will be. I promise I'll be happy here. You know
what?"

"No, what?"

"Now we each have a school to go to. Let's go tell
Grandma Alice and then go swimming in her pool." Chris
bounced up and down on the truck seat several times and
wiggled around as if he had ants in his pants.

"OK, but first let's go back in and register you for
preschool and kindergarten in the fall."

His little face was beaming with excitement as I
signed the enrollment papers. The receptionist introduced
Chris's teacher to us. She was a little younger than I was,
bright and petite with the glow of life radiating from her
cheerful smile.

"Miss Karen, I would like you to meet your new pupil.
This is Christopher."

"Hi, Christopher. I'm Miss Karen. I'm sure glad you
decided to be in my class, because we have the most fun.
You know what?"

"What?"

"Sometimes I take my whole class to the movies in the
afternoon for a cartoon special. Do you like to go to the
movies?"

"Yes, when are you gonna go again?"

"In a couple of days. If you are here then, all your Mommie has to do is give you fifty cents and sign a piece of paper saying that it's all right for you to go."

Chris turned and looked up at me, rubbing his little hands together with anticipation. I placed my hand upon his head.

"Do you send it home with him the day before, or do I need to ask on the morning that I drop him off?"

"No, I'll send something home with him, and Chris can bring it with him in the morning."

"Sounds good to me, Karen, and thank you for all your time. Well, Chris, we'd better be going—"

"Mommie, can I stay here and play for a while with the other kids? Please!"

"What about telling Grandma Alice about your school and going swimming?"

"We can call and tell her tonight. I want to stay here and play, please."

"OK, if that's what you want, then I'll go and get some shopping done and pick you up in a couple of hours."

"Okey-dokey, crocodile! Mommie, will you buy me some bubble gum when you're at the store?"

I nodded yes and smiled. "Yes, my little bubble gum monster, I will." I kissed him good-bye.

6

On Our Own

Karen took Chris's hand, and the two of them started to walk down the hall toward her classroom. He turned around to wave good-bye with a big smile on his face.

"See you later, alligator. I'll buy the gum and see you about two hours from now."

As they walked to the classroom, I asked the receptionist if Karen had hurt her leg.

"No, Karen is handicapped. She has a disease that doesn't permit normal growth on the left side of her body, but she keeps on coming every day to work and going to school in the evening. She loves every minute with the kids and loves giving of herself in any way she can to them. She's a winner in my book."

I stood there at the receptionist's desk not knowing what to say. She excused herself and went to the supply cabinet to get some notepads. I stood silent, listening to children's laughter wafting from various classrooms. She returned and smiled. "Chris will love it here with Karen. She's very special."

Swallowing the lump in my throat, I responded. "She sure is, and she's a winner in my book, too. Well, take care, and I'll be back in a couple of hours for Chris. Thanks."

I turned and walked out the door to the truck with tears in my eyes. I knew Karen and Chris were going to be very good friends; I could just feel it in my heart. They had a common bond between them, something that words just couldn't describe, as they walked hand in hand, talking and laughing down the hall to the classroom.

With Chris safely and happily settled in his school, I decided to drive over to Scottsdale Community College (SCC) to register myself for classes and hopefully to talk with a counselor. I waited about an hour, watching many kids wander in and out of the student union building. Its shelves were packed full of books, and large tables housed a sea of studious faces reading and doing research.

When my name was called, I headed to the reception desk. The receptionist handed me a piece of paper and pointed to a room down the hallway. I knocked on the door, and a man's voice answered. Opening the door, I walked over and sat down in the chair beside his desk.

I explained my entire situation to him and asked for his honest opinion. We talked for almost another hour, finally deciding on Sociology for the first summer session and Art History for the second. I wasn't sure what I was in for, but I was willing to try.

With schedule in hand, I paused to have a cigarette and to think over everything the counselor had said. I walked around the campus for a little while to get the feel of it, then grabbed a cola and took a seat at one of the picnic tables outside the cafeteria.

I gave more thought to what the counselor had said about getting an associate degree in business, then transferring to Arizona State University for a bachelor degree. I was happy to have enrolled that afternoon in both classes. I picked up my books and relaxed in the cafeteria with a cup of coffee before I headed out to pick up Chris.

As I glanced through my Sociology text, part of me drifted back to my old friends back home. It crossed my mind that I would probably never see those old chums again.

The Illinois farm I had grown up on had been subdivided into new homes, and the home Tony and I had worked so hard to build would be sold shortly.

As I watched the kids come and go between classes, wearing shorts, T-shirts, and sneakers, I thought of springtime back home. The cold winter weather with snow frozen so hard that you could walk on it had melted away by now. The trees were surely thick with lush foliage, and the green grass covered the hillsides. The arrival of summer was just around the corner. I was thinking about Dad, too, and how much I wanted to put some flowers on his grave. I knew that it would be a few years before I would make it back there. It consoled me to know that he would understand.

The longer I sat there with my thoughts, the more I started to think about the name "Lynn." A student who stopped to chat with me had suggested that I adopt this new version of my name to go with my new life in the big city. Something was beginning to feel right about it. Although I remained Linda Joy to my family, and in soul and spirit, that afternoon, as I walked off the campus, part of me escaped into a new person—Lynn.

Chris loved his school and all his newfound friends. Karen would take the kids for weekly visits to movies or for a picnic in the park. She had a very special love for each child.

In time, summer session began for me at college. Everything went right over my head. Although the instructor was a doctor in the field of sociology and a very pleasant and intelligent woman, I didn't understand a word she said.

Two fellow classmates, Kay and Ed rescued me. We immediately became friends. Although the class was packed with students most seemed to just sit and listen. While on the other hand, it seemed like we were the only three in the class that offered an opinion on any subject that the instructor was talking about, although mine was more in question form than in opinions.

Kay invited me to study at her house, and it sounded good to me, because I needed all the help I could get. She was a little shorter than I was, with short red hair and a happy smile on her face that said, "welcome any time." We studied for several weeks together, which really helped me pull my grade up.

One evening during our study session, Kay's husband, Tommy, came home from work. He was a tall, lanky man with short, graying, wavy hair. He spoke with a southern Texan-style drawl. Chris was sleeping on the sofa wearing his trusty police badge, detective holster, and pistol. By his side lay his back-up toy rifle and riot helmet.

"Tommy, this is Lynn from my class. Remember I told you she has been studying with me?"

"Yeah, nice to meet you, Lynn. I'm Kay's poor deprived husband that never gets any respect around here," he joked.

"I'm sure that's not true. You have a wonderful family and a very beautiful home," I responded.

"Who is this little guy sleeping on my sofa?"

Tommy rested a hand on the back of the sofa and leaned over to regard the snoozing little boy decked out in police gear. Suddenly, Chris woke up, stared Tommy down, and then drew his gun.

"Freeze. I'm a cop." He surprised the grown man. "Stand against the wall over there, so I can frisk you."

Tommy had a hard time restraining his laughter, while Kay and I covered our mouths to withhold our own. While Chris frisked him, Tommy turned around and informed Chris that he, too, was a cop. He asked Chris's permission to reach in his pocket to get his badge.

Chris's eyes widened with excitement as he held Tommy's badge in one hand and shook Tommy's hand with the other. Chris had found another buddy. Me? I'd found two new friends.

The semester was over, and my sociology grade finally arrived in the mail. As I held the envelope in my hands, I prepared for the worst. Then I reminded myself that I had stuck it out until the end and that, regardless of the grade, I'd given it my best. "You won't know what you got unless you open it," I whispered, tearing open the mail.

A big beautiful B met my eyes. I felt extremely good about that and now was ready for the next summer session. I had three credits under my belt, with only sixty-one credits to go!

During the break between classes, Chris and I visited Old Tucson Movie Studios, Pioneer Village, and took long drives to explore the state of Arizona.

Back at the apartment complex, we found most of the people to be very friendly. One couple had a little boy named Derrick. Our boys became terrific friends and played together almost all the time. Some of the other children became playmates until they found out Chris had leukemia. Their parents wouldn't allow them to play with Chris anymore, in fear that their children might "catch it," although the disease was not contagious.

During dinner one evening, Chris looked up at me with a sad, puzzled expression.

"Why won't the other kids' moms let them play with me?"

It was hard to explain to an almost-five-year old why he couldn't play with certain children, but I tried.

"Mommie, they said their moms won't let them play with me 'cause I'm sick, and they might get sick, too. Is that true?"

"No, it's not true, Christopher. Derrick is your friend, and so are his Mommie and Daddy. They know that you have leukemia. If the other kids are afraid, then just let them be afraid." I paused. "Christopher, nobody is going to catch anything."

Clearing the table and stacking the dishes in the sink, I was hoping the topic of conversation would change.

"Mommie, how did I get leukemia anyway?" he asked me. "And when are we going to go home where Daddy lives?"

"I'll tell you what. You go and wash your hands and face, and we'll talk about it, OK?"

As I leaned up against the kitchen wall, closing my eyes, his tiny legs scrambled up the staircase.

"Oh, Lord, please help me find the words to answer his question. Lord, what if he asks me if he is going to die? What do I say? Yes, in about three years, or no, everything is going to be terrific, then when the time comes, have him say, 'You lied to me, Mommie'?"

His tiny legs scrambled back down the stairs almost as fast as he had gone up them.

"Here I am, Mommie, with Billy Bear. He's been sick, too. Do you think we need to take him to see Dr. Baranko, too?"

I picked him up and carried the boy and the bear to the sofa. We sat together talking, and he repeated what his friends had said. The little tears trickling down his cheek spoke louder than his words.

Brushing the hair from his forehead, I asked, "Chris, you like your doctor, don't you?"

"Sure I do; he's my friend."

"Yes, he is your friend and buddy, and he gives you the best of himself, doesn't he?"

Chris wiped his eyes with Billy Bear's ears, nodded, and turned to listen some more.

"Your doctor gives you medication, shots, and tests. I know you don't like them, but it is the only way he has to check your blood and make sure the good guys or cops are fighting the bad guys."

"Mommie, I know, like when the police fight the bad guys. They have guns, cars, choppers, and stuff."

"That's right, Chris. The medications Dr. Baranko gives you are kind of like that, helping to fight off the bad guys, the bad leukemia cells. See that book on the end table? Can you get it for me?"

He jumped off my lap and returned in seconds with the book, snuggling back into his original position.

We found an illustration of the entire blood system, and I showed him where the blood was produced in his body, where it went and what it did. Chris pointed to the leg in the picture.

"That's where my doctor gives me the bone marrow test, Mommie. Right there."

"That's right, because that is where the blood is made. See, he has to get some of the blood before it goes to your body to fight the bad guys. This way he can find out how strong it is and if he needs to give you different pills to help your good blood get stronger."

"Mommie, why does he have to give me pokies in the back? Are the bad guys there, too?"

I gave it some thought, and then I replied, pointing to the drawing.

"Well, this is the spinal column. There is fluid inside it, and sometimes the bad guys get inside and hide there. So your doctor has to find out if they are there. The doctors don't know why people get leukemia," I continued. "If they did, they could cure it." Chris and Billy Bear listened intently. "Don't worry about the other kids playing with you. You have lots of friends at school and Derrick to play with here."

He seemed to be satisfied with our talk. At least he didn't have any more questions for me, just a final statement. "But, I still don't like those two pokies—the bone marrow one in the leg and the spinal tap one in the back. They hurt!"

By this time, most of Chris's hair had fallen out from the chemotherapy and radiation treatments over the past several months. This created a problem at times with the other kids making fun of him. I had no idea how to resolve this dilemma.

"Chris, do you want to go horseback riding Saturday? Mommie found a stable not too far from here."

"Can we go get a cowboy hat, boots, and stuff?"

"I think I might be able to arrange that, just for you. After all, we don't want to look like two city slickers, now do we?"

At the top of his lungs he shouted, "NEATO!"

The Saturday morning shopping spree was filled with laughter. We managed to round up a cowboy hat, boots, jeans, Western shirt, and a belt. Saturday afternoon we were off to the stables. He was thrilled by the prospect of the horse ride. He stood up in the truck hoping to get there sooner by telling the cars to get out of our way. Once we arrived at the stables, Chris rode a little pony with a lead rope next to the guide. I followed behind on a gentle horse. The two of them got along famously as we rode for about an hour.

They weren't very busy that day, so the guide gave Chris the grand ranch tour. He showed him the tack house, then the big barn where all the horses were kept.

Chris had a ball with the guide, and I got the impression that the guide enjoyed it, too. Too soon it was time for us to leave. I thanked the guide for his time and kindness and Chris shook hands with all the cowboys. "We'll see you later," Chris told the guide. "Save my horse for me when I come back. He's a good horse."

Chris kicked the dirt with his cowboy boots as we traveled the parking lot towards the truck. "Mommie," he asked, "Can we go get some pizza? I know we ate out last night, but can we? Please!"

"Sounds like a winner to me, Chris. Come on. I'll race you to the truck. The last one there has to drive."

"Mommie, you're losing it," he joked, "I can't drive."

We stopped at our favorite little pizza place just up the street from home. While listening to Chris talk about his adventure-filled day, all I could think about was peeling off those boots, sliding into a hot bubble bath, and then falling off to sleep.

Once we'd made it home and I got Chris ready for bed, I tucked Billy Bear in beside him then rubbed his little bald head and kissed him goodnight. A little later I settled in myself, but not before having a talk with my friend.

"God, help me make each day special, like today, for my Chris."

On a hot July day, Chris arrived home from school announcing that he wasn't going to go back to school ever again. When I asked him what was wrong, he just lay in his bed and cried.

"I don't like those kids any more! I hate them, and I'm never going back there, Mommie. Never. And you can't make me."

"Chris," I began carefully. "I'm not going to make you go back there. I just want to know what happened."

I picked him up and held him in my arms, rubbing his back and trying to take the hurt away. He looked at me with tears streaming down his face, his checks flushed from anger. I carried him into the bathroom and got a cool washcloth to wipe his face. I took him into my room and sat down in the big overstuffed chair.

"Mommie, please take me to another school where there aren't any kids."

"Sweetheart, stop crying, and tell Mommie what happened today at school."

Chris sniffled in the tears and told me his story. "The kids called me names and made fun of me because I don't have any hair. I wish I wasn't sick, then I'd still have my hair, and the kids would play with me."

I took a deep breath and tried to explain that many people were bald. I told him that his hair would grow back in no time. My words were sincere, but they didn't help take away the hurt or dry any tears.

"Jesus, help me!" I silently pleaded for his help.

"I hate it there! I hate it there! I'm never going back there again, and you can't make me!"

"Chris," I attempted playing an ace I'd suddenly found up my sleeve, "Who is your favorite television person?"

"The bald cop that eats lollipops."

I pointed out that his favorite policeman was bald as the globe and nobody dared to make fun of him. Chris defended his side of the case.

"He's a movie star and a policeman. Nobody is going to make fun of him! He's not a little boy like me."

"Well, aren't you a policeman, too?"

Chris nodded his head and wiped his tears with the washcloth as he sat on my lap sobbing.

"Then why don't you play 'the bald cop' for a while, until your hair grows back? Then you can go back to being a policeman driving a squad car around the city."

He looked up at me with confusion, anticipating my next phrase.

"I'll tell you what. Let's go to the shopping center and get a brand new hat or stocking cap and a big bag of lollipops. You can wear your police stuff to school, and when they start calling you names, you just give them a lollipop, smile, and tell them to have a nice day. Remember what Jesus said in the Bible? He told us to 'love our enemies.' "

"But what if they still don't like me?"

"Chris, they won't say bad things anymore. Mommie has lots of faith that Jesus will be right there beside you. Just remember that we both love you very much. Now let's go shopping! OK?"

He was a happy little boy again, especially after the con job he did on me in the toy store.

The next day, I had a talk with Miss Karen, explaining Chris's situation and the extra police stuff that accompanied him that morning. She smiled and understood completely. I thanked her and said good-bye to my "mini cop."

Chris was a bigger hit at school the next day than I had ever expected. Even after the lollipops had been devoured, the kids just wanted to be his friend.

"Thanks, Jesus."

7

A Family Apart

August 8, 1977, was Christopher's fifth birthday. Of course there was a grand celebration commemorating the occasion. Along with a cake homemade by my mom, the presents piled on the table were just waiting to be devoured.

The new clothes didn't excite him, but the police helmet, little plastic police car, toy police badge, and gun set were a hit. The grandparents had chipped in to get a battery-operated patrol car, and it got all the attention. On all fours, Chris chased the car all over the kitchen floor, under the table, through the chairs, and even into the laundry room.

His birthday was a special day for all of us, but most of all it was a day of smiles and laughter from Chris and for Chris.

That night he had all his new toys lined up beside the bed waiting for his awakening in the morning.

"Mommie, which present did Daddy send me?"

"Well, honey, your Daddy is probably bringing his present with him when he comes."

"I wonder what it is?"

"Well, we'll just have to wait and see, won't we? You go to sleep now; it's been a busy day, and you're a tired little boy."

"I love you, Mommie. Good night."

"Good night, Chris, and happy birthday, sweetheart. I love you, too, very much."

Our first summer in Phoenix was slowly ending along with the blistering heat. Chris's hair grew back. He continued to attend the same school. It had a kindergarten program in which I had enrolled him for the fall. Karen was still teaching, and their friendship had grown even deeper. Our home in Illinois had sold, and Tony had come for a visit and brought a present. He stayed for about two weeks.

During this time I made a peculiar discovery about the house that Tony and I had sold to his parents. Years before, we had sold our house to them and moved away hoping to put our marriage back together. A year or so later, Tony and I built them a new home and bought ours back, or so we thought. Apparently, the deed to the house had remained in his parents' name.

"Linda, I don't know what happened," Tony began as we were sitting at the kitchen table filling up the ashtray. The sound of country oldies provided the background music.

"All I know is, when it came time to sign papers at the bank, Mom told me that I didn't have to go to the bank, that my signature wasn't needed. Our house was solely in their names."

Listening to him, it came back to me. I recalled the urge to personally go through all the paperwork myself and make sure that it was right; I'd chosen not to because they were part of my family, and I trusted them.

I took a deep breath and looked out the window, watching Chris play on the patio with his friend Derrick. My eyes turned to Tony as I offered a sad smile.

"Tony, I know you don't know what happened. I don't either, except that it happened. Do you want some more coffee?"

"Yes, please."

I poured us another cup, wondering what to say next. Tony broke the silence. "There is a profit on the house. Mom and Dad gave me $10,000 of it, and they somehow figure the rest belongs to them. When I get back home, I will send $7,000 to help you and Chris."

"That will help us all right, and thanks. I know you feel bad, but there's nothing we can do now. What's done is done, Tony. Don't worry about it, OK?"

We sat sipping our coffee until Tony blew my mind yet again. "Linda, did you know that I had rented a house for us when we came back from our honeymoon, but that Mom talked me out of it? She said that we could save money by building a house and living on the farm with them."

I was shocked. "Tony, why didn't you ever tell me this before?"

He shrugged his shoulders and shook his head, the regret leaking through his brown eyes.

"I don't know. I guess I didn't think about it until now."

Tony's face was full of anger towards the situation about our house and remorse that he hadn't moved into that rented house when we were starting our marriage. I could see he felt badly enough about everything as he sipped his coffee.

Once the tensions had faded, we changed directions and sat talking about keeping our little family together, at least while Chris was still alive. We talked about living situations and money. Tony was a welder with a big company back home, and he farmed with his parents.

"My uncle has made some contacts and lined up some interviews if you want to try to stay here. All I have to do is call him and let him know that you want to stay."

"I don't know if I can do it," Tony said. "I don't know if I can handle it because our insurance won't transfer if I quit my job in Illinois, Linda, but I'll try if you want me to."

Chris opened the door and informed us that Derrick had to go home and asked "what's for dinner?"

The next morning the three of us set our sails to the wind, driving down the streets of Phoenix looking up addresses. In the truck, Chris climbed up and sat on his father's lap, happily watching and chatting away about all the places and things we'd done and seen, as I drove.

The three of us spent the next couple of days, worn-out city map baking on the dash of the truck, going to interviews, but nothing came of it. No job was found.

In the evenings, we were the happy little family unit, playing, laughing, and reading bedtime stories. After Chris fell asleep, Tony and I spent almost every night of the two weeks talking.

Tony spent most of the time crying. He just couldn't handle what was happening. I couldn't blame him. Our seven-year-old marriage was pretty much over now. It was just a matter of time. There was never any anger or bitterness between us. We just grew in two different directions, and now we were living in two different states.

One night just before Tony was scheduled to fly home, we had a good heart-to-heart talk.

"Tony, I know you are hurt by everything that is happening to you. You're trying to make the right decision to please others. You're still torn between your parents and Chris and me. What do you want to do? What is going to make *you* happy? I know what I have to do. I have to stay here and see Chris through this, but you don't. I will not hate you if you decide to go back to Illinois."

He looked up at me with tears in his eyes, trying hard to find the right words. Then with a shaky, tearful voice, he said, "I think I can do more good from back there. I can't handle it out here. I can't even handle driving in the traffic. I don't feel as if I'm needed here. You have always handled everything so well. You just seem to know what to do. I love our son, and I want so much to be with him, but I can't watch him die."

I reached out to him and we held each other. There we sat on the floor crying like two little kids. I felt so much pain coming from him. It was upsetting for Tony, wanting to be with us but frustrated by the knowledge that he couldn't be. After a few minutes, I finally found the words to speak through the tears.

"Tony, I think it's best that you go back home and help us from there. Chris and I will be fine out here. I have Mom and the grandparents to help me. Your parents need you on the farm. They won't make it without you. We have had our problems—I can't deny that—and our marriage isn't the best. All in all, I feel it is for the best for you and me. We will call, and you can talk to Chris on the phone. If his health permits, maybe he can visit you back there. You know that you can visit anytime and will always have a place to stay. I'll send you his school pictures, and I'll take snapshots of him so you will have something to hold onto."

That night we parted as good friends, with Chris the only bond between us. I knew once Chris's life was over, I would never see Tony again.

Shortly after Tony returned home, I received a check for $7,000. In his letter he said, "It should be more, but at least this will help make things right."

I called Illinois, hoping to reach Tony, but his mother answered the phone. I could picture her standing in the kitchen, stirring something on the stove. Just as I'd seen her do many times before, I imagined her stretching the phone cord over the table and across the room as she pulled out a chair to sit down by the double kitchen window.

Tony's mother was a short, dark-haired woman who always seemed to have a three-cornered, red handkerchief tied around her head. Behind the smile she usually had on her face was a very determined woman who was going to get what she wanted. She usually wore pants and a large blouse with the shirttail out.

"Hi, how are things back there?" I said, projecting a happy state.

"We're fine, just fixing dinner. How is my little Chris?"

"He is doing much better now. The doctor is encouraged with his progress. I guess Tony filled you in on everything that is going on out here?"

She paused for a moment before answering. "Yes, he did, and I can't believe it."

"Is Tony there? I need to talk to him about the insurance papers."

Her tone went from bad to worse. "No, he isn't, and I am not sure when he'll be back home. I'll tell him you called."

I figured now was as good a time as any to ask the big question. "By the way," I attempted, "I have a question for you. What happened to the rest of the money from the sale of our house?"

A long silence followed, and then she cleared her throat. Our conversation lasted only a minute, then I hung up the phone. Sadness for her washed over me—the only feeling I had at that moment.

I had tried to explain once again that I couldn't take Chris back there, because he would die. There was no medical help available in the small town of Kewanee to handle leukemia. The closest help was in Chicago or at St. Jude in Tennessee.

She told me she didn't believe Chris was even sick. I got the feeling from the conversation that she thought I just wanted to stay in Phoenix and that I was making the whole thing up. My heart was torn for her.

I felt that maybe she was in denial and this was the only way she could deal with Chris's situation. Someday, she would have to face the truth, but by then it would be too late.

After Tony's check cleared, I returned the money I had borrowed from Mom while living with her, plus the $500 she'd loaned me to get into our own place. I knew she wasn't worried about getting the money back, but it was something I had to do.

Chris was such a little man, at times, I truly thought he was taking care of me more than I was him.

On Sunday morning at church, Chris's brand new suit had him scratching like mad. The more I asked him to stop scratching, the more the pants itched. Finally, with the entire congregation in total silence, Chris voiced his opinion.

"But, Mommie, they itch me!" I couldn't help smiling as light laughter filled the church. The priest was leaving to walk down the aisle, and he turned and gave Chris a wink. Naturally, Chris repaid the favor.

Chris and I had lunch out that day, and later we went for a ride in the mountains, but not before we went home to change clothes.

In the fall, Chris started kindergarten, and I obtained a part-time job through Scottsdale Community College working in the accounting department at a hotel in Scottsdale. It didn't pay much, but it was a start. My first paycheck was $87.38, and to Chris and I it seemed like a million.

Every Friday night, Chris and I would dress up and go to a little restaurant or our pizza place. He had his own wallet, and I would give him money before we left home to pay for our dinner that night.

He'd get the biggest kick out of paying the check and leaving a tip. I would always check and see what he'd left because he wasn't too experienced at figuring out the value and denomination of the bills.

The wait staff would joke with him, gifting him with extra mints and asking Chris if he would be back to see them again next Friday. We didn't have much, but what we had was much more than anything money could buy.

The insurance covered most of the medical bills, and Tony took care of the rest. Although, the bills never stopped coming, I finally got it straight with the hospital to send the statements directly to Tony. There were numerous extras that the insurance didn't cover. I had to pay up front for most of it and then wait for reimbursement. It was becoming quite apparent that I needed a bigger paycheck. I feared that I would have to quit school and work full time. I hoped that I might stretch things out enough to at least finish the semester.

The woman who owned our complex had decided to sell it. Chris and I had to move, but we eventually found a huge one bedroom, where both beds would fit, which was also cheaper.

I took Chris over to Mom's for a couple of days, so I could get moved more quickly. I managed to get almost everything moved except the bulky, heavy stuff like the television, sofa, beds, dresser, and kitchen table.

After returning to the old place, during a last run, I walked in, looked around, and sat down in the middle of the room wondering how I was going to get the rest of the things moved by myself.

The missionary boys that had come to call a few days prior phoned and asked if they could stop by and visit.

"It's kind of a bad time," I explained. "I'm right in the middle of moving. Maybe another time, guys."

"Do you need any help? We'll be happy to lend some manpower if you need it."

"I sure do! I was just wondering how I was going to get the heavy stuff moved. I've got a pickup truck but can't lift the stuff by myself."

The boys arrived within thirty minutes, and in about half an hour we finished moving. I thanked them for their help, and they were gone.

Chris and I spent the next couple of days getting everything in order again. We set up beds, put away dishes, and hung up wrinkled clothes. My little helper had fun opening all the boxes and unwrapping everything, toys first, of course.

Chris held the screwdriver and bolts while I fumbled to put the beds together. He had fun kicking the newspapers out of the way as his little suntanned legs carried the sofa cushions, which were bigger than he was.

He helped me in the kitchen, putting things away in the bottom cupboards. I eventually found all my dishes, cookware, bathroom towels, and a couple of shoes that I thought had been thrown out with the newspapers.

In general, we had a lot of fun making a home out of a simple apartment. Again, we enjoyed our hamburgers, fries, and colas as we watched television before going to bed exhausted.

The complex was in an older two-story building, with a horrible lime-green trim. Two L-shaped buildings surrounded the pool and play yard. The place looked as though it had been an old motel in its better days. Still, it was cheap and clean.

I kept trying to tell myself that after the kitchen rugs were done and the place was fixed up, it wouldn't look so bad. I didn't have enough rugs to cover the whole floor, but at least they hid part of it.

The manager had just replaced the rug in our unit with a light tan carpet. The big kitchen included plenty of cupboard space and storage. I thought he should have replaced the kitchen tile when he did the carpet. They were ugly tan with orange, pink, and green speckles, probably dating back to the Fourteenth Century.

The living room window was a problem. Anybody walking by on the sidewalk could glance in. I had to either keep the drapes closed all the time or keep the living room cleaned up all the time. Somehow I'd adjust. I learned later why it was so affordable. We were living in a high crime area. Wonderful!

8

Life in the Big City

Chris loved the new place, especially the play yard and swimming pool. We hadn't been there forty-eight hours before he stood in the living room with his swimming trunks on and a towel around his neck. "Mommie, can we go swimming now?"

About two weeks after we'd moved into the apartment, I came home from school, walked into the kitchen, and found candy and a toy on the kitchen table. I couldn't figure out where it had come from. I went up to the manager's apartment and asked if he had seen anybody around my place.

"No, just me."

Feeling like I'd been vandalized, I stared at him, stunned. His wife came from the kitchen and stood in the doorway holding a dishtowel as she listened to our conversation.

"What do you mean, just you?"

"I went into your apartment and put some candy and a toy on the table for Chris. I wanted to check on the apartment and make sure everything was OK."

I tried to remain calm and explain the situation with Chris's health to him. After all, I didn't want any trouble from him or his wife.

"Chris isn't allowed to have candy unless I give it to him." Trying to hold my temper, yet keep a firm tone of authority, I added, "The toy is fine, but could you please wait and give it to him when you see him in person? Please!"

I was hoping he had gotten the message. We lived about six doors down from his place. I closed the drapes and sat down on the sofa, feeling violated. I looked around the apartment to see if anything was disturbed and then felt guilty for even thinking he would take anything. I tried to convince myself that he was just a nice old man trying to do something for Chris. As caretaker, he had the right to inspect things, but he should have asked me first.

I didn't like the uncomfortable feeling I felt, though, when he would sit by the pool and watch us swimming. I consoled myself that we wouldn't be renting there forever. I left to pick up Chris and headed over to Mom's for dinner and a much-needed family visit.

A week later, the same thing happened again, this time without the candy. I couldn't believe it. This time I checked to see if anything was missing. I didn't go up and have another talk with him, because I really didn't know what to say. I left to go and pick up Chris, then drove over to Mom's again for dinner and a visit. Mom and I talked while Chris entertained the grandparents.

"You know, I think I need some help around here. Taking care of the grandparents and this house is wearing me out. I hardly have time to sit down before it's time to cook another meal. I just don't know what to do about anything anymore."

"Why don't you hire someone to come in and clean a couple of times a month or so? That way you won't be tied up so much."

"Yes, I've thought about that. I called a couple of people today to see what they charge, but it's the cooking, shopping, and waiting on three people all day long, Linda Joy. It's getting me down. I can't help it, but it is."

"Listen, why don't you think about Grandma Vie coming to live with Chris and me? That way you only have your parents to take care of, and you could hire someone to come in and clean this house for you."

"Boy, wouldn't Vie like that! She'd think she was in heaven having Chris around all the time."

"Mom, it would be helping me, too. I would have a built-in baby sitter and could cut back on the day care center. I could even get some extra hours at work and save a little money."

I figured it would also discourage my "friendly" apartment manager from doing his thing, but I didn't tell Mom about that; she had enough to worry about.

A few weeks passed. Mom called and said that they talked it over with Grandma, and she loved the idea of moving in with us. I told the apartment manager that I would like to move into one of the two-bedroom apartments as soon as possible.

That afternoon, I started carrying things to the upstairs apartment. It was the same layout except with dark green carpet and, of course, an extra bedroom.

One of the maintenance men from work offered to help with the heavy furniture. Within a couple of days, we were resettled and ready for Grandma.

Grandma used her walker most of the time to get around. A heavyset woman, rather large boned, with blondish-silver hair combed straight back, she always wore a gray hair net. She liked dressing in pink and blue flowered cotton dresses with a full kitchen apron. There were a few minor adjustments to make in sharing a two-bedroom, one-bath apartment, but we managed very well.

When we had lived in Moline, most of the neighbor kids loved to play on the big hill and in the ravine behind Grandma's house. She would sit and watch us for hours and sometimes come down to help us build a camp or take us for walks in the woods. She never failed to have a big pitcher of our favorite drink, cookies, and sandwiches for all of us.

Grandma offered to kick in some money every month to help with food. She enjoyed taking care of Chris, and he loved waiting on her, because she would read him stories all the time. They had fun playing school, counting numbers with Chris's large blackboard that I had bought for them.

Things went smoothly for the next two months. We took Grandma with us when we went exploring. Sometimes she had a hard time walking due to a lame leg. Chris loved the zoo, so we would rent a wheelchair for

Grandma and push her so she could share the experience and enjoy everything.

The weather grew chilly. Christmas was quickly approaching, and the snowless streets were decorated with red, green, and silver holiday trimmings. The stores were trimmed festively with decorated trees and many beautiful things to buy. The three of us looked at the window displays while walking through the malls.

We trimmed a little tree that year with our handmade decorations. With some glue and a rainbow of construction paper, we had a ball making a paper chain long enough to go around the living room twice.

Chris cut out and colored the bells I'd drawn. Grandma laughed and joined in the fun of coloring, painting, and pasting.

Together with the multicolored lights and tree ornaments Mom had given us, we decked the halls with our handmade treasures. By the time we'd finished, we had a very merry apartment.

When the fall semester ended, I accepted the offer of a full-time position at work. We needed the money more than I needed an education at that time in our lives.

I still had some of the money from Tony left, but I knew it wouldn't last long. Besides, I felt guilty about studying at night instead of being with Chris. I became tired of rushing through dinner so I could clear the table and study. I found myself wanting to be in the living room with him and Grandma, sharing what time they both had left together, enjoying the laughter and fun of being a family.

A week before finals, I had made my difficult
decision; school would have to wait. I would have to
forget about an education for a while. I resigned myself to
get through my finals with what little time I had to study.

To my delight, I passed with a B average. It was
bittersweet walking away from school. But it was the right
thing to do.

There weren't many presents under the tree that year.
Mom had brought Chris a couple of toys and some
clothes. I wished I had more for him. Then just before
Christmas Day, a check came from the Leukemia
Foundation for $50. I couldn't believe it! What a gift from
heaven it was! (I later found out that Sister Madonna
Maria was the instigator.) Before I picked Chris up from
school the next day, I bought presents, wrapped them up,
and placed them under the tree.

After school we all went out to eat. Chris was thrilled
upon arriving home to find all the presents beneath the
tree. He whole-heartedly accepted the story that Santa
Claus had came early that year.

"There are so many kids and presents that it is very
hard to do everything in one night," I'd told him.

I had saved a few special packages for Christmas
morning, so Chris would be surprised to find even more
presents when he awoke and rushed out to the Christmas
tree to open his gifts.

By Saturday, we were back to normal again. While
cleaning the apartment, I noticed Chris putting a pile of
toys in the center of his room.

"What are you doing, Chris?"

"I'm cleaning my room; can't you tell?" The pile continued to grow. "Mommie," he said. "Can I give these toys to those two little boys in the other apartment?"

A few doors down lived a family that hardly had furniture to sit on, let alone money to buy toys for Christmas. I had talked to them many times, and I didn't think they would mind if we showed up with a box of toys and some clothes that Chris had outgrown.

"Tell you what. Let's get that big box from storage, and you can put the toys in it. Then we will ask them. OK?"

"Go get the box, Mommie. I'm not done cleaning yet. Can we go and get the hamburger in the box that the toy comes in?"

"I think we can do that. I also think we have earned it. Don't you?"

Chris's face lit up with a big smile. He clapped his hands and sang to himself as he piled up more toys for our two little neighbors.

After we had stuffed the box full, we took it to our neighbor family. The two little kids were totally thrilled, and the parents were completely overwhelmed. Chris showed them how everything worked and which little toy people, cars, trucks, and cows went with each set of toys.

Over a cup of coffee, I got to know Carol and her brother Mike better. During the conversation, I asked them if they'd had any problems with the manager coming into their apartment.

"No, but others have." Carol explained, "I don't work, and that's probably why he has never come in here. He only goes into apartments when nobody is home. I watched him one day in that apartment across from us. I saw him opening drawers and going from the living room to the kitchen."

Shocked, I listened in awe to her story. "I guess he wandered into the bedroom, because I didn't see him again until he'd left the apartment. I knew the girl that lived there. Some money and a ring were missing. She moved out shortly after that and filed a police report."

About two months later, Carol and her brother moved, too.

The following Sunday, our apartment was honored by yet another visit while Grandma, Chris, and I were out exploring. This time he walked off with a camera that I had borrowed from Mom, some loose change, and Chris's piggy bank. The bank was filled with silver dollars we had been saving to take a trip to an entertainment theme park. I would buy the dollars from work and give them to him for his bank. We had about $110 saved.

I called the police and made out a report, but they said there wasn't much they could do. Although the police had a talk with the manager, nothing came of it.

That night as I went to sleep on the sofa, I had a hard time sleeping. I figured that the perpetrator must have known my schedule, because Sunday was the only day our apartment was ever empty. But something didn't sit right. It wasn't like the manager to take things that someone might see him carrying from the apartment. But who else could have gotten in without a key? The door showed no signs of forced entry, and the window's wooden rods were still in the track.

I was rapidly becoming a basket case, trying to work and make ends meet, fearing for our own safety, and wondering how long Chris would stay in remission.

I had filed for divorce a couple of months earlier, but there were some details to work out. With Tony's out-of-state residence, who should pay the medical bills for Chris's illness that the insurance didn't cover?

One night, everything seemed to hit me at once. The entire year raced through my mind at lightning speed as I lay trying to ease my back, which ached from sleeping on the sofa for the past two and one-half months. Most of the time I would put the cushions on the floor and sleep. At least I could straighten out and fall asleep faster that way.

We'd already spent one year of our "ball game" together. I knew that Chris's first strike, the time when he would go out of remission, was rapidly approaching. Chris and I tried to live through our explorations of the state of Arizona. He danced and laughed, while I dug in my heels, as we played that baseball game together. I dreaded the second strike, which put us that much closer to strike three—the end of the game.

I'd heard about an opening at work at one of the other properties and asked if I could transfer. It paid a little more, and I thought it I would be a great opportunity to get away from the memories of everything that had happened. I got the job as a front-desk clerk in a beautiful Scottsdale resort.

On February 7, 1978, I got my divorce in the Superior Court of Arizona, Maricopa County. A couple weeks later, I got to thinking heavily about Dad's death. I asked

Grandma to watch Chris for a while, as I needed to take care of some business. I drove to the parish that Chris and I attended and parked the truck directly in front of the huge wooden double doors.

I sat there resting my arms on the steering wheel, gazing at the door. I rolled down the window and had a couple of cigarettes trying to get up enough nerve to go in. A myriad of thoughts ran through my mind.

"Go back home. The doors are locked at this time of night. You're just making a fool of yourself sitting here at 8:00 p.m. in the dark. Just go home, stupid."

Then my thoughts changed. *"You won't know if the doors are locked until you try them. You have to get out of the truck and try. You have to make yourself do it. Don't let yourself be defeated by doubt and unbelief."*

I opened the door of the truck and walked up to the double doors. To my delight, they were unlocked.

Inside, the church was dim and had a calm, loving spirit about it. I stood just inside the second set of doors looking at the statue of Christ hanging on the cross at the far end. Small lights on each side of Christ made the image appear live.

With my knees shaking, I walked down the aisle, skipping all the formalities that went with Sunday morning mass. As I stood before the cross looking up at Jesus, tears fell down my cheeks. I didn't speak for a while; I only listened to the quiet, soft words that spoke slowly to my heart.

"I love you very much, my child. I have heard your prayers and seen your tears. Trust in me; I will make you strong."

I wiped my face with my hands, then wiped the dampness off on my blue jeans. I spoke in a weak, shaking voice.

"Why is all this happening to me? Why does Chris have to be sick? Why can't we have a happy life? Why did you give me a son if you are only going to take him away? Lord, I guess you never intended me to be a mother, did you?"

By this time, I was sitting on the floor looking up at the cross of Jesus, still wiping my cheeks. Only a few tears came now. I was more calm.

I stood up, still looking at the cross, smiled, and then turned and walked out the doors to my truck. Driving home, feeling both physically drained and emotionally peaceful, I just wanted to climb into bed and go to sleep without dreaming.

Once inside the apartment, I peeked into the dimly lit bedrooms, checking on Chris and then Grandma. Quietly closing the doors to their bedrooms, I tossed my cushions from the sofa onto the floor and lay down. Staring up at the ceiling, I listened to my heart pound and wondered what adventure awaited tomorrow.

As Grandma Vie always said, "A little bit of good comes out of everything, if you look for it." The sentence kept repeating itself through my mind. My mental response was, "It's going to take a long time and a lot of hard looking to find any good in this situation, but then again, I know we should be thankful for what we have, because there are many people worse off than we are. And I am thankful."

9

A Trip With Daddy

I made some new friends in connection with the new job and learned many new skills. It was such a lovely and peaceful resort, Chris and I often strolled the grounds on my days off. The resort was mostly for winter visitors taking up residence for several months at a time, so we got to know the guests personally. It was set on three gorgeous acres, dotted by a variety of beautiful, mature trees. A little bridge spanned a brook running beneath mighty tree branches. Part of the brook was blocked off to form a little pond that housed several giant goldfish.

Rich, lavish flowers were bordered by bluish green grass manicured to perfection. Each guest "casita" boasted a rear private patio with desert landscaping. The front of each patio faced the courtyard of this oasis in the desert. The buildings were a mixture of Old Spanish and Southwestern architecture, especially the restaurant located in the center of the property surrounded by lush tropical plants nestled under palm trees.

The tall pillars and round domes that stretched towards the light blue sky reminded Chris of his favorite bedtime story of magic lamps, flying carpets, and genie sailors.

I worked in a building with white stucco walls that had Spanish tile and large windows framed in old mahogany. As Chris and I walked down the hallway, we would breathe in the rich aroma of the Old World, mixed with the sweet scent of flowers filtering through the open windows. I envisioned being in another part of the world. The heels of our shoes would click against the Spanish tile floor as we made our daily stroll to the goldfish pond.

Oversized double doors guarded the entrance to the lobby as if to keep out the fast-paced world. Another set of doors opened into the lush courtyard and sprawling grounds. It was sunny almost all the time in Arizona so both sets of doors were left open to let the warm spring breeze flow through the building. The aroma of the flowers filtering in provided a peaceful, tranquil atmosphere.

I used to wonder what it would be like to walk through those doors as a guest, to enter the resort without a care in the world, to really relax by the pool, to dine in the fancy restaurants whenever I so desired, and then to return to a little villa fixed up just as Chris and I wanted.

Chris liked to climb up into the huge, brown leather wing-back chairs offering cheery "hellos" to the guests as they waved to him en route to their villas. I would often ponder the beaming smile on Chris's face as he sat like a proper little gentleman wearing an uncontrollable grin as he watched the guests pass by.

Chris always had a special "hello" for the two women I worked with, Kim and Christie, as well as a hug for Joyce, who ran the little gift shop in the corner, and Jane, who juggled reservations.

The tennis courts were behind the main lobby. One day the manager gave us permission to use the courts. "But, if the guests want to play tennis," he explained, "you will have to give up the court."

Chris rubbed his hands together with excitement and accepted on behalf of Kim, Christie, and me, as we proceeded to the courts. That day, as well as most others to follow, we did more chasing than hitting the ball across the net. We provided such entertainment for the guests that they wouldn't let us turn over the courts to them.

Several tours came through that summer, mainly European. Most of the tour members spoke English very well, so we got along fine although I didn't speak any other language. I found that I enjoyed learning about their countries and customs as much as they enjoyed sharing them with me. Since the tour guides made trips about every three weeks, the staff got to know them pretty well.

Joyce, who ran the gift shop, was like a second mother to all the girls behind the desk. Although she gave us the same advice that our own mothers had given us, somehow we would listen to her. Chris talked to her for hours as he sat on the stool behind her counter, watching her arrange the display case.

Joyce was short, heavyset, and middle-aged, with straight black, short hair. Something about her expression made you believe that if she asked you a question, you were compelled to tell her the truth. When it came to

Joyce, there was no getting away with anything. One day, during a slow period, I sat, with my arms crossed, on a stool behind the front desk, daydreaming out the window.

Joyce walked by and said, "Everything is going to be fine. Trust in Jesus. He loves you very much." I looked up and smiled as she continued on her way to the gift shop, doing more talking with her hands than her voice. At that point, she knew very little about my life, but from then on we talked a lot.

Grandma Vie was doing pretty well, but the steps to the apartment were getting to her. It was getting harder and harder to help her up and down the staircase. I knew it was time to move again, but I really didn't want to move back downstairs. Most of the people I'd made friends with had left the complex, and I'd had it with the manager.

Cleaning and back-flushing Mom's pool one day, I mentioned that I was going to start looking for another place.

All the "kids" were in the pool playing. Chris had become quite the swimmer. The two grandmas were lounging in their plastic rings. They never ventured out far from the side, but they enjoyed the water.

Grandpa Pete liked to just sit and watch all the action. Chris enjoyed showing off his diving and swimming skills as much as the grandparents enjoyed watching him. Since Mom had never learned to swim, nobody used the pool until I visited, which was about twice a week to clean it and play lifeguard.

"How about if I put a down payment on a house, and you make the payments to me?" Mom cleared her throat, then continued. "Chris could play in his own backyard, Grandma wouldn't have any steps, and you could sleep in a bed in your own room."

"Wow! I don't know what to say, Mom." I stood in shock as she continued.

"I don't know how you can get the proper rest sleeping on the sofa cushions on the floor. Why don't you look around for something and let me know when you find a house that we both can afford?" I was ecstatic.

One month later, I found a nice little three-bedroom house in Scottsdale. There was a grade school one block down and around the corner. Chris could walk to school with the neighborhood kids. With three bedrooms, there was one for each of us. I gave Grandma the master bedroom because it had its own shower and would be easier for both of us when I helped her bathe.

Chris wanted the front bedroom so he could see who was at the door. I really didn't care which one was mine, just as long as it had a bed in it.

The L-shaped, slump-block house was a dream come true. Complete with hookups for a washer and dryer, the house had a double garage, a big picture window in the living room, and a fine yard. All the homes on Solano Street had well-maintained yards.

The neighbors behind us had huge pine and orange trees that hung over on our side of the fence. When I looked out the sliding glass dining room door, the trees framed a beautiful picture against the blue sky.

The covered patio had two areas for planting flowers. In the front yard, a good-sized fan palm nestled by the curved driveway entrance.

Chris arranged all his toys in his new bedroom, then he staked out territory in the back yard for his dump trucks and future swing set, which I learned about that evening when he unpacked his toy catalogs. That time, it was fun to move. Everyone was happy, content, and enjoying life once again. Before long, the entire house was ready for action. Sometime during the moving, I celebrated my twenty-seventh birthday. Another year older . . . and a whole lot wiser . . . but best of all, Chris had "his" backyard to play in, and I promised to buy him a swing set for his birthday.

Life was actually fairly normal that spring and summer, like the calm before a storm. I continued to work at the resort and learned the hotel business quite well. It was fun trying to make the guests' stay as pleasant as possible and sharing their day's adventure about town, in the desert, and through mountains. I got good tips on where Chris, Grandma, and I could go exploring.

I worked a great deal with Jane, who handled the resort reservations. Her husband, Dale, was a deputy sheriff for the county; Jane had taken a keen interest in Chris's police enthusiasm. One afternoon, Jane asked me if Chris would like a ride in a real police car. My mouth dropped open.

"Are you kidding? The child would never forget it, and I would probably never hear the end of it!"

"Well, then, that settles it. I'll tell Dale to make the arrangements. He'll drive over to your house on Saturday. OK?"

"Hey, any day would be fine with Chris, so tell Dale to just do it when it's convenient for him."

I could hardly believe it. I hugged her and thanked her. I almost cried.

"I know how these kids are," she said laughing. "I have a little three-year-old boy who is nuts about police cars, too. When he is riding his bike on the sidewalk, he makes siren noises. He sounds so real that cars actually stop in the middle of the street and look for a police car with flashing red lights. But it's just Adam, doing his thing at the top of his lungs."

Later that week, Dale stopped by in uniform to meet me and confirm the directions and time he would arrive.

"I haven't mentioned anything to Chris yet, because I didn't want him to be disappointed if you couldn't make it."

"Everything is a go. I'll see you guys Saturday. Are you going to tell him that I'm coming?"

"No, I think a surprise will be better. Don't you? I can't wait to see the expression on his face when you drive up to the house."

Dale laughed. Shaking hands, we agreed to keep it a special surprise for Chris.

The big day came, and I tried to keep Chris close to the house. I told him that somebody was going to stop by with a surprise for him. He was hyperactive anticipating what the surprise was and who could be coming to visit.

Suddenly the police car pulled into the driveway, and Dale whipped up his siren a couple of times. Chris and I were standing in the kitchen when he heard it. He ran to the front living room window and then out the door before

A proud little five-year-old deputy sheriff,
reporting for duty.

I could dry my hands, which had been plunged in dishwater.

As Dale stepped out of the car, he introduced himself to Chris. By the time Grandma and I got there, Dale had opened the car door, and Chris had already climbed into the driver's seat and seized control.

Dale explained what everything was and let Chris talk over the radio to the dispatcher. I took lots of pictures as the two of them checked out every aspect of the patrol car. Then Dale asked if it would be all right to take Chris for a ride down the street. Chris didn't wait for an answer; he was in the car all buckled up before I could speak. They were off in an instant, patrolling the city streets in the search for "the bad guys." They disappeared for about an hour, and I was beginning to think they had actually found some!

When the cop and his shadow returned, Chris informed me that they had pulled over a speeding red pickup truck and presented the driver with a warning ticket. Dale shook hands with Chris and told him that he had to get back to work.

Chris stood at the end of the driveway, waving good-bye as the police car backed out and disappeared down the street and around the corner. I heard every detail of the afternoon ride in the police car until Chris finally fell asleep that night.

Not long after Chris's "run in with the police," I traded the truck in and bought a nice minivan. The van enabled Chris to lie down when he wasn't feeling well, plus it made climbing in easier for Grandma. After church, we'd spend the day taking long drives through the desert or head north to Flagstaff, Arizona, which was fifty-eight hundred feet higher in elevation, to enjoy the cooler weather.

Chris Greicius was a collector. He'd collect stickers, drawing paper—even pamphlets. One pamphlet depicted the Old West glory of an authentic pioneer village a few miles out of town. Chris had picked up the brochure during one of his many visits, "where Mommie works." He wanted desperately to go there.

One day, my little son came out of his room, snuggled close beside me, and handed me the infamous pamphlet, with a smile in those hopeful blue eyes.

"Mommie, can we go to this place?"

He showed me the pamphlet, and after I'd read it through and considered the time, I told him, "Chris, let's go another day. OK? By the time we get there and back it will be dark. Mommie really doesn't want to be driving around in the desert at night not knowing exactly where she's going."

His little face was filled with disappointment as he jumped from the sofa and raced into his room. A few minutes later, he came out dressed in his police gear from top to bottom.

"Mommie, you know I am a policeman, and policemen take care of people, especially their mommies. So it will be OK to go there, because I will protect you."

How could a mother say no to a five-and-a-half-year-old "policeman"? We went after all, singing along to our favorite tapes and exploring the pioneer town together. We had a ball. We even made it home just before dark.

Although Grandma Vie wasn't with us for the pioneer adventure, she had a great time listening and laughing as Chris described the events of the afternoon. He used his hands and body to act out different "cowboy" situations. Poor Grandma had tears in her eyes, and her side hurt from laughing. This encouraged Christopher to demonstrate even more, making facial expressions and honing his acting ability.

In May of 1978, I took a part-time job at a plant nursery to earn extra money. It worked out well until the following month when the resort where I worked was sold to a developer, and we all lost our jobs. The nursery put me on full time and asked if I would work in the greenhouse. I jumped at the chance. It was cooler, for one thing, and I could read all the plant books I desired.

I figured since I couldn't go to school, I'd make my work a school. Education is learning anywhere you can. I lasted until July, when I was informed that part of my job would be helping to unload the semi-trucks that delivered the plants. I survived for two weeks, but this kid finally gave out.

I was coming home at night stressed out to the max, and I had lost my temper a couple of times. I knew at that point, I had to quit the landscape nursery and find a job that didn't demand so much from me physically.

Grandma Vie was starting to get sick, and she could hardly move about even with her walker. I would make breakfast and a lunch for her before I left for work in the morning and once I got her to the living room recliner with the phone and an insulated container of water, she was pretty much settled until three o'clock when Chris got home from school. I'd arrive home from work at about five, then start dinner and attend to their needs.

One night, I heard Vie stirring, so I knocked on her bedroom door whispering, "Grandma, are you all right?"

Her voice was weak as she welcomed me to join her. "Come in."

As I opened the door, the light from the moon shone in through the open blinds of her dark room. I could see her sitting on the end of the bed hunched over a little, resting her hands on her knees.

I sat down beside her and placed my hand on her back.

"Grandma, what's wrong? Are you sick? You haven't been feeling well. Maybe I'd better get you to a doctor, don't you think?"

She reached over, took my hand, and patted it.

"No, Linda Joy, I don't need a doctor. I'm just getting old. Sometimes it's hard to breathe, and I need to sit up for a while. Everything will be fine. My legs will get strong again someday, so I can walk again. Promise me something, Linda Joy."

"Anything, Grandma. Just name it."

Tears welled in my eyes as I sat on the end of the bed in the dark and listened. The tone in her voice told me it was "truth time." I knew in my heart that I had to be prepared to accept the request she was about to make of me and to fulfill it to the best of my abilities.

"Promise me that, whatever happens, you won't ever let any doctor operate on me. I'm too old for that. I have had a good life, and when I'm buried beside Grandpa and my son, Wally, I will be at peace. We have had some good times here in this little house and on the farm. I always said you were just like me—stubborn—and . . . well, Linda Joy, I'm counting on that."

A smile and laugh broke through the tears as I wiped my eyes.

"Grandma, how long have you been sitting up at night and having trouble breathing?"

"For a while. I know you need to call your mother in the morning, because she will want to take me to Dr. Sam.

But remember your promise. I trust you and know you will do it."

I made the promise to Grandma Vie that night. Grandma was taken to the hospital for a few days, and then we had to put her into a nursing home.

Dr. Sam confirmed that if she lay down in a bed, her lungs slowly filled up with fluid. I arranged to have her recliner replace the nursing home bed. She was content.

The following week I interviewed at a Scottsdale resort for switchboard operator and front desk clerk. I was hired on the spot.

The summer of 1978 brought Tony out for a two-week visit with Chris. Tony slept in Grandma's room, and we had a great time revisiting all of Chris's favorite places.

With Tony carrying the picnic basket and Chris in the middle holding onto each of our hands, we spent the time as a family. We enjoyed the warm sunshine as we walked in the park together tossing the baseball back and forth and playing hide-and-seek.

Christopher was filled with love and excitement. He enjoyed the freedom to be a normal kid as he sat atop the picnic table throwing a baseball and watching his father scamper after it.

It has been said that laughter is the best medicine, and I believe it's true. Chris proved it time and time again beyond the shadow of a doubt.

A few days before Tony was scheduled to head back to Illinois, I asked him a question. "Tony, do you want to take Chris back for a visit with you?"

At first, Tony's face lit up, but the joy was immediately replaced by serious concern. "Yes, I do, but what about the doctor and Chris's medication?"

"I have already asked the doctor if it is all right for him to go. He seems to think that there isn't any reason for Chris not to go as long as you keep to his schedule. I don't have the money for his plane fare, but if you do, I will let him go.

"I know your folks would love to see him again, and Chris should see them, too. I'll write down what days he takes which pill, so you won't have any problem. Please remember, do not give him anything else—not even an aspirin—because it will kill him. Give Chris only the medication that I send back with you. OK?"

The sunshine returned to Tony's eyes. He was thrilled to have two more weeks with his son. When we told Chris about going back with Daddy on the airplane and seeing his other grandma and grandpa again, he was ecstatic.

The day came to drive them both to the airport to board the plane. I had made arrangements with the airline for Chris to fly back ahead of time if an emergency arose.

I hugged and kissed Christopher good-bye and told him to be a good boy for Daddy. Waiting to board the airplane, Chris's little face gleamed with excitement. The boy could hardly stand still, let alone sit still. This was Chris's first airplane ride; he raced from window to window thrilled by the huge plane waiting outside. Tony knelt down beside him and went to great length to explain the jet engines. They watched as the baggage was loaded and supplies were restocked.

Tony's excitement equaled his son's. I knew that it was right. I knew that the trip meant a lot to both of them, and I was pleased to see them happy.

Before they boarded, I confirmed with Tony that he understood all the instructions I had given. He picked up Chris in his arms, and the loudspeaker announced it was time to board. With tickets in their hands, the two waved good-bye.

I watched them walk down the ramp. Chris turned back, looking over his father's shoulder, and waved good-bye again. He had an empty ticket folder in one hand, fiercely flapping in the air, and Billy Bear clutched in the other. A tear trickled down my cheek as I thought to myself, what a happy, precious sight.

10

We Have a Herbie

All of a sudden, I felt so alone. Chris would be gone for two weeks, and Grandma Vie was in the nursing home. Headed down the empty airport corridors, I wondered what I would do with two full weeks of free time. The solo ride home was awfully long.

Despite the loneliness, I managed to keep busy. I spent a lot of time at work, volunteering for as much overtime as I could get. On weekends, I visited with Grandma, and I'd visit Mom, catching up on her day-to-day activities, while I cleaned the pool and played lifeguard.

Three days after Tony and Chris left, I became worried. I didn't want to intrude on their time together, but I hadn't received a phone call letting me know they had arrived safely. I was reluctant to call but felt I had to put my mind at ease. I called in the evening, hoping to catch them after chores. Tony's mother answered the phone.

"Hi, did Tony and Chris make it home all right?"

"Yes, they made it just fine." The tone of her voice told me that this was going to be a repeat of our last conversation, short and to the point.

I was waiting for the next sentence, but it never came. I asked, "Is Chris there? Can I speak with him, please? How is he doing?"

Her reply was short.

"They went to dinner, and I don't know when they will be home. Chris is doing just fine."

"Will you please tell him I called and have him call me when they get in?"

"I'll tell him." With that, she hung up the phone.

I sat at the dining room table for a while, staring at the receiver in my hand.

When Tony called the next night, he said that Chris was doing just fine, but that he wanted to come home. I had Tony put Chris on the phone.

"Hi, Chris. How's my boy?"

"Fine, Mommie, but I want to come home. I miss you."

His voice grew tearful as he chose his words carefully.

"Chris, are you sure you want to come home? Remember we talked about your getting homesick and that this might happen."

I wanted him back with me desperately, but I knew that this would probably be the last chance he would have to visit with Tony and his family.

"But I want to come home, Mommie. Tomorrow."

"I'll tell you what, Chris; I'll make you a deal."

"What Mommie?"

I could hear Tony in the background talking to his mother. Tony was disappointed that Chris wanted to go home but knew that he was homesick.

"Honey, if you want to come home, that's OK, but how about if you give it two days longer? Then if you still want to come home, you tell Daddy. He will call me and tell me which plane you will arrive on, and I'll meet you at the airport. Okey-dokey?"

Chris listened and repeated it back to me, so I knew he understood. "Okey-dokey, Mommie," he replied, his voice much calmer, "but I'm going to call you to come home in two days."

I chuckled a little under my breath, thinking he sure had a mind of his own. Maybe he was a little stubborn—like me.

"That's OK, sweetheart. I miss you very much and want you home with me, too. I love you."

"I love you, too, Mommie."

I talked to Tony for a minute and we tried to figure out what was going on, but he claimed he didn't know. I think Tony knew but just didn't want to tell me in front of his parents. We agreed that in two days Chris would probably be on his way home to Phoenix.

After hanging up the phone, I couldn't help but remember how happy the two of them had been while waiting to get on the plane. What could have happened to change things so much, so quickly? I had a good idea, but thought it was better to leave well enough alone.

The plane was due at about two in the afternoon, some forty-eight hours later. I switched days off with another woman so I could pick up Chris at the airport.

Standing outside behind a chain link fence, I watched everyone get off the plane but Chris. I wondered if I was at the wrong gate.

Then a flight attendant appeared holding hands with a little boy and his Billy Bear. There was Chris, smiling from ear to ear. I was so relieved to see him safe and sound. The tears tried to come. As they reached the bottom of the stairs, Chris took off running towards me.

Chris grinned, dropped everything, and jumped into my arms.

"I was up in the pilot's seat!" he cried out. "The pilot showed me everything, and guess what, Mommie?"

He patted his jacket pocket and pointed to the wings pinned to his shirt pocket.

"I got a whole pocket full of these wings." Chris grinned from ear to ear as if he were the richest boy on earth.

"What are you going to do with all of those wings?" I managed a look of astonishment to add to his excitement.

"I'm going to wear them and give some to my friends. OK?" I was happy to have him back in my arms again.

"Okey-dokey by me, anything you want to do with your wings is fine with me."

That evening, after bath time and our nightly snack in front of the television, I picked Chris up and sat him in my lap. I didn't want Chris to have any bad feelings about his father, and I hoped that by talking about it, Chris might be able to get a few things off his chest.

"Honey, why did you want to come home so soon from visiting with Daddy?"

"I just wanted to." Chris's facial expression, voice, and body language indicated his reticence. He was protecting me for some reason.

"Chris, tell me the truth. We don't keep secrets from each other. Do we?" He was quiet for a few minutes, fiddling with the bottom of his shirt. His eyes darted off to one side as if he were whipping up a good answer.

"Mommie, I just didn't want to stay there. I wanted to be with Daddy, but Grandma asked me questions that I didn't understand."

"Maybe you misunderstood her questions," I suggested.

Frustrated, Chris broke into a shout. "No, I didn't misunderstand." I decided not to pursue it any longer. I knew why Chris had wanted to come home.

Emotionally spent, Chris leaned his head on my shoulder and put his arms around me. I rubbed his back, kissed his cheek, and whispered how very much I loved him. He perked up, grabbed my face with his hands, and laid a big kiss on me. He giggled and wiggled his head so much I started to laugh, and that encouraged him to kiss me harder and harder.

Within seconds, we were both laughing and tickling one another. Carrying him off to bed over my shoulder, I tucked him in with Billy Bear. I kissed him good night as I turned out the light.

Standing in the doorway, I regarded the little policeman who was snuggled beneath the covers with his Billy Bear, probably dreaming of tomorrow's adventures, handing out his pocketful of wings to the kids on the block.

Chris celebrated his sixth birthday with his purchase of a new two-wheeled bike. He had been saving his money from doing extra chores around the house. He was the highest paid kid on the block for taking out the trash.

He was so proud of himself when we went to buy the bike. He eyeballed the entire stock, then he told the salesman, "I want that one."

While the man went to get one in a carton, Chris rubbed his hands together, glowing with excitement. The little guy could hardly contain himself while waiting for his brand new two-wheeled, red-and-white bike to appear.

I was thinking, how am I going to put a bike together? I know they have instructions, but, Lord.

The man came back empty handed. All of Chris's excitement vanished. His sad little eyes looked up at me with all the disappointment that the entire world could hold. I knew at that point that there was no way we were going home without a bike, even if we had to hit every bike shop in the state of Arizona.

"I'm sorry, son, but I don't have any more in stock. We will be getting more in about a week."

Chris stood listening to the man talk. The poor guy could see the disappointment on Chris's face. Wheels turned in my head figuring how to make this little blond-haired boy happy again. I explained to the salesman that it was Chris's birthday and asked whether he might check in the back room one more time.

"I'll tell you what. I can sell you the display model. It will be $10 cheaper, too. And you know what else?" The man tugged the colorful handlebar streamers.

"What?" Chris listened intently.

"These streamers usually cost extra. I'll give them to you as a birthday present. How about that?"

Chris's little eyes opened wide, and his smile made a welcome reappearance. I stood there silently thanking Jesus that I didn't have to assemble one from a carton.

Chris attacked his new bike, testing the pedals, making sure that the streamers were perfect and attempting to ride it through the store and up to the checkout. I encouraged Chris to let the salesman take it up.

"Ring this up for the young man. It's his birthday today, and he has a very special new bike to celebrate with."

The lady rang up the price on the register and Chris, with wallet in hand, took out all his money and gave it to her. She looked at me and smiled back at Chris.

"I don't need all of this money. I just need two twenties and this ten-dollar bill."

Chris started to push his bike out the door when the cashier laughingly asked him, "Don't you want your change?"

"OK." Chris thought of it as a bonus. As far as he was concerned, he just wanted to go home and ride his new bike around the block. For this birthday boy, money was not important at this stage of the game.

He stuffed the money in his pocket. He didn't have time to get the wallet out. The bike was on its way out the door and into the van by the time I finished paying for the training wheels.

All afternoon he practiced riding his new bike in the driveway, venturing out onto the sidewalk from time to time. The neighborhood kids rallied around as Christopher demonstrated the special features of his new rough-and-tuff, off-the-street bike, complete with matching streamers.

With Grandma in the nursing home, my funds were a little short. The new job was OK but didn't pay enough to cover all the bills, let alone buy Chris a new swing set for an added surprise. Something had to go. Chris and I discussed selling the van and buying a used car. We wanted something with affordable payments that didn't take so much gas.

In about two weeks, we sold the van, and in the deal we got a couple of thousand cash and a used car. The car was way too big for our use, but it was fine until we found what we wanted.

One Saturday, we dropped by a car lot to browse. Chris made a beeline to a little gold Volkswagen Bug. When a salesman approached us, I came directly to the point.

"How much is this Bug?"

The salesman explained that the car had been traded in about a week ago. "The lady bought the Bug for her college-bound daughter. I guess the girl parked it on the side of the house and walked to school, because it only has eighteen hundred miles on it."

Chris and I inspected the car, looking for dents and dings. Suddenly, Chris lifted the engine hood, placed his right foot on the rear bumper, and stated in a manly fashion, "It looks pretty good to me, Mommie. Can we take it for a spin?"

The salesman looked at me and grinned at Chris. He reminded us that the car had only eighteen hundred miles on it. It was practically new. He carried on without end about how great of a deal the car was. It wasn't hard to see that Chris had fallen in love with the little gold Volkswagen and wanted to take it home.

While the salesman disappeared to fetch the keys, Chris investigated every nook and cranny of the car. He tested the doors, explored the back seat, poked his nose in the glove box, and even tried to crawl beneath the car.

The salesman hurried back and handed me the keys. Chris and I were full of anticipation as we buckled in for a test spin. But when I turned the key in the ignition, nothing happened. I let the salesman have a go at it. Nothing. Chris climbed out and stood by my side. He looked up with the same disappointed expression he had the day we bought the bike.

"You're not going to buy it, are you, Mommie?"

I looked down at him, placed my hand on his head, and said, "We'll see."

I didn't want to disappoint Chris, so I told the salesman that I would like to buy the car, but that it had to be in excellent running condition. Chris had hope again, and a faint smile appeared. We talked business as we walked over to the salesman's office.

"I can assure you that we will have the car running in top condition before it leaves the lot. You can count on that."

Chris sat in my lap, leaned back against my chest, and turned his head waiting to hear the word "yes" come out of my mouth.

"Can I have photocopies of everything that you do to it? I want to know exactly what's wrong with it." Chris leaned forward with anticipation as the salesman replied.

"You sure can. No problem."

Chris must have figured that we were both taking way too long to get to the point, so he asked the big question that both of us wanted to know anyway. "How much does it cost?"

The salesman leaned back in his chair, a little surprised at Chris's question but humored by his masculine directness.

"Well, son, it costs $3,300."

I choked and started to get up from the chair when the salesman added, "But it was going to be advertised for $2,700, this weekend only."

I sat back down. Chris knew there was still a chance as he waited patiently on my lap. His little head turned back and forth like he was watching a tennis match as the conversation continued between the salesman and myself.

I thought beyond the certificates hanging on the wall that promoted the integrity of the dealership. I knew that the automotive capabilities of this little car might mean the difference between life and death for my son.

As the salesman wrote up the paperwork, I point-blank asked him, "Is this a good car, or is it going to need a bunch of work on it a few months down the road? I'm asking because I can't afford to have a lot of mechanic bills. My son has leukemia, and I need a reliable car for transportation to and from the doctor and hospital. I would appreciate it if you would be totally honest with me."

He sat behind his desk, leaned back in his chair, and just gazed at us for a minute.

Then he leaned forward and folded his hands on his desk. "Young lady," he asserted, "the car will run perfectly, and you won't have any problems with it. I will see to it myself. I *promise* you."

I nodded my head and looked him straight in the eye. "OK, we'll take it."

Chris clapped his hands and shouted with all the enthusiasm of a Heisman Trophy winner. "We got it! We got it! We got the little car, Mommie!"

We returned a week later to pick up our little gold Volkswagen. A neighbor gave us a ride to the car lot that evening because we had sold the other car a few days earlier for the exact price I was asking. I now had more than enough money to pay cash for the little car.

The dealership had put five hundred dollars worth of repairs into the engine, according to the copies of the paperwork. It had also been washed, waxed, and totally cleaned inside.

We brought the little Volkswagen home that evening in October of 1978, and parked it in the garage, but only after celebrating our purchase with dinner of our favorite hamburgers, fries, and colas.

We actually could turn it around in the garage, but didn't. It took me a few days to get used to driving such a tiny car, but within the week, I had it down pat.

A couple of weeks later, we took in a movie after a Friday night of dining out. *Herbie the Love Bug* was playing. When we came out of the theater, it was raining heavily and very dark.

Our little car got a name that night. As I started to back out of the parking space, the other bigger cars were having trouble dodging each other. Brake lights flashed in the rain, and horns sounded, as drivers tried to fight their way through the crowded parking lot.

We simply put our car in reverse, backed out, and drove off. Chris nearly exploded through the rooftop as he pounded on the dashboard. The excitement in his voice mixed with the gleaming smile on his face was worth more than money could buy.

"Mommie, Mommie, we have a Herbie! We have a Herbie!"

I turned to him, smiled, and laughed with him.

"We sure do, Christopher. We sure do."

He kept jumping out of the seat to look backwards at the parking lot full of cars honking their horns trying to get out. He laughed with joy, repeating, "We have a Herbie."

Chris could hardly contain himself as we drove down the wet streets towards home. The little car became a part of our family that rainy night. "Herbie" not only had his own garage to play in but found a special place in our hearts as well.

Just as Herbie the Love Bug took care of his owners, Chris and I knew that our little Herbie would take care of us, too, no matter what.

11

Strike One

It was nearly the end of September, and Chris was in the first grade. Grandma Vie wasn't feeling much better. She remained in the nursing home, and Mom was stressed out from running back and forth taking care of Grandma, plus her own parents.

I had signed up for college again. I thought I would give it another try. It was only three classes, but I could take them in the evening and still work during the day full time.

Chris was bruising more easily and growing paler. Fear clutched my heart. I was afraid he had gone *out* of remission.

The doctor confirmed my fears on our next visit with the results of a blood test, which was standard on every visit. Chris had gone out of remission. The leukemia was rapidly spreading throughout his body. The doctor didn't waste any time. He called the hospital across the street to notify them that we were on our way.

I sat in the emergency room while they gave Chris a transfusion and platelets to help build up his system. The sister had been informed that Chris and I were in the emergency room. In no time, her sweet smile emerged from behind the heavy door. That morning the doctor had arranged for a room in pediatrics, and I revisited my little room several times that week. I was reliving the memories of February 4, 1977.

It seemed that we had come so far, and yet we were right back at the beginning again with one exception: Chris now had one strike against him. All the hopes and fears I had first felt came back, only now they were even stronger. The doctor's words haunted me as I sat and watched the nurse change the IV bags.

"We can get him back into remission. He will be fine in a few days." All I kept thinking about was that the second remission was usually about half as long as the first. Like a baseball game, three strikes and you're out. My mind drifted back to the first time I had met the doctor in my little room.

I cried out in silence as I stood by the nurse watching everything. I watched Chris's complexion change from pale to peach as the drugs took effect and his color returned.

Within three days, Chris was released from the hospital, but the whole series of treatments started all over again. It seemed like a repeat of the previous year. But this time around, he bounced back more quickly, which astonished the doctor.

Chris wanted to go back to school and see all his friends again. He seemed to have a remarkable ability to accept everything, almost without question. I was the one who had all the questions.

I called Tony to let him know what was going on. He asked if it would be all right to visit at Christmas time. I thought that it would be a good idea and encouraged him to make arrangements.

I wasn't concentrating much on school those days. My mind was on Chris and on trying to make a living. I remember sitting in class trying to take notes from the lecture. I don't know what hit me, but before I knew it, I had closed my book, put away my paper, and gotten up and walked out.

I headed straight for the admissions office and withdrew from all my classes. I left my books, paper, and notes in the trash can beside the brick building that held my dream of an education captive. As I walked down the sidewalk towards the parking lot, an education didn't mean much to me anymore. My only thoughts were of Chris and the reality that he was going to die. We'd hit the first strike; he only had two more strikes to go before he would be *out*.

As I walked to the car, I kept talking to myself, *"I quit. That's it. No more school. I give up. I'm not going to even try to do this again. I'll just wait for that someday, and if it doesn't come, well, no problem. I really don't care anymore. It's not important anyway."*

I found Herbie and drove home, and as I sat on the back patio that afternoon thinking, I continued the conversation from the college parking lot. I could get a part-time job now that I was not going to school, or maybe a better job would come along.

While working at the hotel the next day, I was talking to one of the bellmen, Kevin, about getting a second job.

"That's what I do," he replied with an encouraging voice.

"Kevin, what do you mean, that's what you do?"

"I work two full-time jobs. This one here, as a bellman, and over at the Sheraton as a night auditor. Hey, we need another person there. Have you ever done any kind of hotel audit work before?"

"No, Kevin, I haven't." My tone portrayed discouragement and a lack of confidence that I could possibly learn the work, but Kevin kept talking, and it wasn't long before he had built my confidence.

"You could do it. I know you could. It's easy. I'll talk to Mr. Montilla. He's the general manager. We'll get you set up for an interview, OK?"

I agreed and went back to my work, consoled that this opportunity might solve another problem. It paid a little more, but more than that, I could work at night. I figured I could take Chris to Mom's house before I went to work and pick him up in the morning. If I had to, I could take him and the sleeping bag to work with me. That way I could see Chris off to school, sleep during the day, and be with him in the evening. Plus, Mom was talking about selling her big house, because she was tired of the upkeep. Maybe she'd take over my little house, and I could sell all the furniture, then move into another apartment.

Kevin came back shortly and said he had set up an interview for that day, after I got off work. I was to go to the hotel and ask for Mr. Montilla.

I did just as Kevin had told me. His secretary said, "Go ahead and wait in the dining room and have a cup of coffee. Mr. Montilla will be there in a minute."

Mr. Montilla spoke with a fast Puerto Rican accent. He was a handsome man, tall and slender, with black hair slightly graying at the temples. His flamboyant personality erupted as he sat there telling me jokes. The man was a walking joke book. It was the strangest interview I had ever encountered. Suddenly, he asked. "Have you ever audited before?"

"No, I haven't, but I know I can do it. I'll tell you what. I will work for you for two weeks, and if at the end of that time, I can't balance the audit on my own, you don't have to pay me for the two weeks of work."

He sat sipping his coffee and listening to every word. He set his coffee down and leaned on the table.

"You've got guts, kid. You're on. Tomorrow night Kevin works. Be here; he'll train you."

Then he got up and left. I took my cue from him and made for the exit door.

I almost drove myself crazy during those two weeks trying to learn everything and asking Kevin tons of questions. I made copies of everything and scribbled notes all over them. I spent a couple of hours each evening before work studying the papers that I had copied. The big night came to balance the hotel accounts on my own. We weren't running a full house, so that helped a lot.

Things went pretty well that night—not too many check-ins. By 1:30 a.m., I had finished posting the bar bills and was running room and tax. By 3:30 a.m., I was done; I crossed my fingers and closed my eyes as I took a reading, praying that it would be in balance. By 3:31 a.m., I was looking for the problem, going back through every restaurant ticket, bar ticket, banquet ticket—any ticket I could find. Any receipt or piece of paper that had been run through the register, ran through my hands. Anything that had been tossed in the trash, had lain on the counter, or had fallen to the floor beside the trash container was now organized in the hopes of finding a seventeen-cent error.

By 5:45 a.m., I found the problem and corrected it. I took another reading and "Thank you, Jesus." It balanced. I finished cleaning and setting up for the seven o'clock shift, then started making wake-up calls. The phone rang at 6:30 a.m., and guess who? With his unique charismatic charm, Mr. Montilla snickered, anticipation in his voice. I could envision the grin on his face.

"Good morning. Did you balance?"

"No problem. I am just finishing up with the wake-up calls. The reports are on your desk," I replied in my most confident tone of voice.

"I guess this means I have to pay you?"

"Yep, for the whole two weeks." I was relieved that I hadn't worked two weeks for nothing.

"If you want to know your hours, I have a schedule in my top desk drawer. Make a copy so you know when to show up, and don't be late. Good job, kid, I'm proud of you."

Mr. Montilla hung up the phone before I could say anything. I was so tired by this time, that I let out a big sigh of relief and only thought of climbing into bed and going to sleep after I got Christopher off to school.

12

A Special Red Rose

In November of 1978, Chris and I moved into a little furnished studio that I sublet from Kevin. It was located in a very posh part of Scottsdale, but Kevin made the price right, and the change was wonderful.

The place was even more beautiful than the resort, boasting a shopping center within walking distance and a lush green golf course a short walk in the opposite direction. Most of the locals drove expensive cars bearing prestigious emblems. Herbie wasn't quite up to their standards, but he had an emblem. It wasn't like their posh cars', but Chris and I loved him just the same.

I advertised an "Everything Must Go Sale," and everything did go in three short days. All the living and dining room furniture made it out the front door on the very first day. Garage-salers were buying the pictures right off the walls. I cleaned out the kitchen and linen closet, keeping only the items I needed to start over again. I left my bedroom set for Mom and stored Chris's in the garage.

Mom and her parents moved into my house the following week. She also had been cleaning out unwanted items and brought them over for the big sale. All in all, things worked out pretty well for both of us. I was happy that I didn't have to clean the pool anymore, and Mom was happy no longer having to clean her big house.

In the evening, I would take Chris over to Mom's, along with his school clothes for the next morning. He entertained the grandparents and kept Mom busy. She had fun catching him as he jumped on the bed, trying to touch the ceiling. After a while, he would fall asleep in bed with my mother as I worked throughout the night. I stopped by to get him ready for school each morning before I went home to sleep. After school, Chris would walk back to Mom's and wait for me to come and get him.

One time, Christopher decided to walk all the way home, about three miles. I awoke to the sound of little knuckles tapping on the door. I grabbed my robe and opened the door to find Chris standing there grinning from ear to ear.

"Mommie, aren't you proud of me? I walked all the way home all by myself!"

I stood there stunned as he walked over to the kitchen table to set down his backpack. He was excited about accomplishing such a major task on his own. "Did Grandma bring you home?" I asked. "She's sitting outside in her car somewhere, and this is a joke on Mommie, isn't it?"

"No. I told you. I walked all by myself, Mommie."

I sat down on the sofa. Chris came over and gave me a big hug then sat beside me.

"Mommie, I walked the same way that you drive to Grandma's. I crossed the bridge over the canal and then walked in the ditch by the busy road. I figured that way the cars couldn't get me. Aren't you proud of me, Mommie?"

I was searching for just the right words. My mind raced with images of what might have happened. "Yes, I'm proud of you, but please don't do this again. OK? We had better call Grandma, because I'll bet she's wondering where you are. We don't want to make her worry, do we?"

"No, Mommie, but she wasn't home, so I came here."

"Well, I'm sure that if you waited for a minute, Grandma would have been there shortly. Don't you think so?"

Chris was really thinking at this point. He knew I wasn't angry with him. He understood that I was simply trying to explain that we have to think before we do something that might cause another person to worry.

"Mommie, can I call Grandma and tell her I'm here with you?"

"Yes, you can, and please tell her that you have no intentions of ever doing this again. Okey-dokey?"

We were both laughing by this time, and the message got across, plain and simple.

A couple of weeks passed, and Chris made no attempt to walk home from school, although he did make his smiling presence known at the hotel one afternoon. I had to attend a front-desk meeting at three o'clock on a Thursday afternoon. Chris, having only a half-day at school, came with me to the hotel that afternoon. I accepted his promise that he would sit quietly in the lobby until I returned from the meeting. My friend behind the desk agreed to watch the precocious boy.

I sat Chris down on the sofa in the lobby, gave him a pack of bubble gum, and told him I would be gone about an hour. Little did I know what would take place in the owner's office shortly after the meeting started.

Chris had gone to the restroom. Upon his return to the lobby, he spotted an open door and a man sitting behind a rather large desk. He marched into the room, walked up to the desk, and leaned over it with his hands clasped. "Do you know where my Mommie is? I'm getting tired of waiting for her."

Sam, the owner, stopped what he was doing, leaned forward on the desk, and clasped his hands, mirroring Chris. "No, not offhand. What is your Mommie's name?"

Once Chris had told Sam my name and that I worked nights there, he caught on quickly.

"Chris, I'm sure your Mommie will be out of the meeting soon. I have an idea."

"What?"

"Are you thirsty?"

"Yeah!"

"How about if you and I go to the dining room and get a cola?"

"OK!" Chris clapped his hands with excitement, agreeing that this was a neato idea.

The two sat down, ordered large sodas, and talked for quite a while. Sam returned to his office a little later but not without leaving instructions to give the young man *anything* his heart desired. "It's on the house!"

The waitresses kept him happy for awhile, but Chris's patience was wearing thin, and he soon found his way back to Sam's office. Once again Sam looked up from his paperwork to find a little blue-eyed, blond-haired boy clasping his hands as he leaned on the desk. "Isn't my Mommie's meeting over yet?"

Sam cracked a smile, got up from behind the desk, and took Chris by the hand. "They've had long enough for their meeting, don't you think? Let's go find her, OK?"

"Okey-dokey."

Chris and Sam strolled together through the grand hotel, down the hallway, and past the ballrooms to our meeting room. When the door opened, every head turned to spot the culprits that dared interrupt a meeting. Sam and Chris advanced hand in hand to the head of the table. Sam introduced Chris to Mr. Montilla and told him to wind up business for the day.

"This young man has been very patient and polite about this whole ordeal of waiting for his mommie."

Sam cracked a smile as he made eye contact with me. He shook Chris's hand and bid everyone farewell as he closed the door behind him.

Mr. Montilla placed Chris on his lap and spoke very seriously.

"Chris, have you known Sam a long time?"

Chris delivered a rather serious response of his own. "No, we just met today. Is this meeting going to be over soon?"

"Well, Chris, now that you're one of the big boys with important friends, you call the shots." Chuckling, Mr. Montilla glanced around the table. Chris raised a confused brow as he turned to ask Mr. Montilla what he meant.

Mr. Montilla explained in great detail about the agenda and then pointed to the bottom of the page, asking Chris if he could read the sentence.

"I'm only in first grade," Chris replied, "but you know what it says, so why don't you read it?" The whole room burst into laughter.

The merriment continued as Mr. Montilla told Chris, "Repeat after me. 'If there is no further business, this meeting is adjourned.'"

Chris repeated the words, the meeting adjourned, and my little executive son and I were soon on our way home in Herbie.

Soon after, Chris made another friend, closer to his own age. He lived in our complex, was a couple of years older than Chris, and was a very nice boy. One Saturday, a few weeks before Christmas 1978, I was taking a nap on the sofa. Chris sat quietly watching cartoons and playing with toys. There was a light tapping at the front door, and Chris answered it. It was Timmy, and he had plans for Chris.

"Hi, Chris, can you go to the shopping center with me?"

"Mommie, can I go to the shopping center with Timmy?"

This is good, I thought. With the boys at play, I could get some real sleep for an hour or so.

"Chris, it's OK, but I want you two boys to stay together. Both of you guys be good in the stores. Promise! Chris, you can get a dollar out of my wallet."

Chris pulled out the money, stuffed it in his pocket, and the two boys raced out the door, down the steps, and across the yard toward the toy store. I closed my eyes and drifted off to sleep.

A few hours later, I awoke to the sound of little scratching noises. When I rolled over on my side and opened my eyes, I saw Chris sitting on the floor with a sack beside him. "Chris, what is that noise?"

"Look, Mommie, it's a hamster. Can we put him in the empty fish tank?" Suddenly, I was wide-awake!

"Chris, what else do you have in the sack?" I asked apprehensively.

"Mommie, you wouldn't believe all I got. I got this first." He said, revealing a paper airplane. "And when I paid for it, the lady gave me back a whole bunch of money."

Now he really had caught my attention. I was wide-awake and listening to his every word. Chris reached into the paper sack, and two more toys appeared in his mitts.

"Then we found this big toy soldier and all these colors of clay to make stuff with. Each time the lady gave me more money."

By this time, I had a pretty good idea as to what had happened. I grabbed my wallet. Sure enough, the twenty-dollar bill was missing, and only the one-dollar bill remained. I stood there for a few minutes listening to Chris tell me all about his day and the new toys he purchased for only a buck.

I wasn't angry with him, only with myself. Now, how was I going to solve this and explain it to him?

"Chris, sweetheart, I'm sorry, but the hamster has to go back to the store. We aren't allowed to have pets here."

"OK, Mommie."

"So we will have to return it." And that wasn't all. Quite innocently, Chris had spent a week's worth of cash. I was in no position to take the loss. I sat down with my little big spender. "Now, I give you one dollar a week allowance, don't I?" Chris wore a confused frown.

"Chris, these toys are going to be put up on the shelf, and when you earn the money from your allowance, you can have them. You may keep two of them to play with now, but the others will have to be earned.

"I know you didn't know that you had twenty dollars instead of just one dollar. That's my fault. I should have made sure before you left with Timmy." We divided the goods into two piles: the "return" pile and the "have to keep" pile.

About that time, Timmy came by, and I asked him to help Chris return the unopened items. The two boys set out once again for the toy store, but this time, they moved very slowly across the green yard.

I lay back down on the sofa, hoping I had effectively explained the money issue to the boys. I fell back to sleep while awaiting Chris's return. When I woke up again, he was sitting on the floor with the refunds before him.

"Mommie, can I go back to the shopping center with Timmy? He is waiting outside. Here is the money the lady gave me."

Growing frustrated from broken sleep, I agreed to let him go, but with restrictions. It was getting late, and I had to get some sleep before work. "OK, Chris, but only for an hour. Come here, and I will show you on your watch what time you have to come home."

We got the cartoon hands settled on his watch, and out the door he went once again with Timmy. Again, they took to the lush green grass like playful ponies.

When I awoke one hour later, Chris was back sitting quietly on the floor with his hands behind his back watching me sleep. The kid wore a dazzling grin.

"Are you all right, Chris?"

"Yeah, I'm fine, Mommie." He smiled from ear to ear.

"What do you have behind your back?"

Chris was still smiling from ear to ear as he held out one beautiful red rose wrapped in white tissue paper and tied with a red ribbon.

"Here, Mommie. I bought this for you, because I love you."

I was trying to hold back the tears as I gazed at him holding out the rose. Chris got up off the floor, came over, gave me a big hug, and plopped in my lap.

"Mommie, it only cost three pennies. I asked the lady in the flower shop how much it was. I told her it was for my Mommie, because I love her. Then I told her about the toys and having to take them back. She asked me how much money I had, and I showed her the three pennies I found in my pocket.

"Then a man in the back of the store came out and said that is just how much it cost. Do you like it,

Mommie? The man in the back told the lady to put the pretty paper and ribbon on, too."

With big tears in my eyes, I hugged him and kissed him, holding the rose in my hand.

"Chris, it is the most beautiful red rose I have ever seen or could ever receive in my entire life. I love you, and I love the rose. Sweetheart, thank you very much."

I held him tightly and as we leaned back together on the sofa, I talked to the Lord in silence.

Thank you for giving me this special child. Oh God, why does he have to be sick? Why does he have to die so young? Why, Lord, why?

Chris looked up at me, and when he saw my tears, his little eyes started getting moist. He asked, "Mommie, why are you crying?"

"Because I'm so lucky to have a special little boy like you. Sometimes mommies cry because they're happy."

His tearful face turned to a smile. He kissed me on the cheek as he climbed down to turn on the television and asked, "What's for dinner? I'm hungry."

13

Cowboys and Other Heroes

With Christmas just a week away, Chris and I decorated our apartment with much the same decor we had enjoyed last Christmas. A few of the paper items hadn't survived the move, so we created new snowflakes, red and green paper chains, and bells.

Chris counted the hours until his father came for a visit. Mom offered the spare bedroom to Tony to help save expenses. She had her big tree up again, and the house was decorated beautifully. A treasure trove of presents skirted the tree, most of which were addressed to one little boy.

After we had met Tony at the airport, Chris helped his dad settle in by unpacking his suitcase.

With school out for Christmas vacation, Chris and Tony were able to spend plenty of time together. We had only one doctor's appointment scheduled for the week, which was nice. The three of us ventured out to the malls, parks, and restaurants, but most of the time, I gave them time alone at Mom's so they could enjoy one another. I continued to work nights and took advantage of the extra time in the afternoon for naps.

On Christmas Eve, we planned to join together for dinner and our gift exchange. But before heading over to Mom's, I stopped in to visit Grandma Vie.

When I entered Grandma's dimly lit room and approached her bed, she recognized me and reached for my hand. I placed my hand over hers and kissed her on the cheek.

"This is not the way to live!" she began. "Lying in a bed all day long and being sick." Grandma Vie was weary, and she had her mind on dying.

I sat at her bedside listening as she spoke of nothing but death. Among her words, I could hear all of the fear and hopelessness brewing inside her. I realized that Grandma Vie was willing herself to die. I knew that if my stubborn grandmother set her mind to do something, she would do it.

"Grandma, I want you to listen to me. You are going to get better. You're not going to die. It's not your time."

She clenched her mouth shut and shook her head. Silence permeated the room as she pretended to drift off to sleep. I sat looking over the Christmas cards on her nightstand. I knew what I had to say to her, . . . but how?

I took a couple of minutes, but it came to me. "Grandma, I know what you're doing. You're willing yourself to die, because you don't want to be here in this place. Well, if you'd start using your will to get better,

you wouldn't be here long. It works both ways, you know.
I'm not giving up and letting the world get the best of me.
You taught me better than that. You have got lots of good
years ahead of you, so just stop it right now."

She opened her eyes, squeezed my hand, and nodded
her head. "Is that a yes, Grandma?" I asked, my eyes
suddenly blurred by tears. "I hope so, because I'm not
ready to give you up. We have got some new places to
explore, and you will just love 'em."

She cracked a smile at that point and laughed a little. I
knew I had her back on the road to recovery.

"I will never be able to do those things again, Linda
Joy."

"Who said you can't? You can do anything if you set
your mind to it, can't you?"

She nodded again, but with a doubtful expression on
her face.

"Well then, start setting your mind right now to do
just that, Grandma." We talked a little more about Chris
and my job, while we held tightly to one another's hands.

No longer in the mood for a festive family dinner,
before going to Mom's, I stopped off at a local restaurant
for my Christmas meal. As I sat there in the pea green
booth sipping coffee and waiting for my hamburger and
french fries, I considered how quickly things change. Last
year, Christmas Eve had been totally different. The year
before that, I was married and celebrating Christmas at
my home with my family. I wondered what lay in store for
us in 1979 and if this coming Christmas would be Chris's
last.

My dinner arrived in the hands of a cheery waitress, very pregnant, wearing a red stocking cap.

"Enjoy your dinner. Is there anything else I can get you?"

"How about the night off of work?" I teased, not looking forward to greeting Christmas morn on the clock. We shared a good laugh, and she wished me a merry Christmas.

I managed to get most of my meal down, although I wasn't very hungry. I knew it would be a long night at work, and the hotel kitchen there would be closed.

I made it to Mom's just in time to see everybody open his or her presents. I even received a couple myself, then changed my clothes and headed for work.

I sat for about an hour in the back office drinking coffee and smoking cigarettes, waiting to go on duty. The hotel was loud with music from several consecutive shindigs celebrating the holidays. The hotel lobby was filled with beautifully decorated flocked Christmas trees.

By the end of the evening, a couple of trees were missing. I wrote on my report to have the housekeeping department clean the trail of flocking from the carpet in the side hallway and send maintenance to the hotel across the street to recover the trees that someone had found in the middle of the parking lot. Another tree was found by the pool and yet another on top of the roof. I had a feeling Santa Claus had nothing to do with the rooftop festivities. All in all, it was one long night. I just wanted to go to Mom's and wish my family a merry Christmas. I would see what the plans were for the day with Chris and Tony, call Grandma Vie, and go to bed.

Tony and I had talked several times with the doctor. Dr. Baranko updated both of us on the seriousness of Chris's condition. Giant neon lights kept flashing in my mind; one day at a time was the only way we could live. For now, Chris was in remission. As each month passed, Dr. Baranko's words echoed: the second remission is half as long as the first.

Chris was getting older, and he began asking more questions about his illness. As hard as it was for me to answer him at times, I feared the day when he would no longer be there to ask any questions at all. But regardless of the illness, our adventures continued as we were living a lifetime in what little time we had left.

One day, Chris and I had an unplanned adventure while we were driving home from the doctor's along Lincoln Drive, a very wide, four-lane divided street. Herbie started to slow down and putt his way up the slight incline in the road. I pulled off to the side of the road, and Chris sat quietly while I tried repeatedly to start the car. I realized that I was out of gas.

"Chris, come on. Mommie will carry you. We're going to have to walk back to the gas station about a mile and a half to get help and gas for Herbie."

Because it was one of the days when Chris wasn't walking very well, I carried him. I was hoping that someone would stop to help us or give us a ride to the station. Chris watched as three police cars drove by.

"Mommie, why didn't they stop and help us?"

"They must have some very important business to do. We'll be all right; we have only about a mile to go."

About that time, a police car did stop to render aid. "What's the problem, or are you two just out for a walk along a busy street?"

Officer David Mann smiled, and I got the feeling he knew what had happened, but I explained. He drove us to the gas station then back to our car and helped us get it started. During the time we spent driving back and forth, I learned that this wasn't even his district. He had made a quick run to a local store for something and was on his way back to the Paradise Valley area. He was also starting an off-duty job in a couple of days as night security for a hotel.

"Thanks for all your help, David, and I'll be seeing you in a couple of days. I'm the night auditor at the hotel." His jaw dropped.

"You're kidding! Great! Then I'll see you later. Young man, make sure that your Mommie puts gas in little Herbie."

Officer David Mann and I developed a very nice friendship from that meeting along Lincoln Drive. We talked about a variety of subjects and interests and life in general. I think he was the only one at the hotel who knew that Chris had leukemia. At least he was the only person I told. Sometimes he'd talk and I'd listen; sometimes I'd talk and he'd listen. It was nice to have a friend.

January 1979—a brand new year filled with brand new adventures just waiting to unfold. I prayed that the Lord would make 1979 a good year for Chris. Mom suggested that I move back in with her to save money. Since the apartment sublease came to term at the end of

January, the suggestion sounded pretty good. I boxed up what possessions I had and moved Herbie to Mom's garage. Chris and I shared a room together, his favorite, the front bedroom with the window, so he could see who was at the door.

In March, Chris helped me celebrate my twenty-eighth birthday in Old Tucson Movie Studios. Many famous Western movies and television shows have been filmed there. It was a fun day. Some of the cowboys remembered us from our previous visits and came over to say, "Hi," as we savored a hearty lunch in the Old Time Saloon. Chris informed them loud and clear that it was my birthday.

"This is my Mommie's birthday; she's twenty-eight today! I'm going to be seven years old on August eighth."

They got quite a kick out of that mouthful. A couple of the cowboys took Chris outside and showed him the "neato stuff that not everyone gets to see."

I sat finishing my lunch while chatting with the eldest cowboy.

"You two sure like to come here, don't you? Haven't you seen everything yet?"

"Yes, and most things three and four times, but Chris enjoys it here, and I want to give him all I can."

I guess my voice kind of cracked because he asked, "What do you mean, give him all you can?"

I didn't really want to tell him that Chris had a short time to live, but it was evident that the cowboy knew that something was uncommon about our visits to Old Tucson.

"Well, you see, Chris has leukemia. He probably has about a year and a half to live, if the doctors don't find a cure before that. So we just do what we can afford and go where we enjoy it most. I want to make his life fun. I try to make all his wishes come true on a limited budget. Somehow, through the grace of God, we always have enough money. I want him happy, and I'll do whatever is necessary to keep him that way."

The cowboy sat there listening to every word. I could see the man choking up as he parted his lips to speak.

"I felt there was something special about you two. You guys are different than most of the tourists we see. That little boy of yours is sure a heart-grabber. Leukemia never crossed my mind. Can't the doctors do anything?"

"Very little, but they're doing everything they know how to do. It's in God's hands now."

An afternoon with "The Cowboys" of Old Tucson.

Later that afternoon, the cowboys put on a show and picked Chris out of the audience to take part in it. Chris was in his glory, all decked out in his brown Western cowboy outfit with the deputy sheriff patch that Dale had given to him. We'd sewn it onto the sleeve of his jacket.

Toward the end of our tour, we were in one of the old Western stores browsing around when Chris found a gun set nicely packaged in a big box.

"Mommie, why don't you buy this for your birthday?"

"Chris, that looks like something you would want for *your* birthday, not me."

"Well, will you buy it for me, then?"

"It's not your birthday yet."

He kept holding onto it and staring at it. I could see the little wheels turning in his head as he negotiated a plan to get me to buy it for him. I walked over to Chris and looked at the price on the box.

"Chris, I'm not sure I have enough money on me to even buy this today."

"Look and see, Mommie, please."

I opened my wallet and found only three dollars. I showed Chris that I was a little short. I explained that we had just enough for a pack of gum and gas to get us home. Heading up to the register, I glanced back at Chris and found him clutching the box. But after a few minutes, he surrendered and put the box back on the self. He joined me at the register. As I dug in my pocket for bubble gum change, Chris looked up at me and asked, "Mommie, can't you use the paper money?"

I looked a little confused and the salesperson that was watching the whole episode kind of chuckled.

"Happy Birthday, Mommie."
Chris and I in fancy Western duds.

"You know, the paper checks that you write on, when you don't have any money. You said it was the same, like money."

I could see in his eyes that he had the entire next week planned, playing cowboys and Indians in the backyard with that gun set. Who was I to take those dreams from him? I smiled and told him to go get the holster set and that I would use the paper money. Chris did say that I could borrow it any time I wanted, but I never did.

Instead, I suggested that as long as I bought him something for my birthday, I wanted our picture taken in the Old Time Photo Place. I used paper money for that, too.

Later, after the show, the cowboys gave us some free passes to Old Tucson so we could save money on our next visit. I thanked them for everything.

It was nighttime when we started back towards Phoenix. Stopping for gas along the freeway, I found that I had only ninety cents in change. The young man at the station, tall with dark, curly hair that bobbed out from under a ball cap said, "How about if I make it an even dollar?"

As he cleaned the windows and checked the oil, it seemed he had forgotten about the gas pumping away. I started to get the paper money when he said, "That will be ninety cents, please." A big smile beamed from ear to ear illuminating the night.

"Yes, but the pump says—!"

He stopped me in the middle of my sentence and grinned. "Don't worry about what the pump says. That's my fault for forgetting to shut it off."

"I don't want to get you in any trouble. I will be more than happy to write you a check for the full amount."

He shook his head as I handed him the nine dimes. We waved good-bye and headed home, singing to our favorite tapes.

By June, I'd managed to save up more money, and we got another apartment. It had a large patio, enclosed by the living room, dining room, and Christopher's room, which all had double sliding glass doors. One end of the patio overlooked the apartment grounds and swimming pool.

Mom had given me two patio chairs and a round metal table to set outside. The apartment had a nice little kitchen and tiled dining room, which I had to scrub to see the color. I bought some second-hand furniture for the living and dining rooms, then moved my bedroom furniture from Mom's house. It was nice to be back on our own again.

Chris was out of school and enjoying his new surroundings, especially the pool. That kid sure loved the water. Many times we spent the day at the pool as he showed off his swimming skills.

From time to time, Chris was weak from spinal taps. This also affected his legs, and they became stiff. I found it necessary to keep a wheelchair handy all the time. Luckily, Sister Madonna Maria found one small enough to fit in the trunk of Herbie. Chris didn't mind sitting and riding wherever we ventured, just as long as he could go!

One of the tour guides who was a regular at the hotel, asked if I would arrange several functions for the tours before he came to town. This would save him from making phone calls and connections long distance. The job seemed simple enough and paid about two-hundred dollars for a weekend of work, an offer I couldn't refuse.

This soon caught on with the other guides, and before I knew it, I was booking all kinds of functions: flights over the Grand Canyon, barbecues, and transportation to and from various scenic interest points in the state of Arizona.

I got so busy, I quit my job at the hotel and hired two of my girlfriends to help drive the vans I rented to transport the tours to various places. The timing was right. Chris was in and out of a wheelchair at this time, for a few months, anyway. It was nice to be home with him and still have plenty of money to support us.

Chris had a ball with the tourists. I took him everywhere I went. Even the Europeans got the biggest kick out of him. Chris certainly wasn't shy, to say the least. He would join in the Western barbecues and ask the people if they were having a good time while he casually sipped on a can of pop.

That summer I became a pretty good assistant tour director, and Christopher enjoyed being Mommie's little assistant. He was also very good, I might add. At least we were having fun, and I was making ends meet, with a little left over, for a change.

14

Strike Two

It was about two weeks before Christopher's seventh birthday, and I had promised him a party with all his new friends in the complex. He picked out the invitations, prizes, and party favors. I was even informed of what flavor of cake and ice cream he wanted.

Chris delivered all the invitations around the complex himself. I took him over to Mom's so he could give one to Dawn, a cute little girl that lived up the street. I called Dawn's mother later that evening to tell her about the party and explain that she could ride over in the car with my mother.

Dawn was a very special friend of Chris's. She was petite, with dark brown hair and big brown eyes to match. Very much a little lady, she was Chris's first crush.

As I cleaned the apartment and hung the decorations, Chris double-checked with all the kids to make sure that they were coming to his shindig. I don't think I ever saw a kid more excited about a birthday party!

On August 8, 1979, his big day finally arrived. The decorations were in place, the cake was on the table, and Chris waited anxiously for the doorbell to ring. About two o'clock, the kids started flooding the apartment. Mom, the grandparents, and Dawn came shortly afterwards. Chris mingled with all his pals, introducing Dawn as his girlfriend. He tried to let the pretty girl win all the prizes.

Being the smart mother that I was, and knowing my son the way I did, I provided enough prizes for each kid.

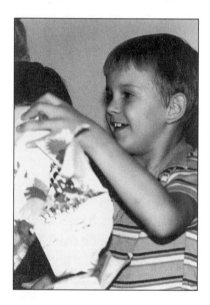

August 8, 1979, "Happy Birthday, Chris."

I was truly relieved when one of the children finally smashed the piñata we had hung on the patio. The swinging of the baseball bat was making me a little nervous with all the glass doors surrounding the patio.

The kids sang "Happy Birthday" to Chris as he blew out the candles on his cake. He was so happy that day and had so much fun. His energy level was at its highest. I hoped he could always be so full of life.

"Neato, it's a tool set to build stuff with."

As the excitement slowed its pace and the kids began to leave, I noticed a few drops of blood dripping from Chris's nose. I didn't make much of it for his sake; I simply handed him a tissue to wipe the blood away.

Deep down, I knew what was happening. Fear gripped my heart. Chris was going out of remission again.

Mom sat and read a new storybook to Chris and Dawn while the grandparents retreated to my room to rest. Tears mixed with soapsuds as I cleaned up the kitchen. I said a silent prayer.

The following morning, I called the doctor. He suggested that I bring Chris in that day. After a blood test, the doctor confirmed what I already knew. He was out of remission; the leukemia was active again.

Chris was switched to different medications and had a blood transfusion in emergency that day. The sister came down to visit us as usual while we sat watching television and waiting for the IV to finish.

As Chris was drifting off to sleep, I told him that the sister and I were going to get some coffee and would be right back. He nodded and we walked to the cafeteria. I got my coffee first and found an empty table. The sister joined me a few seconds later.

"How are you doing through all this?"

"OK, I guess. There isn't much else I can do. Just keep smiling and take one day at a time."

"What does the doctor say about Chris?"

"Well, he really didn't have to say much. I already know the score. This is the third time, and he will be able to stop it for awhile, but there won't be another remission. I guess our time is running out. You remember when we first met in the little room on pediatrics?"

"Yes, I sure do."

"You know, three years seemed like a long time then. Now it seems so short."

We talked for about twenty minutes before returning to Chris in the emergency room. The doctor had again arranged for a room in pediatrics. I ended up having coffee and sitting in that same little room. It happened every time. Nothing ever changed in that room, not the furniture or even the magazines.

Chris's hospital stay lasted about three weeks. During that time, Chris developed a growth on his forehead and right rib cage. The doctor operated to drain the poison. His forehead cleared up fairly well, leaving only a small scar.

His ribs continued to drain for several weeks after I was able to take him home. It was necessary to use the wheelchair more often. Chris's body was very weak from the disease and all the treatments. Luckily, I still had the wheelchair that the sister had arranged; we needed it more than ever now.

I called Tony to tell him of Chris's progress and invited him out for a visit if he wanted to come.

Chris didn't get to start school that year as he spent most of his time in bed. His legs were weak, and I carried him to and from the bathroom, bedroom, and living room. Once in a while, he would get the ambition to crawl on his own.

Twice a day, I would roll him on his side and drain the brown poison from the pocket that developed in his chest. It wasn't painful for Chris, thank God, just time consuming and messy.

Since I had to spend all my time at home with Chris, working a regular job was impossible. The tour business was a blessing. I could make all the phone calls during the week and drive a van on the weekend. I would take Chris with me by hauling his wheelchair in the back of the van and seating him behind me.

Where there's a will, there's a way. Since I didn't speak other languages, I found out what countries I had on board. Then once the people were seated I would ask, "OK, who speaks English?"

A few hands would go up.

"Now, who speaks English *and* German?"

A few hands stayed up.

"OK, up front here. Who speaks English and French? Great, up front here, next to the lady, please."

The Dutch people said they were OK, they understood either language. I started the engine and drove down the road with the interpreters speaking away. The group loved it—three languages going at once. Everyone laughed and tried to speak faster than the other person. It was real team participation. Chris just sat and giggled as they talked, enjoying all of the international attention he could get.

Tony decided to fly out for a visit around Thanksgiving. Chris was feeling better by then, allowing the three of us to go to more places. On one of our shopping trips to the toy store, Chris fell in love with a battery-powered police motorcycle. I split the cost of it with his father. Chris rode it out of the store, drove down the sidewalk, and parked in front of Herbie. He could ride it in the apartment, giving my back a break, and he could play outside with the other kids a little more. By riding the motorcycle, he could keep up with his buddies, and he was the hit of the complex. All the kids wanted to ride it. I had to enforce a few rules in that area, because once Chris was off the motorcycle, he couldn't stand up or even walk more than two feet before falling down.

I can't remember how many times a day I would carry them both up and down the stairs of the apartment building to play for awhile.

Tony and I talked a lot during that visit about Chris and what to do when the end came. He was still having a hard time talking about it, but not as seriously as before. I think it was good for him to see Chris in his weakened condition. Somehow, the truth seemed to hit home, because during Tony's previous visits, Chris hadn't looked sick; leukemia had been only a word.

One evening after Chris had fallen off to sleep, I asked Tony a very important question. "Do you want me to bring Chris's body back to Illinois for burial?"

He was silent for several minutes. Although the topic was extremely emotional for both of us, it also was necessary for both of us to be in agreement. When Tony looked up from the floor, his face portrayed a heart-broken man trying to accept the reality that his son was dying.

"I didn't know if you wanted to do that or not," he said at last. "My folks have a family plot that we can bury him in, if you want."

"I don't want to have him out here in Arizona all alone. I think it would be best if he was buried with family, don't you? At least that way, you can keep the grave up with flowers."

Both of us shed a few tears as we fought to control our emotions. The conversation continued for about two hours. In the back of my mind, I knew Tony still felt badly about not being in Arizona with us. I thought that maybe by taking Chris back home, it would relieve some of the guilt he felt and could possibly provide a closure for him.

We talked about the expense of a funeral and about the insurance policy that we had taken out on Chris when he was two years old. Tony said he would sign it over to me to take care of all the expenses. I agreed. It was a great relief.

Soon after, we changed the subject to more pleasant things, leaving it in God's hands. We would cross that painful bridge when we came to it.

During the last two years, Chris had developed a special place in his heart for Kay's husband, Tommy. We had dinner at the couple's house a couple of times and swam in their pool. Even though Kay, a perky Southern redhead, and I didn't share any more classes together, we shared a friendship. She always knew just what to say at the right time to lift my spirits.

Tommy had called and asked if it would be all right for Chris to go on a camp-out with him and his son's Indian Guide Troop. I explained that the time just wasn't right.

"Chris's resistance level is zero, and he isn't strong enough to walk much like the other kids."

Tommy seemed to understand. "Will it be all right if he comes to a meeting later on sometime?"

"No problem, Tommy, but it will be a couple of months before he will be strong enough to do much of anything."

"How is he doing anyway? Is he getting better?"

"No, Tommy, he is getting worse. He just went out of remission for the second time. The doctor can halt the disease for awhile, but I doubt seriously if he will ever see his eighth birthday."

"Lynn, I can hardly believe it. I tell everybody about Chris and how he wants to be a cop when he grows up. Ron Cox is a DPS narcotics officer that I work with. When we sit on the flight line waiting for planes to land, I tell him all about Chris and how this little guy just wants to be a cop. They all want to meet him."

"Well, maybe someday they can, but right now he needs rest more than excitement."

"Will you keep Kay and me posted on his condition?"

"I'll call you guys if there is a change one way or the other."

The tours were still coming to Phoenix, but I was informed that they were going to be routed through Florida, which meant that my little business would soon be out of business.

15

Golden Stars & Tough Questions

Christmas time was rolling around again. I knew deep down in my heart that this would be our last Christmas together. I decided to go all out that holiday season. We got a real big tree with real "store-bought" decorations.

We bought more presents than we had ever had before. We hung up some of our old decorations and trashed the ones we didn't want anymore. The holiday music played on the stereo while I baked shaped cookies, and then Chris decorated each tin soldier, tree, and star with candy sprinkles.

Mom was doing pretty well herself with Christmas coming again. Grandma Vie had snapped out of her depression and was happy in the nursing home we had found for her.

But the other grandma wasn't doing well at all. It became necessary to place her in the same nursing home.

She didn't like it much, but adjusted to it stubbornly by not speaking to anyone.

When I went to visit once a week, I took Chris because he always made them laugh, along with everyone else in the home. He shook hands and talked with all of them. Mom visited about twice a week to check on them and to pick up and deliver laundry.

My brother, Gary, came out that year for Christmas and brought his son, Jeff. The two boys were a big hit in the nursing home. Jeff was three years younger than Chris, and both boys wanted to wheel all the residents down the long halls in their wheelchairs.

Christmas was good that year. Somehow, Santa brought all the presents that Chris wanted, plus a few more.

One night, shortly after Christmas, Chris brought his *Children's Bible* to me, and asked, "Mommie, what happens when people die, like Grandpa Wally? Is he in heaven?"

He took me by surprise, to say the least. We had talked about Jesus and what it meant to go to heaven, but this was hitting pretty close to home. Careful to conceal my sadness, I gave my son a tender smile.

"Chris, come here."

He climbed upon my lap and opened the Bible to the pictures illustrating Jesus after he had risen from the grave.

"Mommie, when I die someday, will you come with me to heaven?"

His innocent, child-like questions needed to be answered truthfully. With the same innocence with which he had asked them, I answered.

"Chris, if Jesus wants me to, I will, but if he doesn't, then I must stay here for a little while longer until it's time for me to go to heaven."

"What's it like up there?"

I thought for a minute, "Lord, he is really asking some hard questions. Help!"

Somehow, these words came to my mind and spoke from my mouth: "Chris, you know when you're at Grandma's for the day, and I'm here at the apartment, we are apart, aren't we?"

"Yes."

"Well, even though we can't touch each other or see each other, we still feel the love between us, don't we?"

Chris nodded his head listening intensely and waiting to hear what I would say next.

"And, you don't forget me, and I don't forget you, because we know that we will see each other soon, right?"

"Right, because you come and get me from Grandma's," Chris excitedly blurted out as he wiggled into a more comfortable position on the sofa.

"Right, but we can't go to heaven until Jesus comes to get us. Until that particular time we have to stay here."

"But what is it like up there?"

I thought for a minute, watching his face anxiously waiting for my answer.

"Well, I've never been to Heaven, but look here at this picture. There is Jesus holding the little children. There is only laughter. There is no sickness, no tears—only love and joy. You can run and play all you want with all the other children and the angels, too."

"Mommie, will my puppy be there, the one that died?"

I nodded my head yes. "Yes, Chris, he'll be there waiting for you to play with him."

Then I reached out, putting my arms around him, and we started a tickle fight. He seemed to be satisfied that his questions were answered as he climbed down from the sofa and went to his room to get ready for bed. I tucked him in with a big kiss and asked if he had any more questions. With a smile on his face, he shook his head.

I wanted him always to ask questions about anything that was on his mind. I felt it was important to Chris to have that security and freedom. So that evening while tucking him in bed I told him, "Chris, I'm happy that you ask questions whenever you feel like it. I hope you always will. Mommie will always do her best to answer them. Okey-dokey?"

He giggled, "Okey-dokey," as he snuggled in for the night with Billy Bear tucked in beside him.

As we rang in a new year and a new decade, in January 1980, Chris had grown a little stronger. Although he still rode his little police motorcycle around the apartment and out to play, it was mostly for fun now. He was able to play and enjoy some of his favorite outings and activities.

Thank you, big and little Indians, for a special
night with my son.

Tommy was able to take him to an Indian Guide
meeting. Chris received an award from the other kids that
said, "Get Well Soon."

The Guides was totally a father-and-son organization,
but that evening they permitted "Mom" to attend.

A local tour guide friend stopped by one afternoon,
asking if he could take Chris shopping. A few days after
the shopping spree, Chris requested my presence in his
room. I wiped my hands from doing the dishes, wondering
what had caused his serious and solemn expression. When

I entered his room, I found a baseball glove, ball, and an expensive toy racecar laid out on the bed.

"Chris, aren't these the toys that you guys bought the other day?"

Chris leaned on his bed pushing the toys toward me almost robotically, as if he didn't even want to touch them. "Yes, Mommie, they are, but I don't want them." I sat down next to him and picked up the glove. "Why, honey?"

"Because he didn't pay for them. I saw him stuff them in the big box that his golf clubs came in."

Chris leaned against the bed with his hands clasped. Despite his solemn expression, he seemed relieved that he had told me about the "hot" toys. I was shocked, disappointed, and disgusted with the person whom I had trusted. At the same time, I was extremely proud of Chris for not wanting the toys and telling me the truth.

"Well, it's not right to steal. Is it, Chris?"

"No, that's why I don't want them."

I kissed him on the head, told him how proud he had made me, and asked him what we should do about the toys.

"Maybe we could give them back to the store?"

That was my first thought, too, but I wondered how I would explain it to the store. I wasn't sure they would understand.

"Chris, why don't we give them to kids that don't have any toys. The police collect toys for kids. Shall we give these things to them?"

Happy about that plan, he headed into the kitchen to retrieve a paper sack. The next day, we dropped off the toys, then went to have lunch at our favorite restaurant. As a reward for telling me about the "toy caper," I suggested he think of what toy he would like to pick out at the store.

Chris wanted to attend school like all the other kids. He had already missed half the school year, and although his side had healed and his strength was good, I told him it was OK to wait until the fall. I knew that there would be no fall school year for him and didn't want to give up my precious time with him. But Chris insisted.

"Mommie, I can ride my bike to school like the other kids. I want to go, please."

The next day we visited the school. I asked Chris to sit and wait in the outer office while I went to explain his situation.

"Mommie has to go and talk to the principal for a minute. You wait here, OK?"

"OK, but can I get a drink of water over there, and walk around and look at the pictures on the wall?"

"Of course, you can. Just don't leave this room."

"Mommie, what does that say?" I looked at the plaque to which Chris was pointing. "Chris, that says Rose Lane Elementary School. That's the name of this school. OK?" He continued to look around the room and went to get another drink of water. With Chris content, I met with the principal, Mr. Roberts.

I explained about Chris and his desire to attend school. I also explained that I wasn't interested in his grades at all.

"I would appreciate it if you could work something out with his teacher to just let him think he is smart like the other kids. It doesn't matter what he learns; he doesn't have that much time left. He won't need an education after this year. Just ask the teacher to mark his papers with gold stars or whatever they do, please."

Mr. Roberts sat behind his desk with both hands under his chin. He listened intently to every word, as I looked him straight in the eye. The principal leaned back in his chair as he replied with sincerity. "We can do that. I will see to it personally. How old is Chris so I know what grade he will be in?"

"He is seven years old. He completed the first grade last year, but he hasn't attended school so far this year. I don't think he will be able to handle second grade work, but he wants to try."

"You tell me what grade you want him in, and I will talk to the teacher. Just tell me what you want for Chris, and I'll do it."

"Well, as long as he wants to try for second, let him try, OK? We can always put him back in first, if necessary. But he needs to find out for himself and make the decision himself."

The principal cracked a smile and wiped his eyes with a tissue. "Do you want him to start today?"

"Yes, he's sitting outside waiting to go to school."

"Well then, let's show this special young man his new classroom and introduce him to his new teacher."

We found Chris studying all the school's awards, which were displayed in a big glass case. Pictures that the students had drawn were exhibited on the wall behind him.

Mr. Roberts introduced himself and bent down to shake Chris's hand. Chris stood up to clasp his small hand to the principal's. Once the two were acquainted, the principal asked the big question.

"Chris, do you want to take a walk and meet your new teacher and classmates?" Chris grinned, beaming with excitement and pride.

"Yes, and can my Mommie come, too?"

"You bet she can. Come with me this way, and I'll take you around the school and show you everything." The principal's encouraging smile and excited voice made it a special day for Chris.

We toured the entire school. Chris loved every second of it. He asked about the cafeteria, the gym, and the most important part, the entire playground. We finally arrived outside the classroom. Mr. Roberts opened the door of the second grade class and motioned for the teacher to join us outside.

He introduced Chris and asked if she would please introduce him to the class and then return to talk with us. Her puzzled expression suggested she knew that ours was no ordinary situation.

The teacher opened the door, and I could see kids busy at work, coloring and reading stories. Chris waved good-bye, and I told him I would meet him in front of the principal's office when school was over.

When the teacher returned a few minutes later, Mr. Roberts explained Chris's condition and advised her that the only important thing was his happiness, that his schoolwork was irrelevant.

We also discussed the fact that he had lost a half year, and it would probably be necessary to put him in the first grade. She agreed and said she would keep us both posted, If she felt that things were too difficult for him, she would send a note home.

It had only been a few days when Chris came home with a note. We talked that evening, and Chris decided he wanted to transfer into the first-grade class. I went to school with him the next morning. Mr. Roberts was expecting us. He walked us to Chris's new classroom and introduced us to the teacher. She had already been briefed by the second-grade teacher and was looking forward to meeting Chris.

Chris fit in very well with his new class. In no time, all of his papers bore "smiley faces" and big gold stars! We saved them up, and every couple of weeks we'd mail a brown envelope to Illinois for his daddy.

Chris missed a couple of days due to illness, but most of the time he insisted on riding his bike to school.

During the first parent-teacher conference, I visited the classroom and talked with his teacher. "I want to thank you for making this a special time for Chris. I mean, I know he has missed a lot of school and his time is short, but when he comes home, he talks for an hour about you and what everyone did in class."

"I love that little guy. He is a joy to have in the classroom."

"Well, thanks, but I mean allowing Chris to think he is doing the same work as the other kids. You know, the smiley faces and gold stars all over his papers?"

"I've got news for you. That son of yours is at the top of the class all on his own. He is one of my brightest students! He earned those smiley faces and gold stars all on his own." Her face lit up with enthusiasm as she continued to sing high praises about Chris.

I didn't know quite what to say. I was both choked up and very proud at the same time. We looked at each other and started laughing.

"The little squirt is full of surprises, isn't he?"

"He sure is, and all the kids almost fight to play with him. Chris is the most popular kid in the class."

Once the teacher had excused herself to greet other parents, Chris grabbed my hand and showed me his desk where his artwork was displayed.

I went home a very happy and proud mommie. I sat on the patio talking to Jesus for the rest of the afternoon. I thanked him again for a very special little boy.

That night when I tucked Chris in and kissed him good night, I told him that I was very proud of him for doing so well in school. Holding tightly to his Billy Bear, Chris produced a startling question. "Mommie, what's it like in the graveyard at night? Do the monsters come out then?"

I smiled and silently hollered "help" to the Lord. "Well, in the first place, there are no monsters. In the second place, a graveyard is where we bury the bodies of people whose spirits have gone to heaven to be with Jesus, and, finally, Jesus is there in the graveyard, and you and I both know that wherever he is, we have nothing to fear. Right, alligator?"

Chris smiled and hugged his bear.

"Right, crocodile. I love you, Mommie."

I got up to turn off the light then turned to kiss him again. "I love you too, Chris. Sweet dreams and sleep tight."

16

A Walk Through the Valley

About the first of March, Chris was missing more and more school because of illness. I knew that time was running out. Chris had a favorite local kid's television show he watched every chance he got. One afternoon I stopped in to the television station and inquired about how to get Chris on the show.

The receptionist was extremely kind as I explained the situation. She confirmed that anytime I could get him to the television station, Chris would be in the front row, wheelchair and all.

That evening I told Chris where we were going in the morning. His face lit up brighter than white. "You're joking with me, Mommie, aren't you?"

"No, I'm not Chris. You're going to be on television with Wallace and Ladmo. What do you think of that?"

Chris could hardly finish his dinner with all the excitement rushing through his veins but managed to eat a few more bites. He called all his friends that evening and shared the exciting new of his upcoming debut. Some of the kids came over that evening to hear it in person. They played in Chris's room for several hours, laughing and giggling as they all told Chris they would be watching him.

The next morning, I carried Chris downstairs and sat him in the front seat of Herbie. Then I carried the wheelchair down and placed it tightly in the trunk. Seconds later, we were headed for the station, Chris grinning from ear to ear all the way in anticipation of actually seeing his favorite kid-show personalities in person and getting to talk with them. He kept asking, "Mommie, do you think maybe I might get a Ladmo bag like the kids on TV do?"

Upon our arrival, it seemed that special preparation had taken place for Chris. A nice young man gave him a little tour of the television studio. He explained all the cameras and lights while wheeling Chris to a spot just beside the bleachers. Shortly, several kids arrived, and soon Chris was making new friends. I took a seat with the other parents and just smiled with pride and happiness.

The show, of course, was a hit as usual. All the kids laughed and screamed and booed at the villain. The biggest and most special Ladmo bag was given to Chris that day, at least in my son's eyes. All the kids received a bag of goodies, and somehow I felt that each parent and each kid realized, from looking at Chris, why he was given a little more special treatment that day. One of the fathers had thought ahead and brought a camera, which was more than I could say for myself. After the show was over, he approached me and handed me a picture of Chris. I thanked him with tears in my eyes and graciously accepted the photo as I told him of Chris's condition.

Once, I remember Chris, in a tearful little voice, pleading with me, "Mommie, you don't love me. I know you don't."

I asked him, "Why don't you think I love you?"

"Because you don't spank me like the other kids' mothers spank them."

I smiled and told him, "Chris you aren't like the other boys. You don't say bad words, you don't throw rocks, and you don't get into fights. So I can't spank you unless you do something bad that you know you should not do."

He agreed.

I sat on the patio and watched him play with a couple of kids in the yard. Pretty soon I saw him punch one of the boys and say a few words that shouldn't have been coming from his mouth. I just sat and watched, and a few minutes later he came and sat on my lap and told me what he had done.

I took him to his room and asked him if he knew what he did was wrong. He said he did. A couple of taps on the rear end and an hour in his room made him feel better. Later that evening, Chris curled up beside me and asked if I would marry him, because I took such excellent care of him that he wanted me to take care of his kids, too.

One afternoon, Chris and I were walking through the mall on our way to the bank. He usually lagged about five feet behind me, looking at all the things in the windows. When he would fall too far behind me, I would stop and wait for him. I stopped and called to him, "Chris, come on, honey, we'll come back and look at the store window. I have to get to the bank before it closes."

He was standing in front of a display window staring at something. I figured it was a toy he was going to convince me to buy after we had finished at the bank. I waited a few minutes and called to him again. "Chris, please, sweetheart. I have to get to the bank. Come on. We'll come back later. I promise."

There was still no response, which was unusual for him. I headed toward him. Just as I reached him and saw what he was staring at, he turned, took my hand, and said, "I'll be glad when I get there."

"Chris, what did you say?" I asked with wide-eyed wonderment.

I had to ask him to make sure what I just had heard was correct. As we walked down the sidewalk, hand and hand, he looked up at me as if we had never stopped walking and asked, "What are you talking about? You're quacking up, Mommie. Can we go look in the toy store when you're done at the bank?"

I could tell that Chris had no recall of staring at the picture in the window, but I smiled and agreed with him—somewhat in shock—but with partial understanding of what had just taken place. "Maybe I am quacking up, but we still have to get to the bank."

As we stood in the line at the bank, I felt in my spirit that time was short. Chris had been staring at a picture of Jesus. It had held him captive, almost as if they had been talking and Jesus had consoled him that in a little while there would be no more sickness and no more pain. In a short time, he would be happier than he had ever been before.

If Chris had known any fear about death, it passed from him that day. He never asked about death again. He only asked about heaven.

A couple of days later, we had a doctor's appointment. Chris was receiving blood and platelets once a week in the hospital in order to stop the nosebleeds and to keep the color in his cheeks. "Would it be all right if I talked to your Mommie outside while you rest here?" the doctor asked.

We walked into his office, and as we sat down, it was clear that the impending conversation would be an extension of the discussion we had had three years earlier.

"It's coming close to the end, isn't it, doctor?" My voice cracked a little as I searched my purse for a tissue.

His voice was etched with concern. "Yes. There isn't too much I can do except give him medications to control the pain.

"You have to make a decision if you want to let him die with dignity or try to prolong his life through experimental drugs."

I got up and walked around the chair, crossed my arms, and looked up at the ceiling for a moment. He started to get up from his chair when I turned and said, "I'm OK. I think I know what I have to do. I just need a couple of days to talk to my Friend and make the final decision. I know I won't subject him to unnecessary pain and drugs. It isn't going to save his life, is it?"

I knew the answer to my own question, but still I had to hear the words from the doctor in order to let the one clinging shred of hope die within me.

"No, it won't save Chris's life, Linda. It will only prolong the inevitable—at best by only a couple of months." The doctor's voice broke as the same hope was dying within him.

"If I decide to let him die, what will happen then? I mean, can you give him something to keep him comfortable?"

"Yes, we'll increase the blood transfusions to twice a week, and if that isn't enough, we'll give him more. I'll give you some medications you can administer at home in case he is hurting."

I stood wiping my eyes as I attempted to control my emotions.

"We have another appointment in three days. I'll let you know my decision then."

I thanked him for his honesty and even more for being a friend. As we shook hands good-bye, I could see the hurt and sorrow in his eyes. I returned to Chris's bedside to find Sister Maria reading him a story. The platelets were just about finished. Soon we were on our way home, and I tucked Chris into bed. The nurses in the emergency room had given him the empty IV bottles and plastic tubing to take home. Before going to sleep we had to get the tape and hook poor Billy Bear up for a transfusion. They both lay in bed as Chris drifted quietly off to sleep.

That evening was the first of three nights of wrestling with the decision of life or death. No rest would come as I found myself wrestling on the patio all night long, smoking, drinking coffee, and praying.

"Lord, tell me what to do. I need you to help me like you've never helped before."

The doctor's words played like a broken record through my mind over and over again: "It will only prolong the inevitable—for a few months at the very most."

I felt so alone as I gazed out at the pool. All the fun times were over now. No more exploring, swimming, or going to dinner every Friday night. Christmas wouldn't be the same. He had already picked out his birthday presents. He wanted a battery-powered car, so he and his friends could go cruising.

"Lord, can't you make him well? Can't you make me sick instead of him? He is so young, he hasn't even lived yet."

I wept all night long, composing myself only when I went in to check on him. Then I would pour myself another cup of coffee and talk with the Lord some more.

The next day, Chris was still very weak, and he stayed in my bed most of the day. I went about doing my normal daily chores and tried to act as if everything was all right. Exhausted myself, I snuggled up and took a nap with Chris. It was rough enough just making it through the day. Once night had fallen, I found myself plagued by the doctor's words. I knew there would be no sleep for me the second night.

And I knew that I had to come to terms with the decision. I had to feel that it was right. I knew I would have to live with the decision for the rest of my life. There could be no doubt in my mind, no guilt, no question of right or wrong. I had to do what was best for Chris.

I sat on the patio with the three years of memories slowly drifting in and out of my mind. *"It will only prolong the inevitable a few months at the most."* I started to get very cold as more thoughts joined the chaos in my head. Flashbacks of the first night in the hospital with Chris came back. I saw myself leaning against the bars of the window in Chris's room.

I sat on the chair with my arms wrapped around my legs praying and crying like never before.

"Lord, this isn't right. This isn't fair of you. You know I love my son. You know I only want the best for him."

I was shaking as I went inside to warm up and check on Chris. I climbed into bed beside him and watched him sleep. The thoughts continued as I took in the sound of his breath and the warmth of his skin. I found myself wanting to cry again. I slid myself out of bed and returned to the patio. Thoughts haunted me, hour after hour, until sometime close to dawn I fell asleep on the sofa. The next day was pretty much the same as the day before. The following night was not.

It was the third night of my agonizing decision and the third night of memories reliving themselves in my mind with the thought of spending the rest of my life alone without Chris. As I sat drinking coffee and smoking, I seemed to relive the entire three years we had had together.

I sat "listening" to my thoughts for about two hours. I finally spoke them out loud. "I'm a good mother, and I love my son very much. That is why I am giving him to the Lord, Jesus, to take him. God knows the truth. He is the truth.

"Lord, I give Chris to you here and now to take to heaven when you're ready to take him. I'm not going to try to prolong his life. I'm going to stop everything—all medications and bone marrow tests, all spinal taps. I'm only going to keep giving him blood because it helps him feel better.

"Lord, I know I have made the right decision, because I feel good inside about it. Please help me through this time. I know I'm going to need you."

Things became peaceful after that. I sat up until dawn watching the stars disappear as the sun crept over the top of the buildings. I heard the morning traffic in the street. I felt stronger than I had in quite some time.

That morning, I made breakfast and got Chris ready for the doctor's appointment. I told him that there would be no more spinal taps, bone marrow tests, or the shots that made him so sick. Chris was thrilled and asked, "Can I go home to Illinois?"

I looked at him and started to ask what he meant, but stopped myself, nodding my head instead, because I knew to what he was referring.

"Yes, Chris, you can go home to Illinois. Mommie will take you. I promise. OK?"

He smiled and continued building little roads out of his breakfast while he slowly ate. I couldn't eat much and soon just dumped my food in the garbage.

When I informed the doctor of my decision, he seemed relieved and agreed it was for the best.

"I'm glad you decided to let him go in dignity. I would help you any way I could, if you wanted to prolong it, but he has been through enough, and so have you."

A few days later, I took Chris over to Mom's to visit for the afternoon, then went to make funeral arrangements. I thought it best to make the arrangements while I still had some sanity left.

I sat with Chet Hansen, the owner and a director of Hansen's Mortuary, and filled out the paperwork and instructions for shipping the body to Illinois.

As I wrote out the deposit check, I felt I had given up for the first time in three years. There was no hope for my son. The medical world had done its best to save him, and I had to realize that I had done my best, too. Somehow, we had managed to live a lifetime in three years. But it was time to say good-bye.

I was surprisingly calm as I made the arrangements, conducting myself in a totally business-like manner. Every detail had been covered, including the flight reservation for Tony, if he decided to fly out for the very end.

I knew exactly what I had to do and whom to contact when the day came. Handing over the check, I envisioned the time that I would be sitting beside Chris on his hospital bed, praying and fighting for his every breath.

Driving home to Mom's, I felt kind of peaceful about what I had done. I had to acknowledge that the ball game was almost over. Strike three was near.

The bases were loaded now; the batter was at the plate, the pitcher winding up for the pitch, and, like a movie that had suddenly stopped, everything was frozen in time. That's where my mind saw Chris, standing at the plate. I wanted us to stay frozen in that safe moment in time. I knew as soon as the pitcher released the ball, my little slugger would take one last swing, and he would miss. Strike Three, and . . . Chris would be out.

When I drove to Mom's, Chris was riding his motorcycle in the driveway, showing off for Dawn. I sat and had coffee with Mom and Grandpa Pete while filling them in on Chris's condition and the arrangements that I had made. Tears welled up in Mom's eyes.

"I never believed that it would come to this," she said. "I just never did. But I'm glad now that you two did all the things you did, even though I worried about you being all over this state. I don't know how you did it, but you did."

I fought back the tears for Chris's sake. I didn't want him to see me cry. It always made him cry.

"Mom, I'm going to call Tony tonight and tell him about Chris. I think they need to have at least a day or two together. If you don't mind, Mom, can Tony stay in the spare room here?"

Mom agreed with a nod of her head as she got up to grab a tissue.

"I'm going to sell all the furniture and move from the apartment. I can't live there anymore," I told her.

"You can move back here. You know you always have a room waiting for you."

"Thanks, Mom. I was hoping you'd say that. It will only be for a few months until I find a full-time job when I get back from Illinois."

"This is your home, too; you stay as long as you want."

I took Chris to see the two grandmas at the nursing home as much as possible during the next couple of weeks. However, we spent most of our time in the emergency ward with Chris receiving blood and platelets. The sister was always there with a cheery smile and a funny joke for us.

Tony made arrangements to fly into Phoenix. Mom told the grandmothers and my brother, Gary, about Chris's condition.

One day during our weekly visit to the emergency ward, Chris turned to me and said, "Mommie, call Tommy; I want to see him."

"Chris, I'll call him when we get home."

"No, call him now. I want to see him, please."

I looked up the number in my address book and picked up the phone. I wasn't sure what to say to him, but I figured it would come to me. Kay answered the phone.

"Hi, Kay. This is Lynn."

"Well, hi. How are you two doing, anyway?"

"We're fine. Chris and I are sitting here in the emergency room getting a blood transfusion, and he insisted that I call to ask if it would be all right to come over and visit."

"Sure, anytime you want. Is everything OK?" Her voice gave me the impression that she was starting to "hear between the lines."

I took a deep breath and said, "Well, pretty much so. I just have a request from Chris to see Tommy."

"Lynn, he's close to the end, isn't he?" I wanted to cry out loud and tell her everything, but I couldn't. I just kept smiling at Chris as he listened to every word and watched every expression on my face. "Yeah, Kay. He is." She'd understood perfectly.

"Can you come over tonight?

"Chris and I will make every effort to be there if at all possible at about six o'clock. Thanks for understanding, and I'll talk to you later tonight."

"I'll call Tommy at work. Don't worry. He'll be here. I'll make sure of that. We'll see you two when you get here."

"Kay, when you talk to Tommy, would you give him a message for me? Tell him I'm calling in the promise from three years ago. "

"Lynn, what's that?" Her voice sounded confused.

"Kay, he'll hopefully remember. Please, just give him the message, and I'll explain later tonight."

I gave Chris a wink and hung up the phone. His sleepy eyes smiled. I smiled knowing that, hopefully, I had set the ball in motion by calling in that long-ago promise.

"Please, dear Lord, grant me this wish for Chris."

17

Mommie Calls in a Promise

We visited Tommy and Kay that evening, although Chris wasn't very active. He lay on the sofa watching television with the kids. We had coffee in the kitchen while I filled them in on Chris's condition.

I told them there wasn't much time left—maybe a couple of weeks. "There is nothing anyone can do. No amount of money could buy enough medication to prolong or save his life."

I explained that the blood was breaking down. His nosebleeds were a daily occurrence, and he was spitting up blood.

"His liver and spleen are enlarged from the disease, so he's taking codeine for the pain. He just wants to sleep most of the day or just lie and watch television."

Tommy and Kay both listened intensely. I got the feeling that they were wondering how I could even talk about it so calmly. I really wasn't sure myself, except that it was my only option as long as Chris was still with me.

"I have stopped all the medications, and there will be no more tests. They aren't helping him to get well anymore. The medications I gave him at home were only making him vomit, and he is immune to some of them now, anyway. The tests only seemed to make him sicker."

"Lynn, isn't there anything that some doctor can do? Somewhere in this world there has got to be something!" Tommy asked in a desperate voice.

"No, there isn't. The doctor could give him stronger medications and fresh blood while continuing with the tests, but I have decided to stop all of that and let him die in dignity. I will continue with the platelets and the painkillers, and when necessary, fresh blood to stop the bleeding. He had a transfusion this afternoon. In about a week, the leukemia will destroy the blood he received today."

As we sat for a moment, they didn't quite know what to say. Their expressions were a blend of grief mixed with hope that I had overlooked some miraculous cure.

"I have made my decision to let him die with dignity. I will not let him be used as a guinea pig. I know that he had the best medical treatment available. Everything that can be done has been done or is being done. I can't let him go through any more tests. They are too painful, and they aren't helping. Chris is happy that they are over. So now, it's just a matter of time. I'm going to leave now and take Chris home so he can rest, but, Tommy, do you remember a long time ago you promised Chris a ride in a helicopter?"

Tommy replied with a cracked voice and shocked eyes, "Yes, I do."

"Then, if you have any way of doing it, I'm calling in that promise and in light of everything, as soon as possible."

We said good-bye as I carried Chris to little Herbie waiting in the driveway. I prayed that I had done the right thing in asking for the ride in the helicopter. I had never asked for favors, but this was important for Chris and my last chance to make him happy, once again.

Three days later, on Thursday, Tommy called and asked if I thought Chris would like a ride in a police helicopter.

"Hang on a minute, and I'll get Chris. You can ask him yourself." I jokingly added, "I think he'll say yes." I placed the phone to Chris's ear as he lay in bed. Tommy talked about the police helicopter.

Chris drifted back to sleep wearing an enormous smile. A happier little boy I hadn't seen in quite some time.

A few days later, I rushed Chris to the doctor's office. Within minutes, his nurse called to inform the hospital that we were on our way, as Dr. Baranko carried Chris across the street and up to pediatrics.

The doctor and I talked for some time in our little room. He was trying to prepare me for the end. As I sat listening, I also was preparing myself to tell Tony. The helicopter ride seemed unimportant now, as Chris seemed to be fighting for his life with every ounce of strength he had left in his body. I stayed with him most of the day and night, then went home for a brief moment to call his father.

Although, there was no easy way to say what needed to be said, the direct approach seemed the best.

"Tony, if at all possible, I think you need to be here because it is close to the end. I will understand if you don't want to. He is in the hospital now, and the doctor said it would be only a matter of a few days until he is gone."

We endured a long silence. I knew that for three years he had dreaded the day that he would be receiving that phone call. I had dreaded making it, too.

"I'll arrange to be on the next flight out. Can you pick me up at the airport?" He was calm, but I could tell he was shaken by the news.

"Yes, just let me know what time and the flight number. I'll be there."

He called back later that night and left a message with Mom about when to pick him up. I returned to the hospital to spend the night with Chris. The next morning I called Tommy and Kay to inform them of the situation. I thanked Tommy for doing his best with arranging for the helicopter ride, but I knew Chris was not going to leave the hospital. As we talked, I reinforced the statement the doctor had made, that Chris had only a day or two left to live.

That morning I awoke beside Chris's bed. When the doctor came in, he found Chris sitting up in bed and eating all his breakfast. He was confused. We stepped out in the hall to talk.

"I don't know what is going on here, but this is completely out of the ordinary. Chris should *not* be sitting up and eating as he is. I really thought I would find him in a coma this morning."

Dr. Baranko shook his head slightly as he perused the charts once again hoping to find a clue for Chris's turnaround.

"Well," Dr. Baranko continued with a happy smile of confusion. "He asked me if I would take him to the toy room so he could play. I don't know what to say. From yesterday to today, Chris seems normal, healthy, and happy. I think we had better keep him in bed for today and see what happens. If he is like this tomorrow morning, you had better take him home and enjoy the time you have with him."

I suddenly had a spark of fresh hope. Chris sure was full of surprises. The doctor never dreamed that Chris would leave the hospital *alive,* and neither had I. But come tomorrow, I would take him home. Maybe all the prayers had been answered; maybe God had granted Chris a miracle. I was filled with hope for the future.

The following morning, Chris was patiently watching cartoons when I woke in the chair beside his bed. Dr. Baranko, still confused, but gleaming with happiness, released Chris to go home.

Chris and I picked Tony up at the airport, and I took them to a motel nearby so they could be alone for a few days. I had boxed up my things from the apartment and sold the furniture. Mom let me store some things in her garage. I called the motel to check on Chris, then called Tommy and Kay to inform them of the good news about

Chris and, hopefully, get the helicopter ride reinstated. Herbie and I joined Chris and Tony for dinner that evening. In a couple of days, I picked them up and brought them to Mom's house.

The next two weeks were happy for Chris as he had his father with him. We visited the Encanto Park and rode on the train that went completely around the park. Tony and I watched Chris as he went from ride to ride, having fun. We took along bread to feed the ducks in the pond, while we relaxed under a big shady tree near the shore.

Although his spirit was strong, Chris's legs weren't. The wheelchair soon took the place of his legs, which quickly grew tired.

Chris sat beside his father as much as possible during those two weeks. I was happy for them both that they could share these precious weeks together.

During those two weeks, Tommy made a phone call to Ron Cox who was an Arizona Highway Patrol narcotics officer. Ron talked to the boys, G. R. "Doc" Holloway and Steve Lump, who flew on the department's Air Rescue Unit, and W. W. "Duke" More, the Ranger helicopter pilot, and asked if they could do a "show and tell" for Chris of the cockpit. Ron got a resounding, "Hell no; we'll give him a ride in the damn thing." They, in turn, went to their chain of command for permission.

Ron also called the department's Public Relations Officer, Sergeant Allan Schmidt, and told him the story. According to Ron, from that point the "snowball" began rolling.

The director, Ralph Milstead, was informed about
the planned events, but he had a few tricks up his sleeve;
and Lieutenant Colonel Dick Shafer had a few surprises
up his sleeve, too.

Ron contacted Motorcycle Officer Frank Shankwitz,
who was involved with school children throughout the
state and asked if he would meet Chris when he landed at
the department's compound in Phoenix. Among other
events, he had also arranged for a ride in a patrol car
with Sergeant Jim Eaves.

The Department of Public Safety Public Relations
Department went to work notifying the local news
station of the upcoming event. Channel 12 KPNX news
pilot Jerry Foster joined in and rolled the "snowball" a
few more times.

The morning of Chris's wish, he could hardly contain
himself. He had fully dressed himself by 6:00 a.m. and
was jumping up and down off the chair at the breakfast
table, too excited to eat or watch television as he waited
for nine o'clock to arrive.

On April 29, 1980, a few minutes past 8:00 a.m.,
Tommy picked up Chris at Mom's house, then drove to
Scottsdale Memorial Hospital. Waiting there was a
Highway Patrol Ranger helicopter. Chris flew over the
city of Phoenix asking the pilot, Duke Moore, and the
Air Rescue team, Doc Holloway and Steve Lump,
endless questions while pressing his face against the
window and stretching his neck, like a silly goose, trying
to see everything.

Tony and I drove over to meet them at the Highway Patrol Compound in Phoenix, where they landed. Officer Ron Cox took us to the helicopter landing site.

Helicopter pilot Jerry Foster also became involved that day. Chris touched Jerry's heart as he flew alongside the Ranger filming the smiles of a little boy's dream coming true, the story of the soon-to-be littlest trooper in the history of the state of Arizona.

When the two helicopters were within sight of the Highway Patrol compound, everyone in attendance stood, pointing at the sky in excited anticipation of their arrival.

When the crew landed, both Jerry and the Ranger's pilot gave a starry-eyed Chris a rundown on the instrument panel.

They walked Chris over to a real Highway Patrol motorcycle parked nearby. Waiting to meet this little "trooper," Motorcycle Officer Frank Shankwitz put Chris on the bike and placed his big helmet on Chris's head. He showed Chris the various instruments on the bike that every good cop uses. Several officers gathered around Chris, eager to make his every wish come true.

Frank presented Chris with his very own patrol sticker for his little motorcycle. As he sat on the bike, I could see in his face that he saw himself as a big policeman, all grown up. Chris was in his glory being surrounded by all these "big buddies," each wanting to carry him to their own bike.

A patrol car rolled up, and although I don't know how, I think his eyes grew even bigger than his smile. All the motor officers and pilots escorted him over to the police car that waited just for him. They each took their turn shaking his hand and saying good-bye.

Tony and I were invited to get in the back seat for the ride of our lives. Chris climbed into the front with Sergeant Jim Eaves. The sergeant didn't have to ask more than once if Chris wanted to drive the car. He quickly climbed on the sergeant's lap, and off we went. Chris steered the car across the compound and through the gates to the parking lot. The officer grinned and laughed as Chris blew the biggest bubbles ever, from one stick of bubble gum. The department photographer took pictures that captured every happy moment.

The officers followed in procession to the main office building where they escorted Chris into Lieutenant Colonel Dick Shafer's office.

"This young man wants to be a Highway Patrol officer," Ron announced in full authority. "We thought we'd try and help him out. What do you think?"

The colonel extended his hand towards Chris, who continued popping bubbles, and said, "That's what these guys have been telling me. They said you really want to be a policeman? A motorcycle officer to boot."

"Yes, I do." Chris's gleaming smile could have lit up the sky. With a big enthusiastic grin, Chris showed the colonel the patches on his jacket and the sticker that Frank had given him earlier.

"Well, you know, Chris, every officer has to have a Smokey Bear hat."

The colonel reached down behind his chair and picked up the smallest hat they could find in the state.

"Here, try this on for size," he said as he placed a Class A official Smokey Bear hat on Chris's head.

Bright as they were, the flashbulbs that lit up the room still couldn't compete with the smile on Chris's face. Tommy picked Chris up and stood him on the colonel's desk. Then the colonel reached into his desk drawer and pulled out a shiny badge and started to pin it over the U.S. Customs patch that Tommy had given Chris more than two years ago.

Chris placed his hands over his patch while looking Colonel Shafer straight in the eyes. "Not over my customs badge," he explained very seriously. Everyone laughed, especially Tommy. A few seconds later, after a nod of "OK" from Tommy, Chris gave in and allowed the colonel to pin the badge right over the U.S. Customs patch on his little jacket. "Now, Chris," the colonel said smiling, "Raise your right hand, and repeat after me."

Chris raised his right hand with the help of officers whispering "raise your other right hand." He repeated every word like a real trooper, then just looked around at everyone and smiled. Next came the certificate, officially making Chris the youngest member of the Department of Public Safety, State of Arizona, Highway Patrol.

The officers were a little choked up. Someone burst out saying, "He's our little bubble gum trooper." I stood watching Chris hold his certificate, beaming a little myself. He looked at it as the officers explained what it said. Suddenly he looked up at them with surprised eyes and exclaimed, "That's my name! Chris Greicius!"

After the badge-pinning ceremony and swearing in, the officers took turns escorting the newest and youngest patrolman to various departments. Chris was given a tour of the radio room where the supervisor explained all the equipment. Chris was wide-eyed and listened intensely as she explained all the bells and whistles and all the "tricks of the trade" on how to catch the bad guys.

He was getting pretty tired by now, so the officers continued to take turns carrying him around. We went upstairs to Director Ralph Milstead's office, and they sat and talked about the morning's events as Chris showed him all the "neato police stuff" that the officers had given him. Chris blew some big bubbles for his new boss and offered Ralph a stick of bubble gum. The director asked Chris to name his favorite television program. Chris replied without hesitation, excitedly voiced the name of the program, "that's the only one I like."

We stopped outside the main office building to take a few more photos. I knew Chris was getting pretty exhausted, so I asked him if he wanted to rest. He nodded yes, but wanted to stay and talk to his "big buddies" some more.

Tony carried him to the car, and some of the officers went with him. I stayed for a few minutes to thank everyone for what they had done that day. Thanks just didn't seem like enough.

I started to walk toward the car when I met the officers in the middle of the street. I said, "Thanks, special friends. I have to go now, because I don't want him to see me cry. He is too happy, and if I stay any longer, I won't be able to hide the tears. Nothing is going to spoil this day for him. Please tell everyone thanks for making his dream come true."

Ranger and Sky 12 about to land at the DPS compound headquarters. And Chris shuts down the engines on Sky 12.

Jerry's heart is captured as he flies wing filming
Chris's excitement, and "Doc" Holloway escorts
Chris to meet the other officers.

Sergeant Jim Eaves, #227 and Officer Frank
Shankwitz, #1091 familiarize Chris with the rocket while
he plays with all the bells and whistles, then tries the
helmet on for size.

G.R. "Doc" Holloway and Steve Lump tell Chris good-bye,
but there is more to come.

Sergeant Jim Eaves educates Chris in the art of defensive
driving; Chris educates Sergeant Eaves in the art of
blowing bubbles.

Lieutenant Colonel Dick Shafer presents Chris with his certificate of office, various patches, and Smokey Bear hat.

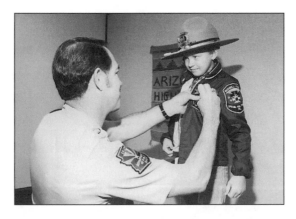

Lieutenant Colonel Dick Shafer pins a star on Chris's chest and tells him, "You are now an official Arizona Highway Patrolman."

Lt. Colonel Dick Shafer and Chris, the newest member of the
Department of Public Safety, Highway Patrol, April 29, 1980.

"Check it out, Mommie. I'm a *real* cop now. NEATO!"

A sworn bubble gum trooper that captured hearts instead of
bad guys certainly captured Director Ralph Milstead's heart as
he talks with Chris about the day's events and Chris shares a
stick of bubble gum with his new boss.

Chris grows tired but takes time for one last photo of the day
with Ron Cox, Tommy Austin, Patrolman Chris,
Mommie, and Daddy.

18

"Hello, Phoenix"

Chris was thirsty on the drive home, so we stopped at Chris Town Mall and went to the restaurant for a soda. Then we headed to a toy store for a police motorcycle helmet, but no such luck; everyone was out of helmets. So then we tried to find a shirt and pants similar to the patrol officer's uniform, but no luck there either. I kept thinking that soon I would be burying him in whatever we picked out.

As we shopped, I couldn't quite believe Chris's sudden burst of energy. I was astonished that his nose hadn't bled all morning. He wanted to browse a few more toy stores, but I decided we had better give up looking for clothes and a motorcycle helmet for the day and go home.

Chris fell asleep almost immediately with his patches and hat beside him. The certificate sat on the dresser and the shiny badge was clasped warmly in his grip as Chris rested his head upon the pillow.

Chris's Highway Patrol certificate

That evening at dinner, he told everyone all about his day and how he was a real police officer now. I asked Chris what he had enjoyed the very best out of everything he had done and seen.

He thought for a minute and then giggled.

"Well, the best part was when the chopper was taking off from the hospital, and it blew the trash cans all over the parking lot, Mommie. The garbage stuff flew all over the grass and cars."

We all got a good laugh from that. I guess it was kind of funny, except to the people who had to pick up the trash.

The evening of April 29, 1980, Ron Cox called to ask me for Chris's clothing size. "You know, every officer has to have a uniform. Since Chris is an officer now, Sergeant Jim Eaves called John's Uniforms; they want to make him a custom uniform of his very own. There are two women that have volunteered their time to work on a full scaled-down Highway Patrol officer's uniform and here's what they need to know—"

Before long I was measuring Chris's arms, legs, and waist as he lay sleeping.

On Wednesday, April 30, 1980, the uniform company was busy making a scaled-down, regulation uniform for their newest and youngest officer. The Apache Junction Police force notified the Highway Patrol that they had a small motorcycle helmet for Chris. Ron was busy talking to friends and to the chain of command making arrangements for one more big day.

Chris played quietly and watched television. He slept most of the day, but he did manage to call his girlfriend, Dawn. She came down to see him for a while. He couldn't wait to impress her by telling her about all the neato police stuff.

On Thursday, May 1, 1980, I received a phone call informing me that the officers, hand carrying a special little uniform, would be arriving about 9:30 a.m. I remembered a store where I had seen a pair of black boots like the ones motorcycle officers wear. So Herbie and I sped in a mad dash to capture the last pair. I rushed to make it home before the uniform arrived.

Squad cars and motorcycles soared down the quiet street of Solano Drive with lights flashing and sirens roaring. The motor officers pulled into the driveway and police cars lined the street at about 9:15 a.m., along with a news crew from the local television station. I came up the street, pulled into the neighbor's drive, jumped from the car, and ran across the yard. One of the guys yelled, "All right! Mom came through with the boots!"

With a grin, another officer said, "You passed us on your way to the store. We tried to catch you, but we couldn't, so we figured we'd wait for you here."

Chris, excited, was beaming from ear to ear. I could only imagine what the neighbors thought.

"Come on in, guys. Chris is so happy and excited to have you guys around to play with."

Sergeant Jim Eaves presented Chris with his uniform. Another officer gave him the riot helmet from Apache Junction Police Department. He was so thrilled, he didn't know which to put on first. After a few minutes, I took him into the bedroom to change his clothes.

When we came back into the living room, the officers just smiled with tears of pride. Chris put his hand on his chest and gasped, "My badge!" He raced back to the bedroom to grab it off the dresser.

The officers got him all fixed up, pinned the badge on, put the police sticker on his motorcycle helmet, and even put his toy gun on the scaled-down police dress belt. The officers had tried to have a complete gun belt scaled down as well, but there simply wasn't enough time.

Chris showed the men his little motorcycle and how it worked, so they showed him their bikes and how they worked.

One of the officers noticed that Chris's bike didn't have an official sticker on it. "All Highway Patrol bikes have to have an Arizona Highway Patrol emblem on them," the officer explained. So several officers reached into their shirt pockets and pulled out stickers for Chris's motorcycle. Everyone laughed and joked with each other while having fun fixing Chris's bike.

Motorcycle Officer Frank Shankwitz had called one of the majors and asked if he would get upset if he heard a little boy's voice over the radio. Once Frank had introduced the little bubble gum trooper, the major gladly replied, "You bet it's OK." Frank called the dispatcher for clearance. Dispatch then set the radio towers to relay the transmission throughout the state of Arizona, to every waiting on-duty patrolman. This had been cleared the previous day.

Chris sat on Frank's motorcycle playing with all the lights and sirens. As Chris continued to eyeball the radio, longing to talk on it, Frank picked up the mic and called dispatch.

"Can I get an OK on a civilian call?"

"That's a great big affirmative. You go right ahead and let our little trooper talk away."

Frank handed the radio to Chris and told him that whatever he said would be heard by every police officer in Arizona. He looked up at Frank, and a split second later, his little voice, full of pride and authority, said the words, "Hello, Phoenix."

The dispatch operator came back with a response. "That's a great big 10-4, we'll pass it on, and you have a great day now, Officer Chris."

Chris, surprised that it talked back to him, quickly handed the mic back to Frank.

Chris still wanted his uniform to look exactly like Frank's but there was one difference: Frank's had wings above the right-hand pocket, and Chris's didn't. Frank wanted to take Chris for a ride on his motorcycle so Chris could get his wings. Chris shook his head no. They all asked him why he didn't want to go for a ride. He very calmly explained to Frank, "Because it doesn't have any door on it."

So he rode his battery-powered motorcycle bike through a course that was set up in the driveway. The makeshift course consisted of the officer's big bikes and a track through the police cars. Chris passed the course with flying colors and earned his motorcycle wings. A warm hug went out to all his new buddies.

The morning went quickly. Although Chris was excited, he was very tired, and I could see that the pain was starting to increase. I took him inside and gave him some pain medication, telling him how proud and happy I was for him as I wiped a small trickle of blood from his nose.

Chris was saddened that he couldn't play with the officers all day. "Mommie, how long can the guys stay here?"

"Not too much longer, Chris. They have to get back to work, but they want to take your picture again. You're their special little buddy. Do you feel up to it?"

He shouted a big "yes" and almost immediately went back out to have his picture taken holding his tissue to wipe the blood. I don't think he cared about the pictures so much as being able to play with the guys again. Soon they said their good-byes, and Frank told Chris that he had earned his wings and would get them in a few days. I took Chris inside so that he could lie down and rest on the sofa.

I went back out to thank the officers again for all they had done. They wanted to know as much as possible about Chris's condition. Looking sad and teary-eyed, I could only tell them what I knew. "I don't know when, only that time is very short."

As the officers pulled out of the drive one by one, Chris appeared in the picture window, waving good-bye.

May 1, 1980, Sergeant Jim Eaves presents Chris with his official Highway Patrol uniform.

Chris takes his place beside his big buddies. "NEATO!"

Chris checks 10-8 with "Hello, Phoenix," and the dispatcher
replies, "OK, Officer Chris, that's a big 10-4."

Chris takes his proficiency tests to earn his wings.
He passed.

Chris gives Sergeant Joseph A. "Fred" Lizarraga a big hug
of happiness and appreciation, then gives a hug to each officer.

(L to R)   Sergeant Allan Schmidt, Ron Cox, Chris,
Tommy Austin, Sergeant Jim Eaves

That evening as I put Chris to bed, he said he wanted to talk. We lay in bed looking at his uniform hanging from the closet door. His boots sat on the floor beneath. The certificate and patches sat on the dresser, and his hat and helmet rested beside his boots. Chris held his badge, rubbing his fingers over it. He turned to me. Looking into my eyes with a mix of sadness and happiness, his voice expressed confusion.

"Mommie, why did the guys do all this for me?"

I put my arms around him while searching for words. Deep down, I knew at what he was hinting. Thoughts of Chris staring at the picture of Jesus reemerged. I felt Chris knew that his time was limited. I had to say something to him, and these were the words that found their way out of my heart.

"Because you are a special little angel. You have always wanted to be a policeman, haven't you?"

"Yes, I am a real policeman, Mommie!"

I nodded my head as I brushed the hair from his forehead and kissed him. Then I said, "Well, lots of the guys heard about this special little boy that wants to be a policeman, so they decided to make it happen. They wanted to give you what you wanted the most. You have always been a good boy for Mommie, and didn't I tell you that when you do what's right, you get special rewards?"

I sat up and kissed him again. As I got up to leave, Chris sat up in bed still clutching his badge.

"Mommie, don't go! Mommie, will you go with me?"

I knew what he was asking, and my heart was breaking inside while I tried to smile on the outside. I headed back to his bedside and took Chris into my arms.

"Chris, I'll go with you if that's what God wants me to do. To be playing with all the angels and to have Jesus put his arms around you and me would be the most special love besides yours that Mommie could ever feel. But if God wants me to stay here and help on earth for a little longer, then that's what I have to do. But I will always be with you in spirit. You know you are the most important thing to me, and where you go, I go. Right?" He nodded his head, and I laid him back down in bed. "Now you go to sleep, and everything will be all right in the morning."

"Mommie, am I a real cop now?"

"Yes, Chris, you're a real cop now, but you always were a little trooper to me."

He giggled a little and then smiled saying, "Good. Then you have to do what I say, and I want you to come to bed with me right now."

"Okey-dokey, alligator, but just until you fall asleep and then Mommie is going to talk with Daddy. OK?"

"OK."

"Then I'll come back and sleep all night beside you. I promise."

"OK, it's a deal."

I lay down beside him until he fell asleep. His badge was still safe in his hand, resting on the pillow beside his head.

19

Wings

On Friday, May 2, 1980, Chris woke up coughing and spitting up blood. His nose was bleeding quite heavily. He complained that his stomach hurt more than usual. I gave him painkillers, trying to stop the bleeding and pain, but Chris lay in bed and asked me if the doctor made house calls.

"No, honey, but Mommie is going to call him. I think we will have to pay him a little visit at his office."

Chris seemed more anxious than ever to get to the doctor's office. I told him that the doctor would probably want to put him in the hospital. He didn't care; he just kept saying, "Please, Mommie, take me to see the doctor. I don't care if he puts me in the hospital, just please take me there."

Within seconds, we were dressed and heading out the door. Tony carried Chris to the car and laid him in Herbie's back seat. He lay quietly as I drove toward St. Joseph's Hospital. Tony clasped his hands tightly while glancing back at Chris, smiling, then at me with a look of despair. We were both silent as we faced the reality that this was the last ride we would take together in Herbie.

The office had been alerted of our arrival and the nurse, Terri, showed us to one of the exam rooms that the doctor had set aside for us. The doctor came in shortly thereafter. Chris was very relaxed as he lay on the exam table with a warm blanket over him.

Dr. Baranko asked us if we wanted to talk with him privately about anything. I shook my head, stating that I wanted to stay with Chris. Tony agreed. The doctor leaned over the table and talked with Chris. He explained what was about to happen at the hospital and then he said. "Is there anything on your mind you want to talk about, Chris? We are going to go across the street to the hospital in a very short time. The nurses are getting a room ready for you right now. I'm sorry but I'm going to have to give you a poky in the hand so I can start an IV."

Chris's veins had pretty well collapsed, and the doctor told us that he might have to start the IV in the foot if he couldn't get a vein.

Chris had only one request of the doctor, "Please don't put the IV in my foot."

The doctor assured him that he would only have one little poky in the hand. Chris lay on the exam table with the blanket over him, eyes closed, trying to rest. Tony and I talked with the doctor in his office for a few minutes.

I knew in my heart that Chris's time was near. There was no more hope, no more reprieves like before. We had had three wonderful weeks together, and Chris had realized his dream of becoming a real policeman. Three years and three months had passed so quickly. The emotional roller coaster ride of hopes and prayers was going to be over very shortly. Chris would not come back home with me. He was going to a new home.

As we sat in the exam room with Chris, waiting for a private room to be ready, I thought about the last three weeks and Tony coming for a final visit. The doctor had told me last time that Chris would not be coming out of the hospital. But two days later, he was sitting up in bed coloring, watching television, and wanting to go home and play. Nobody had quite believed it; it just hadn't made sense. But I certainly wasn't going to argue with fact or fate. I had been more than happy to take him home, rather than see him in the hospital bed. But not this time. I felt death grip my very soul, and I knew that Chris was going to be going to a new home in Heaven.

Dr. Baranko carried Chris across the busy street as we followed. We went directly to pediatrics where the doctor gently tucked Chris into bed. Nurses quietly moved about the room setting up equipment.

By 11:00 a.m., the doctor was starting the IV. Chris's veins were almost totally collapsed. It wouldn't start the first time, so he withdrew it and looked at Chris. With a tear nearly in the doctor's eye, he looked up at Chris apologetically.

"I'm sorry, Chris, but I'm going to have to give you another poky. I know I told you just one poky, and it would be all over, but I have to try another vein."

Chris just rolled his eyes humorously, and in a manly little voice, he told the doctor, "My veins aren't too good in my hand. Try this one here; it's always good."

Chris pointed to his arm, and the doctor smiled at his attempt at helpfulness. Dr. Baranko turned and glanced back at Tony and I, not quite believing Chris's level of maturity.

"I would like to put it in your hand. This one looks good, Chris. I know I said only one poky, but I have to give you another. OK?"

A sleepy Chris raised his eyebrows, gave the doctor a faint smile, and replied in a very weak voice, "You got to do what you got to do."

The doctor was successful on the second poky, and the IV started without delay. Tony and I stayed with him all that afternoon watching him sleep off and on.

Chris wanted all his "neato police stuff" and his stuffed animals, especially Billy Bear. I went home and returned with everything, including a couple of overnight bags. Upon my return, I placed his uniform in the window so he could see it. I hung his gun over the closet door, set the hat and helmet on the dresser, and placed his favorite stuffed toys around his bed. Billy Bear was tucked in beside him, comfy and cozy.

Chris was fighting sleep. Tony sat in the chair beside the bed holding Chris's hand while I sat on the bed with a moist washcloth wiping Chris's face, trying to keep his lips moist. He was starting to dehydrate. The morphine made him restless.

"Are you worried about anything, sweetheart?" I asked.

He only wanted to know one thing. "Mommie, are you going to spend the night here with me?"

"Yes, honey, both Daddy and I will be right here all night. I promise you. Okey-dokey?"

As soon as I reassured him that we would not leave, he fell asleep peacefully. Tony and I took turns with coffee breaks for a couple of hours when he suggested that I go home and get some sleep.

"There is no way I'm leaving this room to go home and get some sleep. I couldn't sleep if I wanted to. I made my son a promise. I haven't broken my word with him yet, and I'm not going to start now."

Eventually I decided to step out quickly to get some food for us. I left about 10:00 p.m. I stopped by the house to pick up some things I had forgotten. As I gathered things together, I filled Mom in on Chris's condition.

At 11:00 p.m., I called the hospital, and Sergeant Eaves answered the phone. Chris was awake and wondering when I was coming back. I talked to him on the phone and told him. "Mommie is on her way back right now. I will be there in about thirty minutes, sweetheart."

He was content with that and drifted back to sleep.

The sergeant had heard the bad news when he called the house that afternoon, and he had stopped in at the hospital after work. Tony had gone for a coffee and cigarette break, and by the time I arrived back at the hospital, Chris was in a deep sleep. I checked him to make sure he was still breathing. As I sat there during the night holding his hand and wiping his face, I thought about our first night in the hospital, just across the hall.

How short three years were! How much more there was still left to show him. I thought about the days we had spent playing and stopping to pick up chicken, with Grandma Alice, for a picnic in Encanto Park. And I thought back on the times we would get up in the morning and Chris would say, "Let's go for a ride in the mountains," or "Let's go over to Grandma's and go swimming."

I smiled over all the hours we had spent shopping in toy stores and how he loved to stop at restaurants for a hamburger.

I could see him in his little cowboy hat and sheriff's outfit. I recalled the times we had spent at Old Tucson Studios. He liked to walk down the street and pretend he was the sheriff.

I closed my eyes and saw his whole life, even the time when he was a baby. He had loved to climb into the freshly folded clothes and go for a ride in the laundry basket as I carried it upstairs to put the clothes away.

I could see his little face, how happy he was when he opened Christmas and birthday presents. When he would sip a drink from Grandpa Wally's beer, he thought he was really getting away with something. All the good times came back so clear, so real.

I guess I drifted off to sleep, because at 3:00 a.m., I woke to the sounds of Chris choking. I jumped up and raised him up. He was spitting up blood. His eyes barely opened, as I helped the nurse clean him up. I laid him back down, brushed the hair from his forehead, and held his hand.

Chris's voice was very weak as he whispered softly, "Mommie. Mommie."

I kissed him and moistened his lips and face with a washcloth. "Mommie is here," I whispered. "I love you, honey."

His voice was so fragile as I held his lifeless hand. He tried to open his heavy eyes as he spoke in a sleepy, shaky low voice. "Mommie, I love you. You've been a good Mommie."

Chris drifted off into a coma, never regaining consciousness again. I sat remembering the nights I had sat up before wondering if he could make it through the night. This time he wasn't going to wake up. He would not have to go for anymore checkups. No more hospital stays, no more tests, and no more wheelchairs. He wouldn't have to feel bad anymore because he couldn't run and play ball like the other kids. He had sure given it one hell of a shot!

Morning was there already, and the city was waking up. The hospital became busier with more nurses and doctors walking in the halls, visitors coming and going.

His "buddies" stopped in throughout the day to see Chris. Frank brought Chris's wings, and I tried to rouse Chris telling him that his fellow patrol officers had come to visit. He awoke a little, looked directly at his uniform hanging in the window, and smiled as Frank pinned the wings on. With deep sadness, they said good-bye and left.

The Ranger's Air Rescue team stopped in to say hi, but Chris moved very little by that time. Once the pilot departed, he flew by the window, sounding the siren to say good-bye one last time. One by one, all day long, the officers came to see their little bubble gum trooper one more time and say "good-bye" to a fellow trooper.

Chris's breathing was erratic. I prayed that he would be out of pain soon. I thought about the decision I had made. I knew it had been the right one.

It comforted me to know that his happy days were just ahead of him. Soon, he would be able to run, play, and do all the things he had always wanted to do. I knew that there was nothing I could do for him other than stay by his side. I had released my son into God's care; the timing was up to him.

I stepped out to the waiting room. There was a little dark-headed boy about Chris's age playing with a racecar. He kept rolling it back and forth under the chairs from one side of the room to the other. I struck up a conversation with him as I caught the plastic car rolling under my chair. While we played, the energy, the questions, and the life in this little boy made me realize how close to death Chris really was.

Joyce, the gift shop woman from the resort where I had worked, showed up at the hospital, to my surprise. She had called Mom and heard the bad news. Joyce told Tony and me, "Now you two get out of here. Go get some coffee or something. I'm going to have a little talk with J. C. and his mother, Mary. Now go; I don't want you here. Get!"

We left and started walking down the hall chuckling a bit, when the sister came around the corner. "Just who I was looking for," she said. "How about some coffee, you two? I sure would love a cup."

It seemed like perfect timing, so we were off to the cafeteria by way of the chapel, where we said a prayer for Chris.

We sat and talked for about an hour reminiscing about old times. I told her I wanted the Leukemia Foundation to have his little motorcycle and all his toys. Maybe there was another little boy somewhere who could enjoy them and get some use out of them.

I wanted to help repay the times the foundation had helped me, such as by paying the rent on my apartment for three months when things were bad. And the check for $50 at Christmas time had meant more than they would ever know.

I told her she had always been there when I needed someone to talk to. She was more than a friend to me, and to so many others. We talked of arrangements. I told her that they already had been taken care of several weeks ago.

We finished our talk, and Tony and I started back to the room to be with Chris. When we walked into the room, the sergeant and his wife were there. Joyce was just leaving. As she hugged me, waving her hands and pointing her finger towards heaven, she promised, "He's fine. Everything is going to be just fine. Trust me; I have his word on it."

"Why don't you two go home and freshen up? We will stay with Chris until you get back," the sergeant suggested.

"I really don't want to go. I want to stay here with him. I promised him I would."

The sergeant assured me that they would not leave until we returned. "You need a break. You've been here all day yesterday, all last night, and all of today. Now, go home, take a shower, and get something to eat, because you will probably be here tonight, too."

I walked over to Chris's bedside, took the moist washcloth, and wiped his lips and face. As I leaned over to kiss him, I told him that I loved him and that Mommie would be back shortly to spend the night with him.

With the sole exception of his shaky breathing, Chris showed no signs of life as Tony and I walked out of the room to the elevator.

When the elevator doors opened and I walked out into the lobby, I stopped and looked at the statue above the doors leading outside, remembering our first day in Phoenix. I looked back at the elevator knowing that Chris was only a few minutes away.

I felt something pulling me back to him, and at the same time, I felt something pushing me out the door. Somehow I knew that if I left, I would never see my son alive again.

I wanted to turn around and see him just one more time. I wanted to hold him in my arms once again and tell him I loved him. I wanted to be with him. I looked at the clock on the wall. It was 8:00 p.m.

"Lord, what do I do? Which way do I go? Forward out the doors or back to the room? Help me, please," I cried.

I suddenly felt a strong push on my back toward the doors with words of peace calmly echoing through my mind:

You are only holding him here. I want you to walk out of the doors.

My feet just started moving, and before I knew it, I was outside. A peaceful embrace came over me that I had never felt before. It was like a huge weight had been lifted from me.

Tony and I stopped and picked up some chicken on the way home that evening. As I pulled out into traffic and stopped at the red light, I rolled back the sunroof and looked at my watch. A very peaceful feeling came over me again.

I looked at the stars, and there in the sky was the brightest star I'd ever seen. On each side of the shiny star, there was another star. The bright star in the middle seemed to light up the sky, while the other two stars seemed to follow only inches away. Somehow in my heart, I knew that Chris would be home with Jesus soon.

I wanted to turn around and head back to the hospital, which was where my heart was. But as the light turned green, my foot stepped on the gas, and I kept heading towards Mom's house.

After arriving home and filling Mom in on Chris's condition, I sat on the end of the bed for a few minutes holding my hands over my eyes.

I couldn't help him anymore. I knew that I had had to leave so he could go home. I had to hold myself together a little bit longer. I couldn't cry yet. I just couldn't. "I have got to be strong. My job is not finished yet." I asked the Lord to help me just a little bit longer.

After being up for two days and sleeping in the chair all night, the shower felt good. I had just returned to my room when the phone rang at 9:05 p.m. Everyone, Mom, Tony, and Grandpa Pete, was sitting in the living room listening to it ring. I knew who it was before I answered it.

"Linda, this is Dr. Baranko's assistant; Chris passed away at 8:35 p.m."

"I will be there as soon as I can. Thank you for calling."

"I have called Dr. Baranko, and he is on his way to the hospital right now."

"Tony and I will be there shortly."

I hung up the phone and walked into the living room. I told Tony, Mom, and Grandpa Pete that Chris was gone.

Then I went back to my room, sat for a moment, looked at his toys and the pictures he had drawn for me. I was happy that it was over for him. I said a small prayer and asked Chris to forgive me for not being there. Somehow, I guess, the good Lord didn't want me there. I knew he would explain it to Chris, and it would be all right.

When Tony and I arrived outside Chris's room, the doctor and the sister met us. The four of us talked for a moment in the hall. Then the doctor slowly opened the door to Chris's room.

The lights were very soft. The bed had been made up with fresh linens. The sheet was pulled back, covering him from the chest down. All the medical equipment was gone. All Chris's things were gone. There was just a soft light above his head as he lay in the bed so peacefully, holding his little stuffed puppy under his arm, which he had named Irene, after one of his nurses.

He looked as though he were only sleeping as I walked over to him and took his hand, kissing him on the forehead. I couldn't hold back the tears any longer. The doctor reached out for me and held me as I cried from the very depth of my soul.

Tony was going through the same thing as the sister tried to comfort him. Wiping my eyes, I regained control. A little laugh escaped as the doctor said, "I have been trying to get you to cry for three years. I have never met a mother so determined or so strong in my entire practice."

"Well, there were a few times I came pretty close in your office. I just never wanted to let anyone see me cry. I did that at night when no one was around."

I took a deep breath and sat looking at Chris while the doctor was talking. I really don't remember what he said, but a few short minutes later, I went back to Chris's bed, sat on the side of it, and kissed him good-bye.

I walked out of the room and leaned against the wall outside. The doctor came out after me; Tony and Sister Madonna Maria followed. We walked down to the little room where Sergeant Eaves and his wife, along with Ron and his wife, were waiting.

As I sat there listening to everybody talk, only one thing kept running through my mind. Three years and three months ago, I had sat in the same little room— where it had all started. Now it was all over, all in the same little room.

I signed the necessary papers that evening and advised the doctor about arrangements. I was glad I had made them ahead of time. At first, I had felt it was a sign of giving up hope. But that day I realized that I made better decisions based on fact and not emotions.

Wanting to help, but not knowing exactly what to do to ease the sorrow, the guys suggested we go for pizza that night, all six of us. Everyone agreed, and we walked to the pizza place hoping to relax a little. I knew that all of them had training in dealing with the death of an officer and the surviving family. Chris was just a kid, but he had been their little bubble gum trooper, and they claimed him as one of their own. I was thankful to have these big buddies on my side also.

When I realized that nobody knew what to do or say, or if they should even mention Chris's name for fear that I would lose it, I broke the ice by saying, "Well, it seems that stories about Chris are in order. You guys want to hear about the time Chris tried washing our blue jeans with bleach?"

Tales of the special times and funny things we did together lightened the sadness that night. The change in scenery and the laughter were great—just what I needed, and all of them knew it! The parlor wasn't busy that evening, so for a couple of hours we sat talking, having fun remembering his special day, while I remembered him as just being my special little buddy.

After we had finished eating, Ron pulled an envelope from his pocket and said, "Lynn, I found this on my desk, and it's addressed to you, so I thought I'd give it to you."

I couldn't think of what it could be, so I opened it. Enclosed I found a check from the F.O.P. Lodge #32 with a handwritten note, "to help cover expenses for Chris's funeral." I sat there stunned.

"Ron, I don't know what to say." A tear came to my eye. Ron scratched his beard, sipped his beer, and in his deep western drawl, he said "Hey, that's OK. You don't have to say anything."

He sipped his beer again and looked around the table at the others who knew what was in the envelope. They had given Chris so much already, I couldn't believe there was any more to give. Ron set down his beer, as I took a good look at the check.

Sergeant Eaves, who by now insisted I call him Jim, took the floor. "Chris was one of us. We take care of our own. I'm going to tell you something else. He gave us guys a whole lot more than we could ever give him. I only wish I could have known him longer."

There was a check made out to me for $500. Tears threatened to flow, but I held back not wanting to put a damper on the evening. Before the evening was over, Ron handed me two other envelopes from different F.O.P. Lodges containing equal amounts.

Not long after, we were walking back to the parking lot at the hospital looking for our cars, saying good-bye to each other as we took out our keys.

Tony and I didn't talk much while I drove home that evening. Somehow it didn't seem necessary. Our thoughts were totally on Christopher.

I don't think anyone got much sleep that night. I found myself sitting up in bed most of the night feeling empty inside. I wanted to cry, but I couldn't.

Things kept going through my mind of what I had to do in the morning, and I kept picturing Chris running, jumping, and playing with his puppy in heaven, laughing and giggling as they rolled in the grass together. As I buried my head in the pillow, the tears that I had held onto for three years, just like my baby boy, had at long last been set free.

20

Arizona Highway Patrol
Salutes
Little Bubble Gum Trooper

Early the next morning, Ron and his wife arrived at
Mom's house to take Tony and me to the mortuary. Ron
informed me that he had all of Chris's things from the
hospital in the car.

"After we had finished with pizza the other night, I
went back to the hospital and asked for his things. They
had them all ready for you, but I told them I'd be happy to
take them to you."

"How about if I take them inside and put them in the
bedroom with everything else? Then we can go."

It's hard to recapture all the emotions that I felt that
morning. Perhaps there are no words that could describe
waking up to a room filled with toys and the remembrance
of a child that was no longer there. Perhaps it is better

not to be able to remember. Perhaps it is a blessing in disguise.

Although I knew that it was real, somehow, it was dream-like. I could neither wake up nor stop thinking about Chris.

My body felt numb as I went through the motions of what I needed to do that day and for several days afterward. At times I couldn't cry even if I tried; at other times, I had no control over when and where the tears would start or stop.

I told Ron that I could handle everything just fine and could drive to the mortuary and finish up the arrangements. But he and his wife insisted on helping us with whatever we might need. Ron opened the car door, pausing for a moment as he turned to me.

"Lynn, let me tell you something. Whenever an officer dies, there is another officer assigned to help the family with whatever needs to be done. I requested to be assigned. So it's settled. Get in the car."

I felt badly because Ron and his wife lived about sixty miles away, and I knew that helping me required a lot of driving for them. Still, I was happy they were there. They were a big help, in many ways.

When we arrived at the mortuary, Chet Hansen, whom I had talked with several weeks earlier was at the front desk on the phone. He recognized me immediately and motioned for us to have a seat. Once he had finished his phone call, he suggested that we all step into his office.

"How are you doing today?" he asked.

"Pretty good, I guess, Chet. This is Chris's father, and these are some friends from the police department. Is Chris here?" I felt my voice quivering slightly.

"The hospital called us last night, and we have Chris here now. I was trying to get in touch with you just as you walked in. Your mother said that you were on your way."

"I decided to bury Chris in his uniform, so I brought everything that you will need with me. If I have forgotten anything, just call the house, and I'll bring it up to you."

I handed Chet a brown grocery bag containing Chris's undergarments, motorcycle boots, and uniform, complete with badge and wings. We talked for a few minutes about the events of the last few days, as there had been quite a bit of news coverage in the papers and on television.

Chet and I talked privately about holding a service for the officers in Phoenix and then a second one in Illinois.

I asked the mortuary to please book our flights to coincide with the arrival of Chris's body in Illinois. I took the checks that Ron had given me at the pizza parlor and endorsed them over to the mortuary as a down payment.

After making the final arrangements that day, I was thankful that I had had the stamina to make arrangements several weeks before. It helped me feel somewhat in control of myself, and I was confident that everything was done to the best of my ability. Christopher would have been pleased with our plans.

Later, after lunch, the four of us—Ron, his wife, Tony, and I—sat for about an hour talking about anything that came to mind, trying to keep the conversation light-hearted. The waitress cleared the table and refilled the coffee cups several times as I listened to the conversation,

staring off into space as the past three years flowed
through my mind. I interrupted the conversation suddenly.
"I feel like I should be doing something. I feel guilty just
sitting here so long and having an enjoyable lunch. I'm
having a hard time believing that it's really over. He's
actually *gone*."

Everyone was silent for a few moments but
understood as I apologized for the outburst.

"I'm sorry, you guys. I don't mean to ruin the
afternoon. I really don't. It's just hard to think about my
life without Chris. He's still very much a part of me. It
just doesn't seem real; it really doesn't. I don't think it
ever will."

"Lynn, it takes time." Ron spoke gently with a quiet
tone. "You have been through a lot these past three years,
and Chris is finally safe and free from pain in heaven.
Why, I'll bet he's looking down and watching you right
now, enjoying yourself and saying, 'That's neato,
Mommie.'"

"I know, but I still miss him very much, and I can't
help it. I'm sorry, guys, but I think it's time for us to go. I
need to be alone for awhile."

"Whenever you are ready." I greatly appreciated Ron's
understanding that day.

We gathered up our things, and Ron paid the check.
He drove us back to Mom's house, and I found myself
with more energy than I knew what to do with. That
afternoon, I packed up Chris's toys in a big box, his
clothes in another. All of his special things I saved and put
in a special place. I will keep those—forever.

I was glad Tony was there so he could pick out what memories he wanted to save. I didn't have to try and pick them out for him.

Cleaning out his drawers and closets, it finally hit me that Chris was really gone. Suddenly, all I wanted to do was be alone somewhere, anywhere, and cry until it didn't hurt inside anymore.

I stopped what I was doing and left the room in a mess. Mom and Tony were on the back patio talking while Grandpa Pete was resting his eyes and listening to the television. I slung my purse over my shoulder, fumbled for my car keys, and quietly closed the screen door behind me. I didn't want anyone to see me; I just wanted to be alone.

I drove around for the rest of the afternoon wanting to find some place to sit and cry—somewhere where nobody could find me, somewhere that was deserted so I could just stand and scream if I wished.

I went out to the desert parks, but every time I stopped to sit in the car, people pulled up beside or behind me with a bunch of kids. Families, excited and happy to be spending a day at the park with a picnic basket in one hand and cooler in the other, surrounded me. Boys tossed baseballs in the air, and little girls carried baby dolls, playing Mommie.

I sat there for a while watching the kids play on the swings and slides, remembering all the times that Chris and I had done the same thing. I flashed back to images of the entire family, including the grandmas and Grandpa Pete, sitting at the picnic table enjoying the afternoon sun and watching the ducks gliding across the pond.

I could still see Chris with a handful of bread, carefully breaking it and throwing it as far as he could across the water so the ducks would see it. He would stand amongst a crowd of quacking ducks, giggling. As they all wanted to be fed, he quickly ran out of bread.

"God, why did his life have to end so young? How could you take my only son away from me? I loved him more than I love myself. I want to see him run and play and splash in the swimming pool. I want to take him on trips and show him places. Lord, why do I keep hearing him calling me, 'Mommie, Mommie, come play with me!'?"

I sat wiping the tears, trying to keep from looking like a crazy woman talking to myself. I started the car and continued to talk out loud. My words turned from the Lord to the sight of my own face in the rearview mirror.

"He's dead. Chris is dead, and there is nothing I can do about it. I only have memories to hold onto now. You knew this day was coming, and you had three years to prepare yourself for it, so snap out of it. This is real life, kid. This is reality, so you've got to make yourself accept it. You have to."

I wiped more tears away and decided to drive home to finish cleaning my room. Maybe it was a way of forcing myself to accept everything, while my heart was denying that Chris was dead.

Maybe I had needed the break to be alone and let some of the hurt and anger out from inside of me. Perhaps I needed to see other families enjoying themselves and realize that life does go on.

Walking back into the house, I could see Mom was a little worried, but I reassured her that I was all right. Grandpa Pete, also worried, wiped his eyes with his handkerchief, but he didn't know what to say either.

"I just needed to be alone for a couple of hours. That's all. Sorry if I worried you, but I needed to get away for awhile. Mom, do you have any masking tape in the garage? I need to tape up some of the boxes."

The following evening came all too quickly; it was time for evening services. Ron and his wife picked up Tony and me, while Mom took Grandpa Pete in her car, so they could leave early.

When we arrived at the mortuary, the sun was just setting. The quiet atmosphere that surrounded the building and parking lot, which was empty, seemed to close off the noisy city traffic. The four of us walked to the front door. As Tony opened it, I walked in first.

Chet greeted us, extending his hand.

"Hi. Do you know which room Christopher is in?"

"He's in the room down the hall. Flowers have been arriving all day. This way, if you please."

Asking Chet to wait a minute, I turned to Tony and Ron.

"I would like to be alone with him for a while. It's just something I need to do. OK?" Both of them understood. As I turned and started down the hall, I kept telling myself to be strong. I didn't want to cry. I didn't know what my reaction was going to be when I saw him. Chet stopped at the doorway and extended his hand toward the room. I took a few steps, then stopped just inside the doorway.

I stood there staring at the casket at the end of a long, large room decorated with elegant light blue drapes and plush blue carpet to match. Beautiful blue velvet wing-back chairs and several sofas were placed about the room, with additional chairs tastefully arranged against the wall. Beautiful big bouquets of flowers in every color stood all around the room on the marble-topped cherry wood tables. Flowers surrounded the casket from every angle and at various heights. Several bouquets were lined up on the floor in front of the tables. The mortuary had anticipated a large gathering and had opened additional rooms for guests.

I wiped my eyes and walked slowly towards my son's casket. With each step, I remembered special times that we had shared together. I thought back to Chris at two years old when he used to crawl into the laundry basket after I'd filled it with warm clothes from the dryer. I would carry him upstairs as he snuggled, giggling.

I remembered when Chris was three years old, and we were at Grandpa Wally's. Chris was playing with a hoe and accidentally nicked the wing of a little bird on the ground. With tears streaming down his cheeks, he pulled me across the yard, begging me to help "the little birdie."

About that same time, Chris also loved to play hide-and-seek in the house. He would unload all the food from the lazy Susan in the cupboard and crawl in, closing the door behind him. I'd soon hear this little voice hollering and giggling.

"Mommie, come find me. I'm where the casup (catsup) is." Of course, it was never hard to find him as the food all over the floor provided a good clue to his whereabouts. His fascination with banging a wooden spoon on my pots and pan led me to wonder if he might grow up to become a drummer some day.

Christmas time with Chris had always been filled with the spirit of wonderment and joy, watching him hand out packages to everyone, his little expressions of excitement as he opened his presents, throwing paper and bows everywhere. I recalled the fun times of seeing Grandpa Wally and Christopher sprawled out on the floor playing with a windup toddler train set and little people just made to fit into Chris's little hands.

The little farm set was a big hit that year also. It wasn't long before the cows were riding the train through the barn. And the little people were all inside the fence where the cows were supposed to be.

Then there was the play acting at bedtime to try and stay up longer, and the many times I would give in and hold him on my lap wrapped in a warm blanket. Within minutes, he would be sound asleep. I carried him to his room and tucked him into bed with his favorite stuffed animal. I would kiss him on the forehead, turn on the night-light for him, and wonder what he would have grown up to be.

Gripping the coffin, I stood regarding my son. Chris was dressed in his little uniform, badge and all. I rested my hand on top of his as I placed my other hand on his head and leaned over to kiss him. I was a total failure at fighting back the tears; they saturated my small hanky.

"It's hard to believe this day is here. But here we are, just you and I, saying good-bye to each other until we can be together once again. I'll miss you very much, but I know in my heart that you are safe and happy, running and playing, making friends with all the other kids. No more sickness, bruises, or tests for my little trooper, just sunshine and fun for all eternity. I never told you this, but I thank you for being as brave as you were, going through all of this.

"I don't know what I would have done if you weren't. I only heard you cry one time—during the last bone marrow test—and that broke my heart. You were a grown-up little man, much more than Mommie was a grown lady. I did the best I could to make you happy and be a good mother. I pray that I made you happy. I know you made me more happy that I ever dreamed possible."

The longer I stood in front of the casket, the more I accepted his death, and the easier it became to stand without holding onto it. I knelt down to pray. My heart was breaking, as I closed my eyes. All I could see was Chris lying in the casket. I stood up, placed one hand over his, the other on his head, and kissed him again, saying good-bye for now.

Somehow, my thoughts returned to happy times we had shared, like Chris jumping on the bed and hollering for me to catch him as we darted off to see our first apartment. I could hear the excitement in his voice when we were playing in the park and feeding the ducks or going on a picnic to the park with lots of rides. I smiled as I remembered driving along in Herbie listening to music, while glancing out of the corner of my eye to watch him snap his fingers and lip-sync to the music.

I turned to leave, and there in the doorway, starting to walk toward me, were several of the boys in tan uniforms with black leather gun belts and shiny badges on their chests. I smiled as they approached, and we exchanged warm hugs of friendship.

Two of the men, Scott Stahl and Frank Shankwitz, stood on each side of me while the others, Sergeant Eavesand Ron, stood behind me. Joined with arms around each other, we stood in front of the casket, each remembering Chris in our own way for the little trooper he really was. As we stood in silence, there wasn't a dry eye among us. Even the big strong boys in uniform shed a few tears as they said good-bye to their newest and most special little trooper.

The silence was broken when one of the guys excitedly said, "Hey, have we got some pictures for you to see! They are so good of Chris, you won't believe it."

"Great, where are they?"

"Over here in the next room. Tony is looking at them now along with a lot of the guys."

Officers and their wives had congregated around a huge oval walnut table full of pictures of Chris's big days. The department photographer had been taking pictures on both days. The gathering admired handfuls of eight by tens and stacks of three by fives.

Before the night was over, almost everyone ended up looking at the pictures and picking out his or her favorite. The shots were just beautiful.

"This is only a sample. We have more coming. Our photographer couldn't get them all done in time for tonight. But just wait until you see those. They are going to be good!"

I was so happy that Chris had been able to have his wish come true. With each photograph, I was reminded of his sensational adventure. He was so happy and proud of his uniform. That's all he had thought about those last days.

Somehow he didn't feel the pain so much, or didn't feel so badly because he couldn't play like the other kids. When he was holding his badge and had all his "neato police stuff" around him, he was happy in his own little world.

Later that evening after everyone had left, Tony and I said our own good-byes to Chris. Side by side, Tony and I knelt before our son and said a prayer. As we rose, we embraced, and the sorrow exploded between us. Our son was gone.

The next morning, services were held for the officers who had been unable to make it the night before. The chapel was filled with uniforms of every color as officers and their families came in from different districts to bid farewell to their "little bubble gum trooper."

Sister Madonna Maria and Reverend McCarthy were in attendance to give the service. I sat listening to the sister speak, with my eyes and thoughts on Chris. I'm glad she handed me a tape of the services afterwards, because I don't remember much of what she said.

Tony and I sat beside each other in the second pew. I still felt close to Chris, as if he were on the other side of me, as he had been so many times before. Tony and I were leaving for Illinois the next morning. Chris was leaving that afternoon.

ARIZONA DEPARTMENT OF PUBLIC SAFETY

2310 NORTH 20th AVENUE   P. O. BOX 6638   PHOENIX, ARIZONA 85005   (602) 262-8011

BRUCE BABBITT   RALPH T. MILSTEAD
GOVERNOR   DIRECTOR

May 5, 1980

Dear Linda and Tony:

My heart goes out to you as you struggle with your grief.

Chris was a brave little fellow. Upon meeting him, we at the Department were saddened and touched by his misfortune, and yet our spirits were lifted as we observed his enthusiasm. I personally feel that my own life has been enriched for having had the opportunity to share a few precious moments of his short life.

Although Chris was small in stature, his impact was tremendous, and we will long remember the courageous little guy who thought cops were great.

Very truly yours,

Ralph T. Milstead

Original letter from Director Ralph Milstead.

As we said good-bye to Ron at the airport the next morning, the men shook hands. I gave Ron a big hug and kiss on the cheek for all the help he and his wife had given us. Our plane left on schedule, and we arrived in St. Louis on time. That's when the smooth side of our journey ended. We soon arrived at the gate of our connecting flight to Illinois only to discover that the flight had been canceled. The airline had gone on strike.

I lit a cigarette and looked at Tony. He leaned against the counter with his head in his hands.

"Well, what are we going to do now? Any ideas?" I asked. "I'm open to any suggestions." A little voice inside of me stated loud and clear, despite the noisy airport,

"Well, kid, pull out the reserves." So I did. "Tony, come on. Let's go get our luggage."

We retrieved it with no problems, then I asked an airline ticket agent to point me in the direction of the commuter flights. Soon we were on our way down the long corridor filled with crowds of people who had apparently had the same idea.

The tiny section was crammed with people trying to make a connection. Tony found himself a seat, convinced that there would be no way we would make it in time for Chris's funeral.

Eventually, I took a seat beside him, racking my brain to come up with a way to get there in time. Looking at Tony, I knew that he could not drive the six-hour distance, and I didn't want to. "There has got to be another way," I said, giving it more thought. At last, it hit me.

I asked Tony for his ticket and he relinquished it with a puzzled look on his face. I waited in line, and when my chance finally came, slapped both tickets on the counter. Looking the ticket agent in the eye, I explained, "Look, I realize that there are at least forty people waiting to get on that plane out there. I would not ask you for any special attention, but I need your help. I have got to get to Moline or as close to it as possible. Our seven-year-old son died, and we are taking him home for burial. He is on another flight going through Chicago. The services are tomorrow afternoon. Please, I wouldn't ask you, but I need to make that flight if at all possible."

The agent at the desk took our tickets and said in a sympathetic tone of voice that it would be about forty-five minutes and that he would announce our names over the loudspeaker. I thanked him whole-heartedly and felt the tears begin to form, but that little voice kept saying, *"Be strong, kid; you can't quit now."*

I took my seat beside Tony and filled him in on the situation. Then I found a phone booth and called my brother who was going to pick me up from the airport. I explained the whole story and that I wasn't sure when I would get in or how I was arriving.

"Hopefully, we are going to get on this commuter flight, but I'm not sure. I may have to rent a car and drive part of the way. I'll call you when I know more."

Tony and I made the flight. The small seventeen-passenger plane hit every air pocket between St. Louis and Springfield. I turned three shades of green, but was happy to be in the air heading closer to Moline. I closed my eyes and thanked God that we were on our way.

We landed at last, and I was so happy to be back on the ground again. My stomach was also pleased to be back where it should be. We found our luggage, then had to find a car. Of course, they didn't have any economy models left, but I finally rented a car for twenty-four hours. At that point, I would have rented a semi or dump truck—anything on wheels that ran.

"I will take one, any one that you have. Just show me where to sign, please."

By this time, we were tired, hungry, and needed to sit and let our stomachs settle. I suggested we go relax with a little lunch before driving for a couple of hours.

21

Home at Last

Once we started our two-hour journey towards Kewanee and then, for me, on to Moline, we talked about old times, Chris, and how the countryside hadn't changed. I enjoyed driving; it was nice to see the places I hadn't seen in three years. Although I crossed a few new roads and spotted a couple of new homes, it was comforting to find that nothing had really changed.

We arrived at Tony's parents' house that evening. I was hesitant about going in, but Tony made me feel welcome. His parents, on the other hand, peered at me as though I were a ghost from the past that had come back to haunt them.

I had never been their favorite person, and they made no bones about reminding me of that, that evening, as I sat remembering the years we had lived there. As my eyes fixed upon the home Tony and I had built across the road, the hopes and dreams I had once had of being a wife and mother flowed back.

I thought back to the good times we had shared as a young rural family at Kewanee, Illinois. I thought of my father doing the vast majority of the building of our home and all the work he did, even after we moved in. I remembered the day that Chris was born and thought of all the things he did as he grew. I recalled the time we poured cement, and the cement guy left a small pile of it in the dirt beside the house. It wasn't but a second later that Chris was standing on top of it, sinking deeper and deeper, cowboy boots and all. He stepped out of his boots and crawled down the pile. The boots, though, were another story. They were goners by the time I got to them.

Then I started remembering the bad times. I had to stop myself from thinking about the past and remind myself that Chris was no longer in a position to suffer. I could picture him playing and running with his puppy once more, throwing a stick as the puppy barked up a storm, running to fetch it.

I phoned my brother, drove sixty miles to meet him along the interstate, then another five miles on back roads to his house.

We sat and talked for awhile, then I had to excuse myself and get some rest. At last, the whole day was catching up with me. I desperately needed sleep.

In the morning, I turned around and drove sixty-five miles back to Kewanee to take care of calling hour arrangements and Chris's burial the following morning.

I stopped by and picked up Tony before going to the funeral home. His parents offered me a cup of coffee. We said good-bye, and Tony and I left to take care of business at the funeral home in Kewanee and to arrange for calling hours that evening.

Some old friends that I hadn't seen in years showed up. Most of Tony's family came to say how sorry they were, as I stood by my son's coffin. I shook their hands and politely thanked them.

Many thoughts rushed through my mind as I met with Tony's family again. Everyone was asking why Chris was made a police officer. I had just begun to explain when a relative of Tony's interrupted me.

"You had services in Phoenix for him; now it's our turn. Why don't you just go sit down in a chair somewhere?"

I stood proudly and held my head high, as she turned to continue telling the story to family members, relaying only what she had read in the newspapers. Just like Moline, nothing seemed to change at all over the years. I did not sit down but, retaining my dignity, politely told them the true tale of Chris's special day. I said my piece and left them to deal with it as they chose. It seemed that my presence at my son's funeral only served to antagonize certain individuals.

As the remaining few people left, I said good-bye to Chris for the night. I would be back tomorrow for the funeral. I thought about how proud and happy Chris would be, knowing that two of his police buddies were coming all the way from Phoenix to escort him to his final resting place. It comforted me as I drove home to Gary's that night to get some rest.

Upon my arrival at the funeral home the next day, Scott and Frank greeted me—two Arizona officers dressed in full uniform. As they gave me a welcome hug, I felt their support. My brother stayed by my side at all times. All three gave me the strength to do what I had to do.

Scott and Frank completed Chris's uniform that morning by placing a black band across his badge. Now Chris's uniform was again just like that of his two buddies who also wore black bands across their badges. Seeing him lying in his casket, dressed in full uniform, his two buddies, Scott and Frank, sitting in the front row waiting to escort him to his grave, told the whole story.

Reverend Remm finished his sermon. The friends and family filed by to pay their last respects. It was only Scott, Frank, and me now. They stood up, walked to the casket, stood at attention, and then offered a final official police salute to their littlest trooper.

I could feel the tears wanting to flow as I walked up to him and knelt down to say a prayer. I stood up and placed my hand on his head and bent down to give him a last kiss before the closing of the casket.

Gary, Scott, and Frank waited for me at the doorway. At that moment, I couldn't hold it any longer. I lost it in every sense of the word. The tears just kept coming, as the three of them escorted me to Gary's car.

I sat in the car with Gary watching the two officers drape the Arizona state flag over Chris's casket, then the state police, Frank, and Scott, acting as pall bearers, placed it in the hearse. I attempted to compose myself a little, but I was far from where I wanted to be.

Frank and Scott mounted two matching dark brown, fully dressed motorcycles. Two different Kewanee residents, Chet Lyle and Gary M. Combs, had donated the highly polished bikes that morning. The generous donors had said that they would be honored if the officers would use their motorcycles to escort Chris's funeral.

The officers pulled out into the street to lead us to the end of our three-year journey. Frank and Scott led the procession followed the hearse, then the Illinois State Police, county police, and city police, each requesting the honor to join in the procession. Then Gary as well; Tony and his parents followed. One by one, family and friends pulled out and fell in line down the street towards the cemetery.

We arrived at the site where everything was set up as I had pictured it in my mind many times before. Gary took me by the arm, and we walked over to be seated under the canopy. I sat looking at the flag draped over the little casket. My heart was pounding, my whole body shaking on the inside. I wanted to scream out, "My God, why? Why my son? Why Chris? Please let me wake up from this horrible nightmare! I love him; he's all I have! He's the only son I'll ever be able to have! Why, God? Why!"

The next thing I remember was being presented with the Arizona State flag, folded into a triangle by Scott and Frank. I held it close to my chest for a moment and almost felt as though I were holding Chris again. As a final salute, all the police officers presented arms to Chris. As the service drew to a close, one by one the attendees began to leave the cemetery and make their way to a hall for a small reception.

I remained seated until everyone had gone except the men who were attending the grave. Gary stood behind me, politely waiting until I was ready to leave. Scott and Frank, along with the other officers, also waited. As I reached down to pick up my purse from the grass, Gary placed his hand on my shoulder. "Well, you think maybe we should head over to the reception?"

As we started to walk to the car, I asked Gary to wait before starting out. "I want to just sit here for a few minutes to say good-bye in my own way."

"Anything you want, kid, it's yours."

Arizona Officers Frank Shankwitz and Scott Stahl talk with news
reporters about Chris's big day at the Department of Public
Safety and how he became the first and only honorary Highway
Patrolman in the history of the State of Arizona.

May 9, 1980, Chet Lyle and Gary M. Combs donate two matching
motorcycles. The Arizona officers gratefully accept with pride
the honor of riding them to lead Chris's procession.

Frank discusses the order of procession with police officers.

The officers prepare themselves for Chris's last ride.

Order of procession: Arizona officers, followed by Chris,
then Illinois, county and city police

With heavy hearts, the officers mount their motors and
prepare themselves to perform their duty.

With grace, pride, and love for their littlest trooper, the officers
pull onto the street, leading the procession, the same street Chris
once rode on in the car with his parents.

Reverend George Remm leads in prayer. Mark Schueneman,
funeral director; the state police; Kewanee Police; and Chris's
"big buddies" escort Chris to his final resting place.

Officers fold the Arizona flag that draped his casket and present
it to his mother in remembrance of her son, a *real* trooper.

Mommie says good-bye to her little trooper.

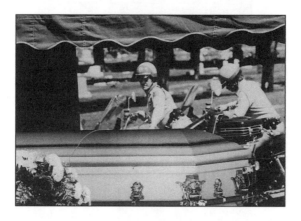

Duties have been performed; a friend and a fellow officer
has been laid to rest. With a glance over the shoulder, Officer
Scott Stahl says good-bye to Chris.

After I had said my last good-bye, Gary, Frank, Scott, and I arrived at the reception hall. As I entered the room and greeted several people with a small nod of my head,. Gary pointed to an empty table and Scott and Frank walked toward it. We sat down together.

Within minutes of our arrival, Tony and Reverend Remm came over, joining us in laughter. For the next hour or so, the six of us sat remembering the good times of Christopher's life, delighting in the snapshots that pictured him receiving his uniform. It was a blessing remembering the fun times we had shared during those remarkable and unforgettable three years.

Scott and Frank told us the story of how two Illinois officers met them at O'Hare Airport holding a sign that said "Looking for Frank and Scott" and helped escort them to where they needed to go. Laughter broke out as the men related the strange looks they had received from motorists on the freeway as they drove a Jeep from Chicago to Kewanee, dressed in full Arizona police uniforms.

The arrangement had been to have their motorcycles flown back to Illinois on a transport plane; Senator Barry Goldwater made phone calls to numerous state officials to arrange for the transport, but his efforts ended in vain minutes before Scott's and Frank's departure from Phoenix Sky Harbor Airport.

Jerry Foster had given the two officers enough money for one round-trip ticket and told them, "You had better take it, because I'll probably spend it on a blond anyway." The rest of the money was raised by donations from the families of officers throughout the department allowing

Frank and Scott to fly back to the funeral and say good-
bye to Christopher one last time. From all of the other
officers back home and all the families that supported
them, it was a final farewell that would be remembered
and cherished forever by a grateful mother. "Thank you,
one and all . . . "

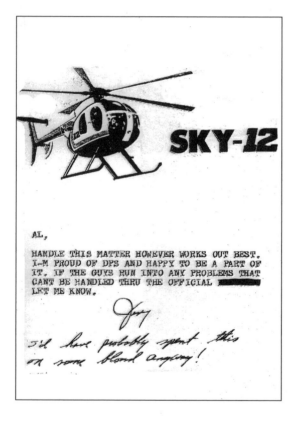

Jerry, thanks for all your help, Mommie.
P.S. Jerry's wife is blond.

I sat sipping coffee, recalling the story of his special wish day with great pride and happiness. I remembered the questions Chris had asked about why the policemen were doing this for him. Could he go back to the police station and visit with them anytime? Could he really keep the badge that the colonel gave him?

If the others wanted to hear the stories, they could. After about half an hour, a few came over to listen. A couple of them joined in briefly to ask questions, while others only thumbed through the pictures in silence. I didn't care anymore what Tony's family thought or said about me. My relationship with them would be permanently severed after that day. I knew that once I left the hall that afternoon, I would never see any of them again.

When I returned to visit Chris's grave, the only evidence they would find of my visit was the red rose that I would leave on his grave, "From Mommie, with Love."

Shortly after Frank and Scott offered their condolences and headed back to Phoenix, Gary and I headed home. We didn't say much to one another on the long drive back to his place. I simply watched the countryside pass by as Gary drove and listened to the radio. I was glad to be home at Gary's, able at last to just kick off my shoes and relax. That evening, I prepared a small dinner for us, and as we watched television, we talked and laughed about our childhood days on the farm.

During the three weeks I stayed in Illinois, I returned several times to my old hometown to meet with Tony. We picked up the cards and the guest book from the funeral home and decided over coffee that he should keep the book from the services in Kewanee. I settled any unpaid bills for the various services and arranged for the headstone to be placed on the grave.

I knew it would be a long time before I would be able to return. While I was in town, I wanted to visit Chris's grave frequently. It never got easier as I drove in the entrance of the cemetery and down the lane to his graveside. The red rose that I carried didn't ease the hurt of losing Chris, but I found it was necessary to kneel and to place a rose on the grave several times during those three weeks . . . to help ease my pain.

He'd been a little trooper in more ways than one throughout three-and-one-half years of illness. I hoped that every time that a red rose was placed on his grave, Christopher would be remembered as the little seven-year-old boy who wanted to be a policeman when he grew up.

Chris was the only Honorary Highway Patrolman in the State of Arizona's history and the only honorary member that the highway patrol would ever have.

Some very special men and women went above and beyond the call of duty at the Arizona Department of Public Safety to make a little boy's dream come true. Their friends and their families contributed to Christopher's last wish. In honor and remembrance of those special men and women, and as a final salute *from* Christopher, to all the men and women in uniform he admired so much, it seemed only proper to have the words "ARIZONA TROOPER" engraved on his headstone.

22

Starting Over
The Conception of Make-A-Wish

During the time I spent in Illinois with Gary, I gained control of my emotions and thoughts. I called and visited with old friends that I hadn't seen for years.

I felt strange, somehow, as though I had gone back in time. The old town hadn't changed much. Neither had the kids with whom I had grown up. I even walked through my old high school. What a kick that was.

The farm had been sub-divided into lots with new homes. Nothing much was left of the good old days, only the memories. I guess it's true that you can never go back. It's just not the same.

Before leaving Illinois, I visited Chris's grave one last time. I wanted to say good-bye. As I placed the flowers on the dirt that covered his grave, I felt such sorrow.

What I would have given to have him back. I couldn't understand why I'd had to endure this loss, but as

Grandma Vie would say, a little bit of good always comes out of everything if you look for it.

I considered the patch of brown dirt outlined by green grass. In a few months, his stone would be there to mark his grave. The grass would cover the dirt.

The little boy buried there was a part of me. Chris was my reason for living. I had only wanted to make him happy, to see him smile and hear him laugh. He was all I ever really needed to be happy.

It was time for the Lord to take care of him. I had done the best I knew how. I hoped I had done it right. I directed my thoughts to the Lord. "I know I've asked a lot of you in the past, but please if I could have just one more request? When the days ahead of me get tough because of missing Chris, please don't let him watch. I don't want him to be sad."

I stood up and headed back to the car. As I started the engine, I took one last glance over my shoulder at the bouquet of flowers and one red rose resting on the small fresh patch of dirt. With watery eyes and the fear of having to make it through life without my son by my side, I blew him a kiss and whispered these words.

"I will always love you, Christopher, and I will always be your Mommie. I hate this part of life and wish I could do something to make it never have happened. But I can't. I wish I could, but I can't. I prayed that this day would never come, but I guess all the prayers in the world couldn't stop it, and I have to be separated from you now. Christopher, I make one last promise to you—that this chapter of our life will never be closed; but for now it's later, alligator. I love you."

The trickling tears rapidly turned to uncontrollable sobbing as I put the car in drive, the gravel crackling under the tires as I coasted down the small road. Huge oak trees lined the cemetery road leading to the city streets. Their image reflected across the windshield as I drove, wiping my eyes with a tissue.

On my way out of town, I stopped by the church where Tony and I had exchanged our wedding vows. It hadn't changed at all. I didn't go inside. I simply sat in the car and remembered the day I had knelt and prayed for a son. Two months later, I was pregnant with Chris.

I'd had enough of the past during that memorable three weeks. There was nothing else to finish, and it was time to return to the world of the living. That night, as I lay awake in bed, I felt ready to go home and start building a new life. I decided it might be fun to take a train back to Phoenix.

I called and made arrangements the next morning. As the day progressed, I became more excited about spending three days sitting and watching the miles of country just roll by. I'd never been on a train, and I figured, why not start my new life with something different? It sounded logical to me anyway.

On the day of my departure, I was up bright and early, excited to be headed home at last. Gary was going to take me to Galesburg to meet my train. There was a slight weather watch for the area until 3 a.m. Massive black clouds hovered across the sky as I boarded the train in a damp, misty rain.

Walking down the narrow aisle, I spotted several empty seats towards the rear of the car. Placing my carry-

on case full of picture albums of Chris in the seat nearest
the aisle, I sat down in the seat next to the window,
hoping that no one would ask to sit beside me. I wanted to
spend my time just staring out the window, watching the
countryside peacefully pass by.

My peaceful three days on train number three ended
all too soon. The porter came and sat beside me, thinking
that I was lonely and wanted to talk. We politely
exchanged conversation several times during the trip. I
found my way to the smoking car and met two sisters on
their way to Las Vegas for a week of fun. They tried their
darnedest to talk me into going with them, but I smiled
and simply told them to have a great time. As the train
slowly pulled into its final destination, Flagstaff, Arizona,
I saw my mother standing on the platform anxiously
watching and waiting for me to emerge from the train.

The three-hour drive home passed quickly as we
talked. Once back at home, I lay down on the bed. As I
tried to rest, my mind actively reminded me of all the
things I had to do. The rest of Christopher's toys were still
about the room, and his clothes hung in the closet.

A few days after I had finished packing up Chris's
toys and remaining clothes, I felt other children might get
some use out of them. I donated them to the hospital, the
Leukemia Foundation, and various other charities. It was
extremely hard to fold his clothes and place them in
boxes, as memories were attached to every small outfit.

My mind filled with images of the times when he
would wear his favorite sweatshirt, and we would play
football in the vacant lot outside our apartment complex. I
could still see him sporting his little sheriff outfit as he

walked the streets of Old Tucson, fantasizing himself six
feet tall as he hunted out the bad guys.

In a couple of days, everything was boxed up and
placed in the garage. I had made arrangements for the
Leukemia Foundation to pick up Chris's things. I stood in
the driveway on a hot June morning watching two
strangers stack the cartons in the back of the truck. One of
the men handed me a receipt as the other man climbed in
the truck and started the engine.

"You can go ahead and write in the value of items
donated for your income tax right here," pointing to the
slip of paper.

As the man walked towards the open door on the
passenger side of the truck, I looked down at the receipt in
my hand, whispering "thank you."

I stood in the grass by the edge of the driveway and
watched the truck disappear around the corner with the
last three years of my life.

Words cannot describe the impact of emotions and
memories that consumed me that afternoon. As I held the
blank receipt in my hand, my entire body started shaking.
I became dizzy, and I felt cold and clammy. I wiped my
eyes with the sleeve of my shirt. I wanted to turn away,
but I didn't want to miss any memory of Chris.

I wondered if I had done the right thing, and I found
myself hoping that the truck would come back. I walked
over and leaned against the palm tree near the driveway to
get out of the sun and give myself a rest.

I could feel Mom watching me through the living
room window. I knew that Grandpa was sitting in his
recliner, as he usually did, half looking at television and

probably holding his daughter's hand as she watched her own daughter standing at the edge . . . of the driveway.

I took a deep breath, consoled that I didn't have to put on a smile before walking back into the house. They would certainly understand if I had just "lost it."

With each step, I seemed to gain strength. By the time my hand touched the doorknob, I had forced all emotions back deep down inside of me. I would have to deal with the grief later, when I could be alone. Putting a smile on my face, I was in control again as I entered the house to continue the day as normally as possible.

That evening, Mom prepared my favorite dinner, and we sat around the dining room table talking and laughing as if nothing had happened. They were doing the best they could to help me cope with everything, while at the same time I was trying to show them that I had everything under control. I retired to my room early that evening, eager to spend a little time on my own.

With emotions erupting whenever they wanted to, I had very little control over my thoughts or feelings. Although it was a relief to spend some time alone where I might laugh or cry, I often wondered if I was the only person in the world that felt so horrible inside.

My dresser was piled with condolence cards, letters, and phone messages Mom had collected for me while I was in Illinois. Later that night, as I sat on the bed staring at the pile on the dresser, a warm appreciation for motherly love filled my heart. Among the cards and letters, sat a large glass of ice-cold milk along with a small plate of munchies with a banana to round out a perfect healthy midnight snack. My sweet mother was always looking out for me.

Once a mother always a mother. Swept up in her thoughtfulness, it occurred to me that I would never get the chance to mother my grown son. I knew I would never again hear the word "Mommie."

I sat on the bed munching away with the television on mute, quietly reading the cards. I couldn't even begin to comprehend what I would say when someone asked, "So, do you have kids?"

I knew I had to go on with my life. I needed to go back to college and finish my degree, find a job, and locate an apartment.

Although I longed to put all the doctor appointments, hospitals, blood transfusions, and hard times out of my mind, there would be no putting the love for my son out of my heart. The eternal bond that we shared would never be severed. I knew that we would be reunited—someday.

That night, the thought of being with Chris again became my only link to sanity. It was my strength, and it provided me with the desire to live. The emotions and memories that raced throughout my entire body as I lay down to sleep in Chris's bed were indescribable.

The delicate new bedspread and the brand new furnishings Mom had purchased couldn't disguise or erase the memory of seeing Chris lying there. I didn't get much sleep that night.

The next morning, the phone in my room started ringing off the hook. Everyone called, including the men from the Highway Patrol. Frank and Scott, the two officers who had flown to Illinois to attend the funeral, wanted to get together and discuss forming an organization to make other kids' wishes come true.

Frank told me that they wanted to name the organization after Chris, in his memory. Frank asked me to meet the two of them for lunch in a few days to discuss the matter, and he asked for me to think it over. I wasn't sure what to think or expect, but I agreed to meet them.

I felt a sense of eagerness the morning I got myself ready to head for the restaurant. A specific time and place to be gave me a purpose for the day, at least. The smile on my face was genuine, and the tears seemed buried in the background as I drove little Herbie to the restaurant.

We sat talking for a couple of hours that afternoon about an organization that would let a kid make a wish that we would make happen. We wanted it based solely on donations and volunteers from every walk of life. Excitement ran wild among us as we came up with more ideas for starting the perfect charity for terminally ill children just like Chris. When I left the restaurant that day, I had made them promise to call me with the details of our next meeting.

I was filled with chills driving home in the blistering sun. I was excited to think that I might be part of helping other families with terminally ill children to have a special day, a day that they could cherish the rest of their lives. It would be a fairy tale day, one in which the doctor and the hospital played no part, a day in which illness and disease dared not interfere, a day when minds could blank out the inescapable end of an innocent child's life.

I loved to share with other families the joy that Chris and I had felt on his special day and the continuing joy that I felt just remembering how happy he had been. Another part of me cherished the idea that maybe, just maybe, his death hadn't been in vain. For the first time there seemed to be a reason for it all. Grandma was right, as usual.

Throughout the next couple of weeks, Frank, Scott, and I talked almost endlessly about the charity. I enjoyed hearing what progress we were making. It consumed my life, but at times, I needed to get away by myself. I would take long drives in the mountains to try and escape my thoughts, searching out places to stop where I had never been before—to eat lunch or to just walk around a shopping center in an unfamiliar part of Arizona.

Occasionally, I'd pass a school and find myself slowing down to watch the children play in the yard. I often remembered a special day when Chris's first-grade class stood in the play yard and released balloons carrying names and addresses into the sky. He came running in the door after school one day announcing, "Mommie, Mommie, guess what this is! Guess what happened at school today!"

"I don't know what it is. Stop waving it in the air, and let me read it!"

"Somebody found my balloon and mailed my name back to the school. Only three kids got their names back in the mail. My teacher put my name up on the blackboard with the other two kids'. What's for dinner?"

My special little red rose, Christopher, was a memory now. Somehow I had to come to terms with it. I knew I had to rebuild my life without him, trying to take one day at a time the best I knew how.

Everything was still so fresh in my mind. I thought it would get easier with each passing day, but the hurt seemed to get stronger as my mind worked overtime to remember everything that we had done over the past three years.

I had never thought a broken heart could hurt so much. I had known I would miss him, but I had never dreamed it would be so painful. Attempting to be strong on the outside, while I felt like I was dying on the inside, it was tough to smile. All the emotions I had stored up during those three years were released from inside me, and the only way they could escape was through the tears that drenched my pillow at night.

Memories replaced dreams as the screen of my mind ran continuous features of our adventurous rides in the pickup truck exploring new territories and visiting Old Tucson. I continued to flash back to the day Chris bought his first two-wheeled bicycle on his birthday and the day we bought little "Herbie." And my most treasured day . . . when I received a beautiful red rose bought for three little pennies of pure love.

For Chris and me, "someday" had seemed so far away back then. Someday—when we would be separated—had seemed more like an imaginary date on a calendar that wasn't really ever going to arrive. Now that it had become reality, the simple word "someday" created the image of Chris, and someday, on another imaginary calendar, I would see him again.

Mom was getting her fill of taking messages for me while I was out driving around. Most of the notes were from friends welcoming me home. One message was to inform me of a meeting at the department compound concerning the charity. I marked it on my calendar and called Scott for details.

Scott shared that he and Frank along with Sergeant. Allan Schmidt, whom they had recruited, wanted to go over some new developments regarding the charity. "We thought we would meet here at our office and see what you think of some of our ideas. I'm eager to see if you like the name we came up with."

"Sounds good to me. What time should I be there? And how do I get to your office?"

After hanging up the phone, I sat on the end of the bed for a minute afraid to get my hopes up for fear that nothing would come of this meeting. I wanted the charity to be all that it could be. Ideas started running through my mind of what a charity like ours would mean to thousands of other kids and to their parents.

I didn't need anymore sad things in my life; I knew that this would not be sad but just the opposite, a happy and fulfilling organization for both families and the people involved.

I envisioned a charity that was really a charity, not a means to make money for a CEO. All the money raised would go for the children. It would be a place where people helped each other, where people could give of themselves, giving their time and love to make a child happy, without asking anything in return. The reward would be knowing that we had helped someone, not in corporate recognition. There was enough bad in the world. The newspapers were full of sad stories. I hoped that by promoting something good, we might change things a little for the better of mankind as a whole.

Among the many calls that I immediately returned, one was to my former employer, Mr. Montilla. He called to offer me my old job back at the hotel. He had transferred to the Sheraton across town, so it meant that I would have to move right away.

23

Labor Pains

Between Mom's big car and my little Herbie, we only had to make two trips back and forth across town. I had sold all of our furnishings, so there were only some boxes of clothes and a few odds and ends. The last trip was marked by my special sense of humor.

I had purchased a set of six-foot Texas longhorns at a yard sale, and Mom didn't want to put them in her car because she was afraid they would poke a hole in her upholstery.

Putting the "old ingenuity" to work, I rolled back the sunroof of Herbie and stuck the horns through it. Then I asked Mom if she had a big safety pin.

"What on earth do you want a safety pin for?" She laughed, shaking her head as she walked towards the house to check her sewing basket.

I stood by Herbie, who was packed to the hilt with clothes, books, records, and a four-and-a-half-foot stuffed animal that resembled a lion called, Puddie, properly seated in the front with his seat belt secured.

"You'll see, Mom, trust me."

Returning a few minutes later with the perfect size pin, Mom handed it to me as I opened the passenger door, bending down to get Puddie's paws. Mom, figuring out what I was up to, stood shaking her head and holding her hands over her mouth to try to contain her laughter. Tears of happiness were coming from her eyes as I pinned the paws around the longhorns, making it appear that he was holding tightly onto them.

"Well, what do you think, Mom?"

"I think I'm glad that you're driving Herbie and not me. Boy, are you going to get the looks driving across town."

"Well, you have to make the good times while you can. Besides it's more fun this way, and I like it."

During our drive across town, I kept glancing in my side mirror; I couldn't see out the rear view mirror, because the back seat was packed full. At stoplights, I caught Mom smiling and trying to pretend that she wasn't with me. With each passing car that honked, she chuckled with pleasure.

Well, if you have to move, you might as well make it fun. Right? So, go for it. Life only goes around once. How well I know that fact.

We dumped the last load on top of everything else on our way to the kitchen to get a cool drink of water. Sipping from a pair of paper cups, we stood for a few minutes and talked before Mom started home.

"I wish I could help you more, but I don't know what to do for you. You always just seem to go and do things so fast, and it works out somehow. You are so much like your father in that way. He always just did things, and they worked out for the best, too. You know I was twenty-nine years old when I married your Dad. I was just starting my life, and it seems like you have already lived an entire lifetime with little Chris."

I was speechless. Mom didn't talk like that much. I knew she was trying to express her concerns for me, and at the same time, she was trying to let me know that she was only a phone call away when I needed her.

"Now I'm starting another lifetime, Mom. Only God knows what this one will bring. It will be good for me to start working again, and I'm going to go back to school again to finish my degree. I don't know if I will make it this fall, but I'm definitely going back in the spring."

"I always wanted to go to classes to try and learn something, but at my age and with taking care of the old folks, I just don't have the time."

"You attend some of the lectures at the community college, and I hope you keep it up. It's good for you, Mom."

"If I can help in any way, you know I will. All you have to do is call me."

"I know, Mom, and you know I love you and my 'oldies but goodies,' and if you need help, all *you* have to do is call, too."

"Well, I'm happy for you, and I need to get back home, because it is getting time to start dinner."

"Thanks again for the help, Mom. I'll call you when I get the phone connected."

We said our good-byes and hugged with wet eyes. Mom turned and walked down the stairs. I closed the door behind her then walked to the only window in my studio apartment. Standing there, I watched her make her way through the apartment complex to her car.

As she drove away, I wasn't sure whether to sit down for a few minutes and cry or to keep myself busy by digging into the piles staring me in the face. As it turned out, I worked late into the night.

By two in the morning, I had all my clothes hung up, books arranged, and pictures and hanging plants perfectly displayed. Puddie found a very perky and, I might add, prominent spot at the small kitchen table, with his very own place setting. I couldn't help but think of the day I had bought Puddie for Chris—just one of our adventures. He had wanted the big lion so badly.

The studio took on a familiar, homey look, and everything seemed in balance, but there was one thing missing—Christopher. I sat down on the sofa bed watching some late show, enjoying a soda and a cigarette. I released a yawn of relief, and a smile emerged colored by happy memories of the day Chris and I moved into our first apartment in Scottsdale.

I remembered playing hide-and-seek in the boxes, watching his little legs scrambling up the stairs as he carried another toy to his very own room, and admiring the way he arranged everything just the way he wanted it. Later that evening, we sat on the floor eating our hamburgers and fries. They sure tasted good.

Coming back to the present, I reminded myself that the little studio would be it for awhile—my new home. It sure hadn't taken me long to put it together, but I didn't have as much stuff as before.

After a couple of days, I settled into my apartment. My phone was hooked up, and I had groceries in the refrigerator. It felt good but a little strange and scary getting back into the flow of life. It was a challenge doing something besides just wandering through each day waiting for night to come so at least eight hours passed before I had to try and figure out what to do with the next day.

One evening while getting ready for work, I had finished dressing and putting the final touches on my hair. As I stood in front of the mirror in the tiny bathroom, I looked myself straight in the eye and made a promise to myself.

"No more bad times, no more hurt. I am going to have a happy future full of life and fun, doing whatever I want, whenever I want, doing all the things that make me happy. The charity is going to be a big success, so put a smile on your face and believe that you can do it.

"You're the only one that is holding you back. You can be anything you want to be. All you have to do is start trying and don't give up until you succeed. You got that? Don't ever give up trying to be all that you can be."

I didn't relish working nights again, but I was glad to have a job and hoped that someday I could move into a day job with the hotel. It was a start back into the reality of life's flow, and that is what I needed.

On the night of the big meeting with Allan Schmidt, Frank and Scott, the latter using his cartoon voice impersonation, greeted me with a warm hug as I met him at department headquarters. We laughed and then hurried to meet the others waiting for me.

In the meeting room, Frank's enthusiastic words kicked off the meeting. "Lynn, have we got something exciting to talk to you about! But I want you to know that the idea that Scott and I have will go no further if you don't want it to."

I looked around the table of the boardroom and smiled as a tear of happiness glided down my cheek.

"I want to hear it all, you guys, every thought and every idea." Their faces and voices broke out into laughter, because they knew I was with them one hundred percent.

Frank started the conversation rolling, "Lynn, when Scott and I were flying back on the plane we still couldn't get over how Chris had touched our lives in the short time we knew him."

Scott jumped into the conversation, "Yeah, we figured that there must be hundreds of other kids out there that are just like Chris. They have dreams and wishes, too. Why can't we do the same for them as we did for Chris?"

"You guys, I'm so excited and happy, and yes, let's make other kids' wishes come true. You have no idea what it did for him. He even went to sleep with the badge clutched in his little hand. You guys know what it was like at the hospital; he wasn't about to go anywhere without his uniform. There are thousands of other kids out there, just like Chris, who need something special in their lives. I've sat in the doctor's office the past three years, and I've seen the sadness on the faces of the parents. I think it's about time we do something about that. Don't you guys?"

For about an hour we talked of what we had to do in order to become a charity. We considered whom we would need to enlist to help us in making kids' wishes come true. Towards the end of the meeting, Frank suggested that we talk to Kathy and see if she would be interested in helping us. Kathy McMorris's husband was a fellow police officer, and Kathy was an energetic young woman who actively volunteered for anything connected with kids.

The evening ended with a joined high five in the air and the question of what to call this organization. A loud and enthusiastic cheer came from Frank and Scott as they shouted out the name together. "The Chris Greicius Make-A-Wish Memorial, Inc."

"We want to name it after Chris in honor of his memory, if that's OK with you."

"I think he would be extremely pleased and honored to have it named after him, because I know I am. Thank you very much for wanting to name it after him."

The evening ended with a little bit of an emotional tone as they walked me to Herbie and we said good-bye until the next meeting. Driving home, I felt that renewed sense of purpose once again in my life. I felt as though I was coming alive again, instead of feeling as though I was in a coma. Energy surged throughout my entire body. I couldn't wait to get home and break the great news to Mom.

The words of Grandma Vie danced happily in my mind. "A little bit of good comes out of everything, if you just look for it."

For the next several months, the five of us met in a variety of spots. (Kathy had agreed to join us.) We would meet at someone's home, my apartment clubhouse, or coffee shops to exchange information and accept new assignments in order to further our goal.

Frank had secured the help of an attorney, Patrick McGroder III, to incorporate the charity, but we still needed another attorney to do some of the legal work for us. We were also in need of a CPA for an IRS status as soon as possible.

Kathy's voice was alive with excitement as she announced, "Hey, my brother-in-law is an attorney. I'll give him a call tomorrow and see if he can help us."

"Hey, my uncle is a CPA. I'll call him tomorrow and see if he can help us with the IRS forms or something." I wanted to contribute my part, but as it turned out, donated my uncle's knowledge and copying machine; he had no objection. Frank later enlisted the services of Doug Bell, CPA, to actually fill out forms and file them for us.

Between the five of us, we came up with several people to contact. We figured if they couldn't help us, at least they might know who could. They did. It seemed that before we knew it, several people from all walks of life were knocking on our "meeting door" volunteering their help in any capacity that would be helpful to forming the organization.

Several months passed. We had met, written by-laws, and filed the papers. Now, we watched our mailboxes for the IRS reply, eager to discover if we were to become a legal charitable organization.

Sadly, the paperwork we agonized over was returned due to missing information. It seemed every time we called a meeting, all we would do was review paperwork, read the by-laws, discuss charters, and drink coffee.

We held elections among the five of us, each taking an elected position and signing our names on the paperwork to be incorporated. Frank Shankwitz, president; Scott Stahl, vice-president; Kathy McMorris, secretary-treasurer; Linda Bergendahl, Wish Child liaison; Allan Schmidt, public relations.

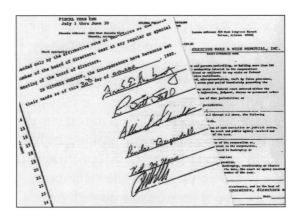

More and more friendly faces showed up or called us with the desire to help raise money, to volunteer for services such as running errands, or to become a charity member.

We explained that until the charity had been granted legal status, our hands were tied. The kind folks understood, and they asked that we take their names and numbers and call once we obtained our status. The five of us—Frank, Scott, Kathy, Allan, and I—remained the original founders of the Greicius Make-A-Wish Memorial, Inc. dba Make-A-Wish Foundation, on the incorporation papers, and we thanked God for his blessings and for all the support from volunteers.

The original banner from our first fund raiser in 1980.

Sometimes after the meeting, I would return to my apartment to get ready for work, thrilled by what we were doing. The possibilities of making a dream come true for a child consumed my thoughts. I didn't know if I was coming or going. The nights passed quickly as the words Make-A-Wish kept dancing in rainbow colors through my mind. Our little group plotted and planned to make the organization one of which Chris would be proud.

I was overwhelmed with happiness and pride about out little group and wanted everyone to know what the

DPS had done for Chris as well as for me. So one evening I sat down with a pad and pen and decided to write a letter to the governor of Arizona to let him know about some wonderful police officers.

Christmas holidays were rapidly approaching, and I don't think a day passed without my remembering our last Christmas together as I watched Chris open his presents. I missed the little boy that loved to dress up in a mini suit and tie for the holidays, because he wanted to look nice, like a little gentleman.

The hotel was decorated elegantly, with garlands and delicate ornaments tastefully arranged upon a seven-foot blue spruce triumphant in the center of the lobby. Empty boxes were colorfully gift wrapped and placed in perfect symmetry under the tree.

When I finished the audit, I often wrote in my journal, pouring out everything I could remember of Chris and our times together over the past three years. At times when I didn't have it in me to write any more, I would sit on the sofa in the lobby and just stare at the tree while planning a little getaway trip to the mountains.

It had been about eight months since Chris's death, and I felt that I had handled his death better at the time than I was now. I tried to tell myself that the ups and downs were just because of the Christmas holidays.

The charity was closer to becoming incorporated. We were getting closer to giving birth to an organization that wanted to make kids happy. We had filled out tons of papers, notarized almost everything, signed every document twice, then sealed and mailed it. Somehow the little group pulled together to accomplished each task because we were all in accord.

The charity kept me on my toes, but nothing could stop me from missing Chris. I thought about the life I had lived over the past four years. So much had happened since that day four years ago, when the doctor took a simple blood test and pronounced my son to be stricken by leukemia. Life from that moment on became extremely valuable.

I can't remember where I heard this phrase but it went something like this.

"Were those days the best compared to the total sum—I guess it depends on how far we've come."

I personally had to answer that statement with, "Yes, they were the best days of my life. The love and simplicity of the life we had shared were gone forever. There was no replacement and no turning back to that time. No two little arms could ever hug me the way Chris did."

The trusting little face that used to look to me for all the answers was now gone. Now it was only me looking back at myself in the mirror, and I didn't have many answers for myself—only a lot of doubts and fears.

Although Frank, Scott, Kathy, Allan, and my mother were always there for me, I couldn't share with anyone exactly what was going on inside of me. I felt that I had to be strong for the charity so that it would succeed and help the other families that we would come to know.

I had made a vow to the Lord and to myself, that for the next three years I would not allow myself to become involved in any personal relationships, and I kept that vow. The charity became my life; helping others became my goal.

One night after I had finished writing in my journal, I closed the book and opened the louvers, gazing out the window into the darkness with a blank mind.

Everything was starting to get to me. The next couple of weeks passed slowly. The hotel wasn't full. The audit, which I was able to complete in record time, left me with too much time to sit and stare at the beautifully decorated Christmas tree in the lobby.

It seemed like the walls were closing in on me. It became harder and harder to think of being alone without my son. Although I had found purpose in the charity, there were times when it seemed there was no point in living anymore. I wanted to escape to some place where there was fun and life again.

I waited for the first rays of sunlight to find their way through the slatted louvers and onto the pages of my journal. Partly laughing, but mostly wiping away the tears, I sat night after night writing down memories and thoughts still buried deep within me. I wondered if other parents of terminally ill children had gone or were going through the same things that I had experienced. I wanted to share with them, or with anyone who would listen and understand, but I couldn't somehow. I didn't know how. The emotions seemed locked up inside. I felt my only release was to be alone and write.

24

A Mountain Escape
to Reality

Journal entry:

August 8, 1980

For the past couple of days I've been thinking about Chris very much. Remembering the places we used to visit and things we used to do. Most of the week I just sit alone and cry. I can't stop remembering the feeling when I'd hold him in my arms.

When I go to sleep, I keep thinking he is beside me, but when I turn over to watch him sleep, he's not there. Then I sit up in bed and have a little talk with God.

I remember his birthday last year and the happy smile on his face when all his friends came. Today is his birthday, and I wonder if he is having a party in heaven.

I had lunch with a girlfriend today, and as we sat and talked, I became very shaky for no reason. My head became dizzy just sitting there in the booth. Sometimes I really don't care if I die. At least I would be with Chris.

August 25, 1980

At night while lying in bed, I sometimes see myself driving over a cliff. A couple of times while cleaning my gun, things that aren't right went through my mind. I feel myself drained of all my energy. I just close my eyes and see Chris's face, and then I hear his voice, "Mommie, Mommie!"

August 27, 1980

This morning I went to register for school, but I was tired and I left. I went to Mom's to change the oil in my car. I think I poured in a little too much because smoke sputtered from out the back like crazy.

Frankly, right now I really don't care. If it burns up, I'll just bury it like I did Chris.

September 30, 1980

I remembered when I got him on the local kid's television program. He was in the wheelchair, and it made him so happy when they gave him the special prize at the end of the show. He talked about it for weeks afterwards. All his little friends watched him that day.

Wallace and Ladmo from the television program even came to see Chris at the hospital. Chris, you never knew that they came to see you, but they did, all dressed in costume for you, little man.

October 16, 1980

I've been practicing shooting, still going to church, and enjoying the world more. I took it up after Chris's death; somehow it relieves the tension.

I think about Chris but it's not in sorrow. It's happy thoughts, knowing I was his mother, knowing I gave him all the love I had to give. That makes me feel very proud.

I was remembering the time before his death when we were walking in the mall on our way to the bank. I couldn't believe what came out of his mouth after looking at the picture of Jesus in the window. I know they had a little talk that day, so Chris would know that there is no pain or sorrow in heaven. I felt that it was a sign to me that the end was near.

I always told him the truth the best I knew how, so he could understand it.

October 30, 1980

One of the officers stopped by today for my signature on some papers for the charity. We're getting closer, and I can hardly wait until we are really moving. I want it to be successful for other kids, Chris. It's hard being reminded of everything almost everyday of my life, and sometimes it takes more than what I have to be able to stand in front of people and tell them of your special day. As wonderful as it was, it can be tough telling them what it meant to you as well as what it meant to me.

The tears feel like a dam behind my eyes as I force my emotions to remain silent while I conjure up a smile on my face. I love what I'm doing or, at least, what I'm trying to do, but it's just hard at times.

November 15, 1980

My head really hurts tonight. I can't remember when it felt like this. I can't seem to see straight and it feels so heavy. I know there will come a day when this life will end and I will be happy. I just have to hold on a little longer.

The time isn't right now. God will tell me when and show me the way. I guess what I want on earth, just isn't here. That doesn't leave me much of a choice, does it?

December 1, 1980

Christmas is almost here. The stores have the trees up, and the malls are full of people doing their shopping and lots of kids getting their pictures taken with Santa.

The closer it gets to Christmas, the more I feel Chris has gone.

December 10, 1980

When I sit in the lobby of the hotel after the audit is done and I look at the Christmas tree, I can almost feel Chris and see him opening presents.

I know some of my thoughts are wrong, and I know he would want me to be happy. I guess my faith, more than a lack of guts keeps me from joining him.

December 21, 1980

I guess I will always think about Chris and wonder what he would be if he had grown up. Would he like to play baseball and football at school? Would he do well in school? Would his hair turn dark or stay blond?

What kind of toys would he have wanted this year for Christmas? Would he still like animals so much and still want me to tuck him in bed at night?

Would he always feel that he could come to me and ask any question on his mind? I wonder if he would have grown up to be a cop someday?

When I look at his pictures and see the smile on his face, I remember how happy he was. How proud he was to wear his uniform, his badge, and his boots.

Dreaming that night of his special days as a little Highway Patrol Officer ready for action, I thank God for the miracle he worked through those men.

December 24, 1980

Christmas Eve is here. The hotel is full of people and parties. I'll be glad when the bar closes and everyone goes home, so I can do my work.

I have Chris's certificate and the flag on the bookshelf in the studio. I do feel happy that my little man got his wish.

When I see kids mistreated by their parents or by other adults, I want to scream at them and tell them how lucky they are to have a little child to love!

I don't understand why and how a person can do those things to innocent children. This world is sick! The more I see it, the more I want out of it.

December 25, 1980

Merry Christmas, Chris! I sat looking at your picture today and came across last year's Christmas card. I remember how surprised you were to get that big semi truck! You had so many presents you didn't know which one to open first.

How handsome you looked all dressed up in your new suit. I still have the present you gave me, and I play the tape you made for me. It's nice to hear your voice again and feel you near me.

Your stuffed puppies are sitting on the end table and Billy Bear is there, too. I gave your little motorcycle to the Leukemia Foundation so that another little boy could enjoy it.

I'm happy for you on this day and how wonderful that you are sharing in Christ's birthday. All the angels are singing, and I know you are among them. So, Chris, sing loud and clear with the angels. Mommie is proud of you.

Some of our friends called to say they were thinking of you and wished me a merry Christmas. Their calls meant a lot to me.

I'm still working nights. It's OK, I guess. Mommie is going to the mountains for a few days; I'm leaving just after Christmas.

A family offered me the use of their cabin for a few days. They will be there when I arrive and show me how to lock up everything when I leave.

It will be nice to sit and collect my thoughts. Maybe this will help.

I don't seem to be hungry or eating much anymore. When I go home in the morning, I end up sleeping until it's time to get ready for work again.

I did go out with some single friends on a weekend, but that whole evening made me sick. It was like some giant meat market of people on display.

I would rather spend my life going from hospitals to emergency rooms, if I could.

It will be nice to get away from the city, to sit in the woods and listen to the birds sing. I'm really looking forward to it.

Herbie is still running well, and I got him all ready for the trip. With his oil changed and bumpers all shined up, down the road we'll go.

Well, my little trooper, I hope you enjoy your Christmas in Heaven. Mommie loves you, and I'll see you soon.

December 27, 1980
Chris, sometimes I can't help wishing I were with you. Dear Lord, if you see Chris watching me and feeling sad, please make him understand that my sorrow is only because of me. Tell him things will be all right.

Please, Lord, give Chris my share of heaven, if I have any. Let him enjoy the beauty and be happy and know the kingdom of heaven to the fullest.

I pray that when I die, I will know your kingdom also.

At last the morning arrived when I would take to the mountains of North Central Arizona. I packed a few cold-weather clothes, but mainly I took memories of Chris. I brought along Chris's pictures, the tape he had made for me, and the gun I had purchased. I left a letter on the table by the door of my apartment. I figured it would explain everything to whomever found it.

I called and talked to Mom the night before, and she said that Grandma Pete wasn't feeling well. I told her I would be back in about a week and that I was just taking a little vacation.

Not a cloud hung in the sky as Herbie and I rolled down the road. I was all set with my suitcase in the back seat, an Arizona road map on the dash, and the instructions for getting to the cabin in my purse.

I drove a couple of hours through the backwoods making my way to the mountains. Giant trees framed the highway, and waterways ran full, splashing against the rocks in the creeks.

As I approached the mountains, a couple of deer emerged from the woods, pausing to eat alongside the road. Feeling hungry myself, I stopped for breakfast in Payson, a small, peaceful country town. The folks were friendly and down to earth. Devouring a hot roast beef sandwich, I glanced around the restaurant, and it touched me just how happy everyone seemed. I felt happy, but yet sad, that I would probably never see any of them again, even though I didn't know them.

I paid for the meal and continued down the road headed for the cabin. After twenty miles of winding washboard gravel road traversed in second gear, I came upon a small village with a neighborhood grocery store and a few cabins.

About a mile in, I found my getaway, a large, two-story cedar cabin with a balcony overlooking the creek and a large stone fireplace, which peeked through the sloping roof. WOW!

The owners rushed out to greet me and helped me carry in my suitcase. Their youngest son, Michael, a coworker from the hotel, was there to greet me, too.

Michael had told his family all about Make-A-Wish and Christopher. He told them that I really needed to get away for the holidays.

He introduced me to the generous family, and we shared hot coffee in the kitchen. As we sat talking, I couldn't remember seeing a family more happy.

They made me feel so much a part of their family that night, and I almost forgot about for what I had gone up there.

By the time the sun had set, a scruffy little old man showed up at the back door. He was dressed in faded old blue jeans and a tattered winter coat. The graying whiskers and snowcap pulled down around his face gave me a fright. As it turned out, the ragged old man lived a few houses down the road. He was warmly invited by the family to come in and join us for coffee.

The family introduced me as a friend who would be staying in the cabin for about a week. It's a good thing he showed up while they were still there, because I never would have opened the door and let him inside that cabin.

Bright and early the next morning, the whole family packed up and prepared to go home as scheduled. Within an hour, I was all alone sitting on the balcony watching the water gently flow downstream.

I took a couple of walks through the woods, down the road, and along the creek, enjoying the peace and quiet. I couldn't hear cars racing by, sirens blasting away, or neighbors fighting and throwing each other against the walls of their apartment. For the first time in a long time, peace and quiet surrounded me.

That night, I made myself dinner and sat by the fire before going to sleep. I thought a lot about why I had gone up there. Chris was on my mind, along with Mom and the grandparents.

In my solitude, I gave thought to living and not living. I wondered what life might be like if I picked up and headed for Dallas, for Japan, or for the moon. I wondered if a move would give me a new lease on life. But then I thought about Mom and the "oldies but goodies." They needed me.

I went upstairs to try and get some sleep but found it was warmer to sleep on the sofa by the fire. Sometime during the night, I fell asleep from the exhaustion of tears.

The next morning I took a drive to clear my head. Among the dense, tall pines, I would pause at a clearing every now and then to gaze out the car window at the endless beauty of the mountains. The rocky peaks, hidden by drifting fluffy white clouds, provided only a glimpse of their strength, the beauty and mystery of several thousand years.

Working off of a makeshift, handwritten map, I decided not to venture off the washboard main road much. There were several small dirt roads leading back through the tall pines that promised adventure, but I figured I'd end up in somebody's front yard, and that wouldn't be too good.

I returned to the cabin after a two-hour drive and made myself a sandwich for lunch. Then I set out on foot down the side road on a mission to find the old man's cabin.

He had extended a "welcome anytime," and I just wanted to see where he lived. There was something different about him, but I couldn't put my finger on it. The old man's cabin was supposed to be situated just down the road and behind a patch of pines, but there was no other cabin in sight. I shrugged my shoulders, gave up for the day, and headed back to the cabin.

Early that evening, I grabbed a gallon jug of wine out of my car and proceeded to drink as much of it as possible, hoping to drown my depression and sorrow. I played Chris's tape and sat staring at the fire, consumed by Chris's voice as he sang songs and spun handmade tales about all his favorite Saturday cartoon characters.

I reached for a stack of Chris's pictures, and tears pelted each snapshot as I thumbed through them over and over. After I'd been through the stack a billion times, I loaded the gun sitting on the coffee table. I stared at it for a long time, as the night grew colder. When I could no longer bear the chill, I threw a few logs on the fire and choked down some more wine. Getting drunk should not have taken so much effort, as I had never really been a drinker and I had only tasted my first alcoholic beverage a few months before.

Forcing myself to swallow the cheap wine, every minute inched by like a day, while every hour crawled by like years. Throughout every morbid moment, I was drowned in thoughts of Chris. I didn't want to live without him anymore. I wanted to be with Chris.

Deep into the bitter, winter night, I struggled with my desire to kill the pain, to set myself free, and to be with my son again. I put another log on the fire and poured another glass of wine. I dumped the overflowing ashtray into the fireplace. At long last, I closed my son's photo album, placed the ashtray on one side and the glass of wine on the other and sat with my legs crossed on the sofa staring into the roaring fire.

The more I stared at the bright flames, the larger they grew. The flames were mesmerizing, and my thoughts snapped and popped with the fire. I didn't want to stop watching the wicked dance, but I knew that I had to look away in order to maintain my self-control.

I drifted back in time to the first night in the hospital with Chris, and I remembered the words of those waging great battles over the landscape of my mind as I'd leaned against the window bars in his room.

The battle had returned, and the voices exploded in my head. One voice told me to beware of the dark thoughts invading my soul. *"Those flames are only a whisper of what hell is like. You don't want that, do you?"* The other voice started in, determined to confuse me. *"All you have to do is pull the trigger, and you will be with your son. Go ahead. Pick up the gun, and do it. All your problems will be over, and you'll be in heaven."* I tried to derail my tangled thoughts with another glass of wine, but oddly enough, the more I drank, the more wide-awake and stone cold sober I became.

I cried out over the roaring fire, disgusted by everything. "God, now I can't even get drunk! I must be the biggest failure you have on this earth. I'm a failure as a mother and a wife. I don't fit into this world, Lord, and I don't like it here!"

I took in a deep breath and stopped shouting. I knew that the Lord could hear me over the desperation of my own despondent thoughts. "Please forgive me for wanting to kill myself, God. I just can't take it any longer. I can't bear all this hurt inside of me anymore, God. Please take me home tonight."

I covered my tear-tracked face with both hands and sobbed. My cries echoed throughout the otherwise silent room, lit only by firelight. As I wiped my eyes and looked again to the flames, a very peaceful embracement surrounded me. It was the same sensation I had felt the evening of Chris's death when I had felt that I was being pushed out the hospital doors only to find myself surrounded by a calm and wonderful serenity that filled me throughout. One voice repeated itself in my mind with the very same words I had heard on February 4, 1977.

"Remember that I said I would never leave you nor forsake you, my child?"

The voice was clear as a bell, and its presence comforted me in my self-imposed isolation. The voice sounded so real that I got up and started walking around talking out loud.

"I want to be in heaven with Chris. Is that too much to ask for?"

A calm and soothing voice lingered through my mind again with words that brought me back to reality.

"If you take your own life, you will never see your son again."

I stopped and stood there in the middle of the room looking around. It didn't seem dark any more. I hadn't turned any lights on, but the room took on a loving atmosphere. The flames of the fire served as warmth and illumination rather than a mesmerizing dance of evil. Reality began to set in.

"I can't do this; I can't kill myself. . . . it's wrong. I have to go on with my life no matter what the path ahead may bring. I will see Chris someday, but not tonight. I will conquer the hurt and sorrow one day at a time. This way out is not an option. The Bible says that God will only give you as much as you can handle. Well then, Lord, you must have more faith in me than I do in myself. I'll try to not disappoint you, but stick close, because I have just proven to you and to myself that I can't do this alone."

With tears of relief flowing down my cheeks, I brushed the hair away from my face, took a deep breath, and continued to talk as I wandered around the room gathering my things.

"OK, then, whatever mountain you want me to climb, I'll do my best to climb it, Lord. You may have to throw me a rope once in awhile, but I'll make it to the top for you."

I dumped the rest of the wine down the drain. I gathered Chris's snapshots, the tape, and my clothes—everything but the gun. The gun remained on the table, as I sat back down on the sofa. Before I had had a chance to fall off to sleep, my eyes popped open, and I jumped up out of my seat as a terrifying image blasted through my mind: the image of the gun suspended in the air pointed at my head.

"Lord, what is going on here? I don't believe this." Total terror flooded my entire body, and all of my five senses were alert to everything that surrounded me. I felt as if something evil was going to emerge from the walls or erupt through the floor. It was like something out of a horror movie.

I sat on the sofa for a few minutes staring at the gun lying on the table. Eventually, I grabbed it and unloaded the bullets, quickly so as not to give it a chance to fire itself at me. I felt a little bit better, but not by much. I stood by the coffee table holding the gun in one hand and the bullets in the other. Gripping the bullets that I might have used that night, I raised my voice to the Lord.

"I could be lying dead on this floor in a pool of blood right now. It would have been all over forever, all eternity—no more hope or the chance for anything. God, forgive me."

I headed out to the balcony and leaned over the railing, tossing the bullets into the creek. I locked the gun inside Herbie, consoled that it couldn't fly through the air, unlock the door, or enter the cabin. I bedded down on the sofa and puzzled over both the terror and the beauty of my night. Emotionally spent, I tried to fall off to sleep, but every ounce of me remained fully alert, eagerly anticipating the first morning light when at last I could go home.

I have heard it said that this earth is as much heaven or as much hell as some people will know. "Well, Jesus, this earth is going to be the only hell I ever know."

By sunrise, I had replaced a night of wine with a morning of fresh coffee. I was dedicated to reviving myself for the long ride home. Downing my third cup, I turned around and saw the scruffy old man looking in the backdoor window. At first, he startled me, but then I opened the door and invited him in to share a cup or two.

As I poured the old man a cup of coffee, he explained his visit. "I didn't mean to frighten you, I just wanted to make sure you were all right. If you need help with anything, I'll be happy to do whatever I can. The family asked me if I would help watch out for things."

The little old man struck me as different. I don't know why, but he was. Maybe he had lived up there too long without much people contact. Maybe he had sensed the reason behind my mountain getaway. Maybe the smile on my face hadn't effectively concealed the perplexed state of confusion churning inside of me. Maybe he had had a loved one, perhaps a daughter, who had succeeded in doing what I almost had done the night before. Maybe I was the one who was different.

"Everything is OK," I cheerfully replied. "I just finished winterizing the cabin, because I'm leaving to go home in an hour or so. Most everything is packed, and all I have to do is put it in the car. Do you want some more coffee? I'm going to have a cup."

"No, I've had enough. I just wanted to make sure you were OK. I'm glad you're going home. Did you have a good stay here?"

I detected a hint of inquisitiveness in his voice, almost as if he had been watching last night.

"Well, it has been eventful, to say the least. A lot happened, probably more than I realize right now."

"Is that good?" A faint smile slightly emerged from beneath his graying beard.

"Yeah, I guess it was good. I learned something important last night—something that I'll take with me the rest of my life."

He didn't ask what that "important something" was. He just seemed pleased and quite happy as he prepared to leave. "Good. Then the time wasn't wasted up here, was it?"

"No, it wasn't wasted. I'll never forget these past couple of days."

"Good. I've got to go now. You drive carefully going back to Phoenix, won't you?"

"Thanks, I will do just that." The door closed quietly and I watched the old man hobble down the road. It crossed my mind to follow him to see where he lived, but I didn't. As he disappeared into the shaded pine tree, I knew I would never see him again. The gentle, concerned love and strength he projected from beneath that scruffy appearance left a lasting impression.

Herbie and I were ready to go home to get some rest and get back to work.

I started down the road relieved to leave the pain, rather than my hopes and dreams, on the cabin floor. I got a couple of miles down the washboard road, no cabins in sight, and headed down a fairly good-sized hill.

The car was at top speed; second gear was a little too fast for the road down the steep hill. I stepped on the brake to slow down, but the pedal went straight to the floor. I reached for the emergency brake and gave it a yank; there was no result. It was no use; I tried it over and over.

I veered off to the side of the road hoping the gravel would slow me down, and, thank God, it did. Shifting into first, I slowed the car down even more.

"God, help me!" I cried out, "I don't want to die!"

Scenes spanning the previous night flashed through my mind. I remembered everything that I had thought of doing as I finally reached the bottom of the hill. I sat leaning my head on the steering wheel listening to my heart pound.

"God, how am I going to make it eighteen miles through these mountains with no brakes?"

Staring at the road in front of me, it occurred to me how much I wanted to make it home safely and how good that felt. "You see? You really don't want to die, now do you?" I said to myself.

The thought of going over the side of the mountain gripped me in terror. My own words came back to me.

"God, help me. I don't want to die. I won't ever think of killing myself again. I know now that I want to live. Lord, forgive me. I'm sorry for last night. I'll never try anything like that again. I promise. I promise, Lord. Just please, get me back to Phoenix. OK?"

I was trying to hold back the tears, but I wasn't very successful. Pushing in the clutch and easing Herbie into first gear, I kept to the inside of the road in the heavy gravel to keep from going too fast.

The road leveled out for a while, so I didn't need to use the brakes anyway. I planned when I arrived in the town of Payson to have the brakes checked out at a service station. About five miles down the road, I started to relax and slipped a tape in the stereo deck. Before I knew it, I was heading down another steep hill. Without thinking about it, I hit the brakes, and little Herbie stopped halfway down the hill in the middle of the road.

"Lord, how do I have brakes now and didn't before? OK, you really taught me a lesson this time, didn't you! I don't understand everything that's going on, but I'm still going to stop at the gas station to get the brakes checked out, if you don't mind."

I sat reading a magazine at the service station waiting for the man to check my brakes. I certainly was not going to drive back to Phoenix without brakes.

"There is nothing wrong with the brakes. They're in perfect condition. You won't have any trouble getting to Phoenix. I sure don't know what could have happened to cause them to go out on you like that. You said the emergency brake didn't work either? Well, I don't know what to tell you, young lady, but there is nothing wrong with them now."

I thanked him, then got back in Herbie and continued on my way home. I wasn't quite sure what to make of the whole experience: the cabin, then the little old man, and then my crazy brakes going out.

Nothing seemed to make any sense except that God really did love me and was there with me in the cabin the whole time.

I knew that my life had a purpose, and I prayed that the charity would be my answer to prayer and would make wishes come true for thousands of other children.

Arriving back in Phoenix, later that afternoon, I turned off Herbie's engine and leaned my head back against the seat accepting that life goes on.

I knew I had to keep moving forward, growing and learning each day. All the things that I had tried to teach Chris, things I wanted him to believe in, came to my mind. It was almost as if I heard him say. "Now you do those things. You live life to the fullest. It's your turn, Mommie. Do it."

I walked up to the apartment carrying my suitcase, unlocked the door, and as I stepped in, a feeling of peace surrounded me. Setting the suitcase down, my eyes focused on the letter I had left on the table. As I reached for it, intending to rip it into tiny little pieces, the phone rang.

"Linda Joy, I didn't know if you would be back or not, but I thought I'd call anyway."

"Yeah, I just walked in the door when you called, Mom. What's up anyway?"

"Well, the nursing home called and said that they took Grandma Pete to the hospital. They don't know for sure, but the nurse said they didn't expect her to make it much longer—maybe only hours."

I stared at the sealed envelope in my hands, after Mom and I finished talking, and felt as if I were holding death itself. I ripped the letter into pieces and threw it in the trash.

On January 5, 1981, Nora Alice Torstenson-Peterson, better known as Grandma Pete, passed away peacefully in her sleep at ninety-five years old. The song "The Old Rugged Cross" was playing softy in the background.

It was her favorite hymn, not only because of its beautiful meaning but also for the memory that the authors had written the song at her parents' home. My grandmother's sister was the organist that accompanied the authors, Reverend Bennard and Ed. E. Mieras, when they sang the song as a duet for the first time in public on January 12, 1913, at the Sawyer Friend's Church, Sturgeon Bay, Wisconsin.

Information taken from: *The story of THE OLD RUGGED CROSS at Sturgeon Bay, Wisconsin* by Reverend John M. Baxter. And my grandmother.

25

The First Wish Kids

By the end of January 1981, our little group had officially become a charity in the eyes of the IRS.

With the addition of a couple of new board members, the group had grown. As time passed, many people volunteered whatever help they could give, in any area. For the first time in a long time, I felt alive, useful, and happy again. Maybe this was God's plan for my life: to help other families that were facing the same situation that I had faced with Chris.

We held a couple of fund-raising events, trying to get the idea known in the community. The acceptance was overwhelming as we spoke to various community groups. Our fund-raisers were lots of fun as volunteers, including me, made snow cones and flipped hamburgers in the hot summer sun. Although we didn't raise much money, what we earned looked like a million dollars to us.

The story of what happened to Chris became quite well known in Phoenix, with all the newspaper and television coverage. They showed the same encouraging delight in covering our fund-raising events.

At first, I was hesitant to speak in front of groups, but I slowly became accustomed to being pushed out onto a stage to tell the story of what Make-A-Wish was all about. Usually someone would ask me the question of how Chris's wish came to be, which led me to tell and relive the entire emotional two days.

My knees shook and my voice crackled as I stood speaking to various organizations hoping to raise money for Make-A-Wish.

I guess it was natural that the group elected me to find our first "wish kid." The first person I thought about was Dr. Baranko. I was hesitant, nervous, and excited to think we were about to make a child's dream come true.

I thought a lot about what the charity wanted me to do. It helped in some ways to talk about Chris and the happy times we had shared, but at the same time, it was very painful remembering the fear-ridden nights when I had sat beside his hospital bed wondering if he would die before morning.

I fought an indescribable emotional battle every time I spoke, attempting to tell the brave story of Chris, while suppressing my tears.

I concentrated on thoughts of what I knew I wanted to say, asking God to give me the strength to do it, as he always had in the past.

I relived every emotion and vivid memory of those days as I stood speaking to groups. I did my best to remain in control, holding my head up high with grace and dignity in order to present a positive image. It wasn't only

for the charity but also on the chance that someone who
was listening was possibly going through the same ordeal
and could gain hope for their own lives.

My thoughts were only to try to give another family
the joy that Chris and I had experienced for his special
day. So I suppose the group was right; the most logical
place for me to start looking for a child in need of a wish
was with Christopher's doctor, Dr. Baranko.

I called the office and talked to Terri, Chris's favorite
nurse. I explained the reason I was calling and Terri's
response was filled with excitement

"Hang on a minute, and let me go and ask him." I
wasn't sure how I would feel seeing him in his office
again, but I committed myself to going through with it for
the benefit of all children.

Terri, still enthusiastic, came on the line. "How about
Tuesday at 10:00 a.m. next week?"

"That's fine, Terri. I'll be there."

"It will be nice to see you again, and Dr. Baranko is
excited to see you again, too. We miss you two guys
around here; we really do."

Tuesday morning arrived all too soon, and I must
admit it was rather a strange feeling driving to the
doctor's office that morning in Herbie, without Chris
sitting beside me, holding his hand out the window trying
to catch a bug.

But as I entered the office building, I noticed a little
boy standing by the candy counter selecting his goodies.
As I continued to walk through the building towards the
little boy, I noticed a bandage across the back of his hand.

I smiled at him and wondered if he would be our first wish child.

It seems all parents do the same things to cheer up their children. I had to smile remembering back to the days when we would stop and get some candy on the way out. Somehow a couple of pieces of candy always turned into a toy and several pieces of candy. I think that's true with any parent who has a terminally ill child. You just don't have the heart to deny them anything.

I walked toward the door that led to the interior of the building, covering my mouth with my hand as flashbacks of past visits to the same candy counter relived themselves in my heart.

It had been almost a year since Chris's death, but the memories were far from dying. The tile floor still had my sneaker's squeaking with each step that I took. Placing my hand on the wrought iron railing that led upstairs to the doctor's office, I paused. With one foot resting on the first step, I stood looking upward at the first door on the left.

I swallowed the lump in my throat and heaved the other foot onto the next step. Emotions from the past flashed into focus as I climbed my way to the top of the stairs. Chris's voice and his endless questions echoed through my mind with each step that I took.

"What is going to happen today, Mommie? How many pokies do I have to have? Mommie, can we get some candy on our way out to Herbie?"

As I drew closer to the doctor's office, my heart went out to the parents and children coming down the stairs, some kids jumping from step to step enjoying the sound of their shoes on the tile steps. Some kids were carried in their mother's arms, with their dad's hand softly and gently supporting from behind.

My hand gripped the rail for security as I walked up the steps. My heart pounded with emotions from the past mixed with hope for the future of Make-A-Wish. I was trying not to let it show that I was having a hard time with this. After all, I had to portray the image that everything was great. At least, that's what I thought.

I took a seat after signing in, and Dr. Baranko opened the door to the waiting room carrying a crying child in his arms. He tried to comfort the child's mother while attempting to reassure her with hope for the future. I remembered very vividly the many times during the three years that I had heard those same words. This doctor was more than a man of medicine. He was also a friend, a person who cared about each and every patient.

Dr. Baranko was a little surprised to see me in the waiting room. From the look on his face, it had obviously brought back memories for him, too. He grinned, smiled, and extended his hand. "How have you been doing this past year? OK, I hope?"

"I've been fine. . . . A couple of times, no, but for the most part, things are going great."

"Why don't we go to my office where we can talk a little more privately? I am curious to hear about Make-A-Wish. Terri was telling me a little, and I would like to hear more."

As we walked toward his office, the cartoon characters on the walls and the smell of disinfectant brought memories of the past visits to life. There was no way I could put it out of my mind and heart, but somehow I had to draw a line between the past and present.

Dr. Baranko closed the door. We sat down and began to talk. His desk hadn't changed much in a year's time. I handed him the small package that I was carrying, hoping he would be pleased as he opened it. I wondered if I had done the right thing, but as soon as he opened it, I knew he was happy that I had brought it for him. He smiled looking at the picture of Chris in full uniform with the same sincere, caring gleam in his eyes that I remembered.

"I never met a kid like Chris before in all my practice. I don't know how to thank you, except to say thanks."

"There's no thanks needed," I replied. "I know Chris would want you to have this as much as I do."

"This will look great hanging on the wall right here, don't you think?"

He stood up and took down a picture, replacing it with the one of Chris. We talked a few moments about how I was getting along with my life, and I reassured him that I was doing fine. I remember telling him that if he asked anyone else they might say differently, so I wasn't going to give out any names.

We laughed, and then I began to tell him about the charity. I told him it was our desire to give a child a wish come true and a lasting memory of happiness, something special for the whole family, no questions asked, nothing asked in return. Just name it, and it's yours. That was what we were attempting to do.

The doctor knew a little boy whose time was short. He suggested that he call the child's family and get back to me with their decision.

Our visit was over in about a half-hour, but I felt that more had taken place in that short amount of time than I realize even today. Innocently, through God's mercy, I conquered something by reentering the past. On that memorable spring day, I conquered the present and at the same time released the past.

As a result of that first visit with Dr. Baranko, one week later the group had its first wish kid. I met with the boy's mother, Vennia, several times for lunch just to sit and chat about anything that came to our minds. We both realized that it felt good to talk about the fears we shared before and after a child's death. A couple of times, I felt a little silly mentioning things that I didn't think anyone else would even think about, but she had also been wondering about the same things.

There were no barriers between us as we shared with each other as two single mothers who loved our sons. As two women about the same age, we wondered what life had in store for us.

Three weeks later, Bopsy, her seven-year-old son, had his special day, and what a wonderful day it was. He wanted to be a fire fighter when he grew up, and that day, he was more of a fire fighter than he had ever dreamed. I think the whole city of Phoenix showed up. The event drew television and newspaper coverage, and I truly believe every fire fighter within Arizona knew about the day's events.

Bopsy had his very own helmet, turnout coat, and everything that a good fire fighter needs to do the job properly. Sliding down the pole was small potatoes compared with riding on the fire truck. The water hose took several helping hands as Bopsy led the charge.

My heart pounded with excitement as Vennia and I stood watching Bopsy.

We suddenly embraced each other, exchanging something that I believe only two mothers in the same situation could share or even understand. No words needed to be spoken, and no pictures were needed to capture the moment—just the simple exchange of love and compassion. I shall forever keep that tender experience engraved in my mind and heart.

When Bopsy was in the hospital for the last time, his mother called, and I joined her there. We walked to the cafeteria much as Sister Madonna Maria and I had, sitting at a table sipping coffee and talking about things that made no sense.

The fire fighters came to see Bopsy one last time by parking a fire truck on the hospital lawn and raising the ladder to his window. One by one, they climbed in through the window to say good-bye to their fellow fire fighter. He was *their* "little buddy" now, just as Chris had been the patrol's little buddy almost a year and a half before.

At Bopsy's funeral, Vennia and I shared in proud tales of our boys and considered what the pint-size angels might have been thinking that day.

"You know, I bet the two boys are looking down at us now and wondering why we're so sad. They know the truth in its full glory, and we are only feeling sad for ourselves because we miss them. They are probably playing together right now, rescuing people and putting out fires."

We hugged each other and said good-bye with a few tears trickling down our cheeks. I have thought a lot about Vennia over the years. To her, I wish to extend a warm hello and to say I miss our luncheons.

The group was on its way; five little people had made an impression on the big city of Phoenix. We were totally amazed by the success of Bopsy's wish. Even more amazing was how people from different walks of life pulled together to make a little boy's dream come true. The joy and lasting memories that it brought to the family filled my heart. I prayed that this could happen again and again and again for thousands of other children and thousands of other families.

At the next board meeting, everyone was eager to learn what was going to happen next. Fund-raising ideas specifically focused on the granting of another wish consumed the majority of the discussion that evening. Before the meeting adjourned, the big question was "Where does Lynn find our next wish child?"

Within one second, the board voted for me to return to the doctor's office and ask if he had any more kids for us. I sat in my chair that evening resting my elbow on the long walnut conference table at the highway patrol conference room, trying to understand why I had a sour feeling in my stomach.

I didn't want to go back to the doctor's office. It didn't seem right for some reason. But I knew our little group wanted to give another child a dream come true.

It wasn't long before another family came to our attention, which released me from having to return to the doctor's office. I was once again elected to go and visit with them, because I could relate to them. I gladly accepted the assignment with the hope of sharing with someone else what Chris and Bopsy had done in my life and Vennia's.

I enjoyed talking with the children, especially visiting with them in their rooms. They would show me their favorite stuffed toy or race car. I would smile watching them rummage through their toy box looking for just the right favorite toy to share with me. The importance was beyond words, sitting on the bed or a chair as they yelled out, "I found it. Here you hold this one. It's my favorite because my grandma gave it to me."

Their little hearts were so eager to please everyone, and the smiles on their faces shined so brightly. So many times we brush off childish words as babbling, and laughingly we tell our children to go play outside because Mommie or Daddy is busy. I wonder how many times we as parents have missed a very important insight into who that child really is or what he or she is really thinking! Next time, just listen, and remember when you were their age, trying to tell your mother and father something you thought was extremely important when you were told to go and play because they were too busy.

Summer was just about over and so was summer school. Working nights and going to school in the evening was taking its toll. I knew something had to change, but what?

It seemed that the board meetings were always on the nights that I had to attend class. I became torn between school and the charity. My education was important to me, but so was my involvement with the kids and their families. Sometimes I would cut class and show up at the meeting late. This presented problems at both ends.

Several board members had resigned by this time, and a couple of new faces joined us. Some of the volunteers had become emotionally involved and needed to back off for a while. Others joining our group were filled with excitement to help make a wish come true for a child. I don't think any of us expected the rapid growth, the eager volunteers, and the wonderful newspaper promotions. Everyone was pleased that the charity was doing wonderfully, except we weren't quite sure where to go from there.

It was about Christmas 1981, when a national television crew came to film the story of Make-A-Wish and cover a child experiencing his wish by filming it. I called the family when I got home to give them the good news and arranged a time to visit them at their home. I remember the five-year-old boy named Ben, who had whispered in my ear one afternoon while sitting on my lap.

"Don't tell my Mommy and Daddy, but soon I'll get to be an angel."

As the crew and I sat in the little office behind the meeting room talking and laughing, they informed me that they wanted to come to my apartment and do a one-on-one interview for the special. They also wanted me to see the family off at the airport.

350   Little Bubble Gum Trooper

"Are you guys going to interview the others? This isn't a one-person operation. Everyone involved helps make this happen."

The crew reassured me that the production would involve everyone, but I was the one that the public wanted to know about. I sat at the end of the table listening as they fired off questions too fast for my brain to answer.

The crew enjoyed the project as much as the family enjoyed the trip. The special was a big success for the group, in more ways than one. Phone calls and letters from all over the United States started to flood our little group at all hours of the day and night. They all wanted to know how to start a group like ours in their city.

Jean Rhodes, Aircraft Registrar for the State of Arizona, a wonderful woman that reminds anyone who meets her of a grandmother; and Theresa Dotson, a supervisor for Mountain Bell Telephone Co. (now Qwest and about the same age as me, with the most super attitude and laugh; and I soon became known as the three musketeers. My two "co-hearts," volunteers in crime, and I were having a ball giving callers whatever information we could in order to help them get started. A couple of times we mailed our charter and by-laws and simply told them to adapt them to their state. The three of us made a lot of new friends during that time giving folks our home phone numbers, just in case they had questions.

One by one, I saw people offering their services to help any way they could, whether it be driving a family to the airport or picking up medications and delivering them to the family. Some people were there to lend an ear and a kind word when times were rough for our precious families.

One morning, Jean picked me up early so we would arrive early at a church in Sedona, Arizona, where we were scheduled to give a presentation on behalf of the charity. We had a ball talking all the way up about the funny times in each of our lives.

"You know, Jean, between helping my mother with the grandparents, going to school, working with the charity, and living like an owl, I'm not sure sometimes about who I really am. Sometime, I feel like I'm being pulled in a hundred directions at once.

"If I could make a wish, I'm not sure what I'd wish for! I think I would like to stop the world and get off for a while. If there was some place where I could just go and relax for a couple of weeks, I would go, but then I couldn't afford to pay the rent when I got back."

After a couple of chuckles, Jean's face lit up with the memory of another time we shared together. "Oh, remember when the governor called Air Evac Services for the thirteen-year-old boy named Andy? He just wanted to come home to Arizona from California. I can still remember the two volunteers running into my office and dropping the piece of paper on my desk. It had Andy's name, address, and phone number in California on it. There was no doubt on their faces that this was definitely going to be the one that was impossible to pull off."

"I remember, Jean. He just wanted to come home to die in his own state. His mother and father were with him in California, but all the rest of his family was here and so was his heart."

"All I could think of was to start calling. You were the first on my list," Jean remembered.

I chuckled. "Boy, was that a day to remember," Jean continued. "My phone rang off the hook that afternoon, and I don't know how, but one of the calls was the governor of Arizona, and I came to find out that a couple of senators were sitting in on the conference call. They were asking me, mind you, if it was all right if they contacted Air Evac Services and told them to charge it." Chuckling, Jean repeated herself. "Charge it, mind you, just charge it."

"That was something else. I do remember that day. What a surprise when Senator Alfredo Gutierrez called you back and said that his office was going to raise the money to pay the bill for Air Evac Services."

"I will never forget when you and I were waiting on the runway at midnight and listening to the communication between the chopper and the ground transportation that was waiting to take him to the hospital," Jean continued.

"It was touch and go there for awhile, but Andy made it home, and that's all that counts."

We continued to laugh about some of the "capers" we had pulled off and some of the funny board meetings, especially the time that I dressed up in a cartoon bird costume to meet a family at the airport who was just returning from the wish trip. The little boy was nuts about this character, and it just seemed to be the icing on the cake to make his wish complete.

The disappointment of returning home after his wish was relieved when he saw his favorite yellow-feathered friend waving to him from the gate.

Theresa was driving the car as I got into the costume and adjusted my beak while we were stopped at a traffic light. The people in the car next to us were pointing and laughing. I encouraged her to get moving—the light was green! But all she said was, "I know, but I can't stop laughing—you look so funny."

We both laughed so hard we had tears in our eyes and our sides hurt by the time we parked the car and made our way into the terminal, then on to the arrival gate.

People just roared with excitement wondering who was the lucky kid that this was all for. Kids ran up and grabbed my yellow hands shaking them and saying, "Hello, I watch you every day."

I politely nodded my beak as we walked on through the terminal. As hot as it was inside the feathers, there was no way I was going to take off my beak.

"The family won't be here for a little while yet, so go ahead and get some air if you want to," Theresa said.

"There's no way, Theresa. Nobody knows who I am, and that's the way I want to keep it. But just remember they know who you are."

"Yeah, the lady walking through the airport with someone dressed up in a bird costume with bird legs."

Moving through the security system, Theresa had no problem. I, on the other hand, had to wiggle and waddle my way through sideways making a total spectacle of myself as the beak caught on the frame and turned my head around backwards. I threw my hands in the air and just stood there.

"I'm blind. Someone turned the lights out. Help! Theresa, help!"

I laughingly recouped when she grabbed my beak and twisted it back around so I could see once again. She was cracking up at that point, and so was everyone around us. She took my feathered hand and led me down the hallway. As I nodded my head at pilots, they tipped their hats and smiled.

The plane finally landed, and ground people pushed the portable stairway up to the door. People departed carrying business briefs, small luggage, and souvenirs. We stood outside the building on the concrete in the hot sun waiting for the family to emerge from the plane and waving at everyone that passed by.

After what seemed like an hour of silence, an attendant carried a wheelchair down the steps of the ramp and, once on solid ground, adjusted it into position.

It was all worthwhile when little Jeremiah from the small town of Casa Grande, got off the plane. His father was carrying him in his arms while his mother followed behind, carrying his younger brother.

I was glad I had the costume on for a couple of reasons. Number one, the excited expression of happiness on Jeremiah's face was worth it all. Number two, it was easier to hide the tears behind the yellow-headed costume.

The "Bird" led the battalion through the airport right past security, with a nod of the beak to security signifying to everyone that the mission was accomplished. Security responded with an astounding round of applause.

While Jeremiah's parents rounded up their luggage, I heard about the whole trip. The excitement in his voice overrode any discomfort from the wheelchair or illness.

For a little while, anyway, he and his family were just that, a family—a family on vacation and having fun, complete with souvenirs, pictures, stories, and memories. That will live forever.

Later that evening, I visited the Sheraton Hotel & Resort, where they were staying. Jeremiah retold tales of the trip and how his favorite cartoon bird had met him at the airport.

Then he asked his mother to pass him the sack on the table. He reached his hand into it, smiling while he watched my eyes. Excitedly, he pulled out a necklace that he had picked out and bought himself.

"Do you like it? It's for you. I picked it out all my myself."

It was hard to hold back the tears, and I didn't have any yellow-hooded costume to hide behind.

"It's the prettiest necklace I have ever seen, and you're a very special young man. Thank you, very much, Jeremiah."

I slipped the necklace on over my head and shared a smile with his parents and little brother. Jeremiah reached over and placed his arms around my neck, giving me a kiss on the cheek as I thanked him again for my hand-picked little necklace that was worth more than a pot of gold to me.

There is nothing that can replace the hug of a child. The smiles on their faces as they share their experiences with you, the whispers of trust in your ear as they sit on

your lap and ask you to be a friend to their mommie, the
spontaneous kiss on the cheek as they present a hand-
picked little gift. . .

Those moments are precious and rare, and I would
like to thank the kids and families that gave these special
moments to me. You made the sad time worthwhile and
the good times even better. Those special moments are
precious because each one is given from the heart with
pure and simple love. I wouldn't trade them for anything.

Another precious moment was our eleventh wish
child, a young man twelve years old from Globe, Arizona.
We learned of his wish to attend the Super Bowl game
just a week and a half before kick-off. Our little band of
volunteers panicked. We called a special meeting at the
Sheraton Hotel & Resort on I-17 in Phoenix.

How could we even get tickets for the game, let alone
a hotel reservation? Since I worked the night audit there,
and Jose Montilla was the general manager, we asked him
for help. The liquor distributor happened to be delivering
that day, and Jose talked to him. Both men disappeared
into the office. They returned about twenty minutes later
with big smiles on their faces.

"We have tickets and hotel accommodations for John
Paul and his father. They are not just going to the game
but are going to sit on the bench with the team and party
at the hotel with them also." Jose continued, "What else
do you need to make this the best of all times for him?"

We sat there with our mouths open in amazement. The
panic was all over. Everything had been arranged in
twenty minutes. We couldn't believe it.

Later that day, Jerry Foster heard about the Super Bowl wish and called to offer his services. Since Globe was about a two-hour drive from Phoenix, Jerry donated the Sky 12 helicopter to fly John Paul to Sky Harbor Airport for his flight. Everything went according to plan. He and his father had a blast, to say the least. Upon their return, I was at the airport to greet them. John Paul's arms were full of treasures and memories of a super three days with the *winning* Super Bowl team. What more could anyone ask for?

But here is a footnote: Eighteen years later, in April 2000, John Paul walked into our local wish house in Phoenix with his twelve-year-old son and said he would like to volunteer his services to make a wish come true for another child. "WOW!"

Today we have several wish parents returning to help grant wishes to other children and wish kids, all grown up, on our National Speakers Bureau. They share their wish and tell what it meant to them, personally. This is the next generation that will take care of Make-A-Wish. Keep up the good work, guys. I'm proud of all of you.

26

Beating the System

Over the next couple of months I finished up the spring semester while continuing to search for other wish children. Our group also continued to plot and plan on how to set up chapters in other states.

At the end of April 1982, I made a trip to Illinois. I had been employed for a year as an Inventory Control clerk at a large government electronics plant in Scottsdale and had two weeks vacation coming. I wanted to get away before summer school started; at least that's what I told myself. The truth of the matter was I missed Chris. It had been two years since his death, and I wanted to be there at the grave on that day, May 3.

I made the rounds between my childhood classmates and old family friends. Gary and I talked a lot about the good old farm days.

I drove by the house that Tony and I had built on his parents' farm. There was a family living there now, but memories and words of the past lingered in my mind as the car slowly cruised to the end of the old blacktop road.

I traveled on the back road into town and drove to
Chris's grave. I placed a bouquet in the vase and a red
rose on the grave. I sat on the ground not thinking of
anything when another car drove up. An elderly woman
got out.

She placed some flowers on a grave about ten feet
from Chris's. With another bouquet still in her hands, she
approached me. "Do you know the little boy that is buried
here?" she asked curiously.

"Yes, I'm his mother. I live in Arizona, so I don't get
much of a chance to visit his grave."

"Well, you don't have to worry. I usually bring some
flowers for him, too. I remember that day of his funeral
very well, and I noticed that there aren't many flowers for
him. So I thought while I cut fresh flowers for my late
husband, I would also bring your little boy some. I try to
make it here once a week or so, but sometimes I'm just
not up to it. It's this arthritis. Some days I tell you—"

I sat listening to her talk about everything under the
sun, not knowing what to say except, "Thank you very
much for the beautiful flowers."

I couldn't find the words to express the feelings I had
inside. There were so many thoughts going through my
mind, but my mouth couldn't speak them. She seemed to
understand as she smiled and turned to walk to her car.
She drove away as mysteriously as she had appeared.

Shortly after I returned to Phoenix, I received a
wedding invitation from Karen, Chris's former preschool
teacher. We met for coffee one Saturday afternoon and
caught up on what had happened to each of us.

Her wedding was the most precious I have ever had the privilege to attend. The attendants were all children dressed in long dresses and little tuxedos.

Karen never looked more beautiful as she walked down the aisle filled with rose petals. Flowers, hung on every pew, made a beautiful border, separating the bride from the world that was watching. Her husband-to-be, waited for her just at the end of the long aisle. Once hand-in-hand, it would be the beginning for them both.

Karen and I shared a few moments after the services were over. With tears of happiness we hugged each other. After we got that out of our systems, we found some tissues so we wouldn't look like little raccoons. Karen told me, "You know, don't you, who I really wanted to be the best man at my wedding. I still miss him. He was special."

"Yes, I do know, Karen. I remember your talking about it when he was in your class. You're a very beautiful bride and a special teacher. I still miss him, too."

We stood there smiling, holding hands, and wishing the best in life for each other. "You know, it's a good thing that Chris didn't have to give you away. I think he would have wanted to keep you for himself."

We both laughed and hugged each other and said good-bye as the other guests came over to congratulate the bride. When I reached the bottom of the steps of the church, I turned to take one last look. We each caught a final wave good-bye, accompanied by a faint smile of happiness. Somehow each of us knew we would probably never see each other again.

Grandma Vie was still in the nursing home and making the best of it. The home was just down the street from where I worked. After work I stopped to visit on the nights I didn't have school.

Sometimes I would stop and pick up fried chicken complete with mashed potatoes and coleslaw. Grandma and I would close the door of her room and just pig out! A couple of times, I joined her for dinner in the large dining room at the nursing home. We both agreed it was more fun eating chicken in her room than being proper young ladies at the table!

I kept the promise I made her the night we talked in her bedroom. Grandma was taken to the hospital because of retinal bleeding. Mom called me at work. That evening I was standing beside Grandma's hospital bed, but she wasn't there.

I made inquiries as to her whereabouts, entertaining the thought that she probably had wheeled herself out the door and was by now halfway back to the nursing home. I rode the elevator down and made my way through several corridors. I finally found her sitting outside the door of the x-ray room.

"Grandma, are you waiting for someone to wheel you back to your room?"

I knelt down beside the wheelchair, placing my hand over hers. Hunched over, she slowly turned towards me. The wrinkled face that once projected strength, now portrayed helplessness.

"Linda Joy, I have been sitting here for a couple of hours. A nurse brought me here for x-rays, but I don't know where she is. I'm so thirsty, Linda Joy."

"Grandma, have they taken any x-rays yet?"

"No."

"I'll be right back with some water for you. Don't run away on me now. OK?"

With that, I stood up, went to get some water for her, then headed for the nurses station. Angrily, I set my purse on the counter. In a calm but forceful voice, I asked the three nurses who were talking and laughing behind the desk, "Do you people have a problem with your x-ray machine?"

The expressions on their faces were confused.

"No, I don't think so."

I not only had their attention but that of several others within hearing distance.

"Well, then you have a problem with whoever is running it. I suggest very strongly to get someone over there immediately! A little old lady has been sitting outside that door for over two hours with not so much as a drink of water!

"Is this the way you run a hospital? Because if it is, I will not take my grandmother back to her room. We're headed out the door and to my Volkswagen!"

A young man showed up almost immediately to take x-rays. I helped her onto the table then stood back as he started to do his job. It was about twenty minutes later, and Grandma was having an extremely hard time lying on the table in the different positions. She called out my name in a weak voice, and as I approached her, I could see tears slowly moving down her cheeks.

"Come on, Grandma, I'm taking you back to your room."

I helped her sit up, then went to get the wheelchair. The young man stood there a minute, in shock, then spoke.

"You can't do that. I'm suppose to take nine sets of x-rays. I'm not finished yet."

Continuing to help Grandma into her chair, I made sure she was comfortable, then I turned to speak to him. I wanted to say more than I did.

"How many have you taken so far?"

"Well, I only have three sets."

"You have enough! If the doctor has a problem, I won't be hard to find. As far as Medicare is concerned, they got a break today. I just saved them the expense of six sets of x-rays that probably won't be needed anyway."

Upstairs, I got her settled in bed, then she told me what the doctor had said and what he wanted to do. I reached over and took her hand and asked her what she wanted.

"I want to go back to the nursing home, sit in my recliner, and have chicken."

"Then that's what you will do."

"I don't want those tests that the doctor talked about or any operation of any sort, Linda Joy."

"Grandma, trust me, you won't! That's a promise!"

No more needed to be said. Grandma knew that as soon as arrangements could be made, she would be back at the nursing home sitting in her recliner, and I would supply the chicken.

The next day I received a call at work from Mom. The nursing home had given away Grandma's room. Long-term care, a division of Medicare, said that there were no rooms available in any facility until the new budget came out, and the hospital said that Grandma was going to stay there at the hospitalfor probably two months or until the new budget was released.

Mom gave me the name and phone number of each person she had talked with. I sat there at my desk a few minutes and thought of what would be the most logical place to start. I decided to call long-term care. The ball bounced back and forth in each other's court a couple of times during the conversation. That evening I paid a visit to the hospital. There was no one who really knew what was going on. The nurse suggested I talk to the social worker. That conversation lasted about ten minutes. With an authoritative tone of voice, my closing statement was, "I will call the chief surgeon, and his response will determine any statement I make to the newspapers or TV station, unless she is released by tomorrow morning and happily settled in the nursing home in time for lunch. Do you have any questions?"

The woman just stood there. As I started to close the door, I glanced back at her. "I'll take that as a 'no,'" I said and shut the door behind me.

The next morning I called my boss to explain why I wouldn't be in to work. Her words of encouragement set me rolling for the day.

My first stop was the administration office, the government agency that takes care of the elderly. A young man, smiling politely and adding "Good luck," handed me a list of nursing homes in the area. We had a short conversation that I'm sure made a long-lasting impression. I interviewed several nursing homes.

That afternoon I returned to the office building of elderly care and handed the same young man seated behind the desk the name of a nursing home complete with the address, phone number, room number, and the name of the director who was waiting for a phone call. As I sat in the chair beside his desk, he looked the information over in utter amazement. He didn't know whether to applaud or get angry. I broke the ice.

"The director of this home is waiting for your phone call to confirm everything."

"You've been busy today, haven't you!" he replied. I politely smiled. "Yes, I have."

He started to stamp his seal of approval on the papers, then looked up and said, "Is tomorrow morning OK with you?"

"That will be just fine." I got up from the chair to leave, extended my hand, and said. "Good-bye, and thank you for your time."

He stood up from his desk and extended his hand with a half grin that turned into a full smile. "If you ever need a job, just let me know. You just beat the system."

Entering the hospital, I made my way to Grandma's room. The bed had been made, and her personal items had been removed. At the nurses station, they suggested I check out the day room at the end of the hall. Confused I checked it out anyway. There was only an elderly man, sadly sitting in a wheelchair staring out the window to the busy street below.

I returned to the nurses station and asked again where my grandmother was. They finally came up with a room number, so I was off to check out this lead.

I arrived at the room and there in a wheelchair, looking frightened and alone, sat Grandma. She was staring out the window. I approached her from behind. She turned, hearing my footsteps, and called my name in a low, desperate voice.

"Linda Joy, is that you? They say I will be here in this room for two months." I took her hand trying to comfort her and spoke to her in a firm but gentle manner.

"That's not going to happen, Grandma. I found you a new place to live today. We're busting out of here, and it had better be tomorrow morning."

She looked happy, but I could sense from the expression on her face that she had her doubts. I began describing the new nursing home to her: the big courtyard full of trees and flowers with picnic tables so we could have our chicken outdoors if we wanted. She started to bite her lower lip anxious to believe.

"Grandma, you will like it there. Trust me! Hey! Have you forgotten with whom you are dealing? Besides, I already left notes at the nurses stations and on all the bulletin boards not to pay the ransom because you don't want to come back here."

That did it. She cracked up. I pulled up a chair, and we both laughed and talked for about an hour thinking up what other capers we could pull off. Before I left, I kissed her on the forehead.

"Grandma, I always keep my promises. I learned that from you a long time ago. You always kept yours to me."

She looked up at me so tenderly, as if she was seeing me as an adult instead of her granddaughter. Perhaps she was seeing herself many years ago protecting someone she had loved very much.

With a hope and a smile she softly spoke. "You learned well."

Mom received a phone call from the hospital and long-term care that afternoon. Grandma was going to be transferred to the nursing home at nine o'clock the next morning. She lived there in peace for the next several months.

On May 28, 1984, Grandma was laid to rest beside her husband in Moline, Illinois. The promise I made her was completely fulfilled now. I didn't fly back for the funeral. I knew she was at peace,

Knowing Grandma, she probably found a picnic table in heaven and is enjoying chicken with Chris and all the kids!

Shortly after Grandma's passing, I took a new job at an aerospace plant in the little town of Goodyear, Arizona. After about a year, I was offered another job, in the same plant. I accepted another position in the engineering department, checking blueprints and reading military specification to verify the bill of materials.

27

Family Comes First

It was summer of 1984. After a long and intense deliberation with myself, my mind was now made up. I called my attorney, asking him to write a letter of resignation to Make-A-Wish for me. I needed to be away from it all for a little while. He understood completely and repeated his earlier question. "How have you hung in there this long with everything else that you have going on in your life? Are you trying to drive yourself crazy?"

I had stopped attending all board meetings and really didn't care to hear about the group at all. He wrote a very nice letter and advised me that when I was ready to submit the letter, I should send it by registered mail to each member that was on the board at that time and watch my mailbox for a reply. I took the letter, neatly folded in the envelope, and placed it in my purse.

Once I got home, I placed it on the kitchen table in front of my four-foot lion, Puddie, who was still sitting, waiting for some dinner. I couldn't mail it just yet, for some reason. I knew that I had to wait a little while longer.

I had few emotions of any sort left to give to anyone or anything. What was left I found myself guarding extremely closely, reserving them for my family.

The pains of letting go of something I loved very much were like burying Christopher all over again. I was facing the fact that I had to start a life for myself, but this time it would be just that—for myself and not the charity.

I tried to separate the two in my mind, but in my heart they remained joined. I knew it wasn't over with the charity, it was just good-bye for now.

I hadn't attended any meeting or functions of the charity for a couple of months. I was beginning to feel halfway normal again, whatever that was. During those months I relaxed, finding time to enjoy myself with an evening out with my friends. Taking time for myself without feeling guilty about it was the hardest thing to do. I was still geared to taking care of someone. Being so involved with the charity, I didn't know who I was or what I was about or even what I wanted out of life for myself.

I still hadn't mailed my letter of resignation. I wanted to attend a board meeting one last time, perhaps just to prove to myself that the only way was to resign from the board of directors.

I attended a meeting one evening, and all the time I was driving there, I debated with myself wondering if it was a mistake to go.

As I walked, unannounced, into the room, the heads turned to stare as if I were a ghost returned from the dead.

Saying "hello" politely, I walked to one of the leather chairs that surrounded the long walnut table.

I sat quietly during the two-hour meeting watching while the past years repeated themselves. In a strange way, while I sat there I knew that this evening was the closing of one chapter in my life.

I felt sad as I sat listening to the echoing voices of the various people gathered around the table. I glanced up and down the table remembering happy times with each of the members. Driving home that night, I thought about the comments made to me that evening.

In the four years of my involvement with the charity, I had the blessing of working with many families. Unfortunately, there also had been thirteen funerals to attend. After talking with the families on several occasions, during the wish and long after the wish was over, I heard the same statement from each of them. "Don't tell me how I feel or that someone understands until you've walked in my shoes and had to bury your child. Then we'll talk."

Still debating posting the resignation letter, I called an old friend who was also on the board, in the hope that by talking to him he would understand what I was going through. I felt that if anyone could understand, he could.

Tommy agreed to meet me at a local restaurant in Scottsdale. After exchanging pleasantries for a time, I explained to Tommy why I felt it was time for me to leave the foundation. At first he was reluctant to accept the idea, but as I explained he seemed to understand my need to remove myself for a time.

He sat leaning back in the booth staring for a few minutes in silence; slowly he leaned his elbows on the table. "You do need a break, and I think this will be good for you. You have too much on your shoulders. We will all miss you, but I understand that your family needs you."

Driving home that afternoon, I felt deep losses within, and at the same time I realized a deep peace and fulfillment that Make-A-Wish was in God's hands and it would survive. I had given the charity my all and the best I knew how to give. I passed a post office and mailed the letter to each board member. Remembering the advice of my attorney, I sent it by registered mail.

In September 1984, I registered for classes at the college and then gave my employer, Jose Montilla, notice at work that I was going to go to school full time and get my degree. Associate Degree or bust!

Fall 1984. At night after homework when Mom and Grandpa had gone to bed, I kept myself positive by thinking about the future. For the most part, I was putting the charity behind me and planning how many credits I needed to graduate, while making little trips to the refrigerator for snacks. Several volunteers phoned me, wanting to know what had happened.

The most frequent question was, "Why did you resign from the charity? It's like the very heart of the organization has been cut away. It's not the same now, nor will it ever be. You have to come back." Most of the people knew the reason.

My heart and emotions still reached out to hold Christopher, or maybe I was reaching out trying to fill the emptiness from missing the charity. It was harder as the years passed to regain the feeling of holding Chris in my arms. I guess time heals all wounds, and maybe that was what was happening with me.

Many a night I would hear my father's voice saying to me. "You make a decision, and you have to live with it, so you had better think it out completely. Try to think of every possible avenue that one decision could lead you down. Think it through to the best of your ability, and you yourself know what that is."

In the spring of 1985, Mom had to put Grandpa Pete in a nursing home. His health was starting to fail at the young age of ninety-eight years old. She decided to sell the house in Scottsdale and move into a condo, something she had wanted, and I thought it was a good idea.

She was almost sixty-eight and for the first time in her life didn't have someone for whom to care. With her newfound freedom, she enjoyed all the amenities of her new place.

Then two weeks before Christmas 1985, Mom and I were having coffee in her condo when she told me that she was going into the hospital for an operation. She tried to disguise the intensity of the moment by saying, "Things will be fine. The doctor says that there is no need for anyone to be alarmed."

The tone of her voice told me just the opposite. This was very serious. We had lunch at her favorite restaurant a couple of times before the operation. Mom asked certain questions that led me to believe she felt she wasn't going to make it. Questions like, "Do you remember where all my important papers are?" and "You have access to the safety deposit box and can sign checks for me. You handle all the insurance stuff now, so I don't have to worry about that."

I asked questions, too, trying to phrase them so as not to alarm Mom with my concerns. "Well, what do the doctors say is wrong? Mom, I know where things are, and I know what to do. Just talk to me."

She would clear her throat and reach for a tissue from her purse as she tried to stall for time. "Oh, it's just a mass in the uterus that the doctor seems to feel shouldn't be there."

It was obvious that Mom, now very frightened, didn't want to talk anymore on the subject. She was to be admitted to the hospital the next morning and asked if I would meet her there. I offered to drive her, but she said that a neighbor would take her.

"If you just meet me at St. Joseph hospital, it will be fine. I don't know which room or where I'll be, but I know somehow you'll find me. You always know how to do things."

"I'll find you, Mom. Don't you worry about that. If I can spot the Caddie in a parking lot full of cars and surprise you and the "oldies but goodies" by sitting down to have lunch with you, I'll find your room. That's a promise."

I arrived at the hospital in the morning, stopped at admitting, and obtained a map and the information needed to find Mom in the new wing, built since I was there almost six years ago. With my trusty little map and my clean, non-squeaky white sneakers, along with pressed blue jeans, I went in search of Mom.

I made my way down and around the corridors, up and out the elevators to her room. The walls were painted a calm, light blue-gray color that enhanced the pictures of medical technology artistically placed at various intervals in the corridors.

Modern lounges for visitors were comfortably spaced throughout the new wing with smiling volunteers waiting to be helpful.

No television noise came from the patients' rooms. They didn't even open into the main hallway. It almost didn't seem like the same hospital. The only sound I heard was the rustling of my blue jeans as I walked down the hallway towards Mom's room.

She was resting quietly in the bed as I opened the door. Somehow this just didn't seem real. She had never been sick a day in her life, and now my mother, the health nut, was lying in a hospital bed waiting for tests and surgery.

"Hi, Mom, how are you doing? Told you I'd find you." I walked over to the side of her bed and sat down beside her, feeling somewhat scared that time was short.

"Are they treating you all right? We can order out if the food isn't up to par. Lobster sounds good to me." Mom smiled and started to mess with her hair while clearing her throat. "Everything is so nice here. The nurses are wonderful. The doctor hasn't been in yet, today, but I guess he ordered tests because the nurses are in here making sure I save everything."

I couldn't help letting my eyes wander around the room to pick up clues to what was "wrong." Her voice tone seemed an attempt to reassure herself that this was not really happening to her. Mom projected a strong sense of the fear through faked laughter as we talked.

"Linda, would you go over to the mall and find me a new pair of slippers and a robe? If you happen to find some nice PJs, that's fine, too. You know what I like, so just buy them. They'll be fine."

I kind of got the clue that she didn't want me there when the doctor showed up. She knew I would start asking questions, and I guess she couldn't handle being in the same room when I got the truth.

Handing me her wallet and checkbook, she described what she had in mind for a robe. "Just write a check or pay cash for them, if you want. I don't care. Whatever you want to do is fine."

I had mixed emotions as to whether she just wanted me out of the way for a while or whether these things were important to her. I think it was a little of both. There wasn't anything shabby about what she had, and being the daughter that I am, I didn't argue.

"No problem, I'll be back in a flash with a little less of your cash."

Before leaving, I stopped at the nurses station and made some inquires. "I would like to talk to the doctor about my mother's condition, if you don't mind."

"We will let him know that you are here. He should be around until 11:00 a.m."

A second later, the nurse spotted the doctor coming down the hall and motioned for him to stop at the desk.

"This is Alice's daughter. She is wondering about her mother and would like to talk with you." I didn't need any further introduction.

The doctor and I stood in the hallway for about half an hour talking. He confirmed my concerns. It was cancer—ovarian cancer. He went into more detail as to the extent that it may have already spread throughout her body. The surgery would tell.

I leaned against the wall during the conversation trying to maintain eye contact while absorbing every word he spoke. I had to look away a couple of times to regain control of my emotions.

I shook his hand and thanked him for the time from his busy schedule and his honesty.

"I've got some shopping to do for a very special lady." Most of my questions had been answered by the doctor, and the ones I didn't have answers to would take care of themselves in the future. At the mall, shopping became a struggle to hold back the tears, fight the fear, and try to find just the right robe, slippers, and PJs that would make Mom happy. A couple of hours later, I returned to Mom's bedside with all the loot. We opened the packages, which were gift-wrapped with big brightly colored bows. The slippers were exactly what she wanted, and everything fit perfectly.

We laughed and talked about happy times in our lives. For a few short minutes, I think we both forgot where we were and what was ahead of us. Mom suddenly changed facial expressions. As she leaned back in the bed to rest, she never took her eyes off of me.

"You know, don't you?"

I stopped folding the clothes. Taking her hand in mine, I sat on the bed and answered in a cracking voice.

"Yeah, Mom, I know. I talked to the doctor on the way out, and he told me everything."

Nothing more needed to be said at that point. I knew what I had to do, and Mom knew that I would take care of it the best I could. She squeezed my hand and cleared her throat. "You've had so much in your young life—more than what I probably know. Maybe this is why mothers have daughters."

"Maybe, it is, Mom. But you just tell me what you want, and it's as good as done."

She seemed to want to be alone to get some rest, so I excused myself and told her I would be back tomorrow morning. When I got to my car, I sat holding the keys in my hand. I was having a hard time accepting what I knew was true. The doctor had given Mom about a year to live.

I knew that chemo treatments would eventually become necessary along with medications to control the pain. A lot would depend on to what extent the cancer had spread. I decided to tell Gary the whole truth. Mom needed hope and encouragement from here on out.

I don't remember driving home that afternoon, because it was like an instant replay of my first day in Phoenix with Chris, now almost nine years earlier. Later that afternoon, I snapped out of it and found myself sitting on the patio crying.

I returned to the hospital the next morning to keep her company. Mom thought of a few more items she wanted to make her hospital stay more pleasant. I ended up getting my exercise by making several trips to the mall.

The following day, I arrived a little before they were ready to take her to surgery. We talked very briefly. It was enough just to see her and to let her know that I was there.

I wandered around the waiting room for five or six hours, waiting for someone to call my name. Many people came and went. Doctors still in their scrubs would enter the waiting room calling out a name, and soon the family or friends would rush over to hear the results of the surgery.

Sometimes the loved one grabbed another loved one and just cried while the doctor placed his hand on their shoulders. Sometimes the loved one shook the doctor's hand and smiled tears of relief. I sat thinking and trying to prepare myself for both situations.

Christmas was only two days away, and somehow I had to pull myself together. Grandpa was my full responsibility now. Mom had asked me not to tell him anything about the cancer. She didn't want him to worry or be upset.

A doctor entered the waiting room and called my name. We shook hands and sat down on the chairs. He talked for about twenty minutes, and I listened patiently for the bottom line.

"She is alive. Critical, but alive! The cancer had spread throughout most of her. Even into the lungs. We got most of it but couldn't get it all."

At this point, the doctor went into great detail at my request. He looked at his watch then took my hand. "Wait here a few minutes. They're taking her to intensive care, and you can see her, but only for a few seconds, all right?"

I reached over to get my purse, then went to the intensive care unit. Mom was still unconscious as I approached the bed slowly. I took a deep breath and, placing my hand over hers, I whispered. "It's just me, Mom. You're going to be all right. I'll be back tomorrow. I love you."

28

Another Red Rose

I went each day to visit Mom, and each day she
improved a little. Gary sent money for me to buy flowers.
I got a brainstorm while on my way to see Mom
Christmas Day. When I arrived at her room, the nurses
were starting to celebrate Christmas in the intensive care
unit. They had a small tree decorated with various
ornaments and had gathered around the tree to open
presents. I figured this would make my plan easier to
pull off.

I went in to say hello to Mom and placed the two
flower arrangements where she could see them. I then
excused myself from her room and went to talk to the
nurses. I approached them slowly with a mild questioning
voice. "Excuse me, you guys, but do you have a phone
that would reach into my mother's room?"

One nurse looked at me kind of puzzled but smiled while looking at the other nurse. "Yes, I guess we do. Here. See if this one will reach in there." I started to pick up the phone and walk toward Mom's room when the nurse asked, "What are you going to do?"

"Well, it's Christmas, and families should be together, don't you think? This is a present to my mother; I'm going to call my brother in Illinois so they can say 'hi' to each other. Don't worry. I'm charging it to my home phone. Trust me."

The nurse just smiled, turned, and joined the others at the party. I got the impression that she didn't care if I charged it or not, as if she were thinking, just do it!

Once inside Mom's room, I closed the sliding door to block out any noise and dialed. A few seconds later, it was ringing. Mom was kind of alert and asking what I was doing. On the third ring, Gary answered. "Hello, big brother, and merry Christmas." Mom's face lit up brighter than the streets of Broadway.

"Well, merry Christmas to you too, kid. How's Mom doing?" His voice was a little tense.

"Why don't you ask her yourself? Hang on a minute." I placed the phone to Mom's ear. She steadied it with her hand while looking at me.

"Well, say merry Christmas to your son, woman!" She smiled and a tear came to her eye. At that point, it was all worth it. I didn't care if they talked for hours, but it was only a few minutes before she became tired and wanted to rest.

She handed me the phone, and I told Gary I would call him later. Mom fell asleep very quickly that late afternoon, with a peaceful smile on her face. I kissed her on her forehead and told her I would be back in the morning.

I returned the phone along with several feet of cord gathered in my hand to the nurses station. Stopping outside the glass sliding doors for a few seconds, I watched Mom sleep before I left the hospital to go home.

Driving little Herbie down the streets of busy holiday traffic, I felt a mixture of happiness and tears, but I was cheerfully smiling all the way, grateful that I had been able to make her happy.

Nothing wrapped in the prettiest paper, with the biggest bow, placed under the most beautifully decorated tree could ever compare to the small, faint smile I received from my mother as she said merry Christmas to Gary.

The doctor released Mom from the hospital the morning of New Year's Eve 1985. She had asked me to find a place where she could stay for a week or two until her strength returned.

I found just that, a private room with all her meals provided and a beautiful lounge area to visit and watch television. One week later, she was ready and raring to return to her condo to resume life the best she could.

I returned to work after the holiday shutdown. Everyone was talking about what they got for Christmas and what their families did. A close friend asked how my holiday went. I filled her in on Mom's condition, and then she asked what I got for Christmas. I told her I got a smile

from Mom that would last a lifetime. I smiled and
continued to work away at my desk.

Mom wanted to sell the Cadillac and get a smaller,
more economical car. I showed up in the parking lot of
her building with a little four-door, baby blue Olds. It was
only a couple of years old and ran like a top. I remember
Mom's comment when she saw it.

"Oh, good, it's got wire hubcaps like the Cadillac! I
liked those so much, and now I have them again. The car
is perfect. I love it! Now all I have to do is get my strength
back and find the nerve to drive it. Someday maybe I can
take all the ladies to lunch in my new car."

Gary came out to spend a couple of months with Mom
and help around the condo. It sure helped me a lot, too. I
would call Mom before leaving work to see if there was
anything she needed me to bring her. Every other evening
I would drive to her place to visit or deliver whatever she
had on her list. So when Gary came out, he took over,
drove her to the doctor's office, and went to the grocery
store. I felt like I was on vacation.

Mom seemed to be improving a little. She enjoyed
having Gary drive her around, but most of all she loved
having him there with her. He would do the cooking,
cleaning, and shopping, and they would spend hours
sitting on her patio just talking.

One day after Gary had returned home to Illinois,
surprisingly, Mom drove over to my place all by herself.
She was so proud of herself for driving and feeling well
enough to enjoy the day out, sporting a little red hat and
matching red vest.

As we sat and visited, I suddenly remembered what I had received in the mail a few days earlier. I got up and went to my bedroom, picked up a five-by-eight-inch hard folder, and returned to the living room.

"Look, Mom. I got a present for you. I finally did it— my Associate Degree in Business from the college."

I just stood there for a minute watching Mom, sitting on the sofa holding the folder. Somehow I think she was more proud than I was. Her smile was the one I remembered from the hospital on Christmas Day.

As she wiped her eyes, she exclaimed, "You really did it, didn't you! You always wanted to go to school. I sure wished your Dad and I had let you go when you were eighteen years old. I bet your life would have been very different, too. I know he would be very proud of you today."

That afternoon that piece of paper meant more to me than all the years of struggle to get it. I went to the kitchen to make some coffee while Mom sat on the sofa holding the folder and talking away.

I remembered the day I sat in the cafeteria on campus thumbing through the fall catalog. I had more than enough credits for the business degree but needed nine more for the marketing degree, my original goal. The longer I sat there, the more I realized that I would not be able to complete those other classes and get the marketing degree before Mom passed away. I went over to the office and requested the necessary paperwork to submit for a diploma in business. I filled it out on the spot, then handed it to the elderly woman behind the counter. She checked it over to make sure that all the information was there.

"Well, congratulations! I guess this means that you will be leaving us at the end of the semester." I smiled while leaning on the counter, feeling happy and excited that I could give this to Mom.

"No, I'll be back in the fall. This diploma is a present for my mother."

The doctor started Mom's chemo and radiation treatments shortly afterwards. The first couple of times weren't too bad for her, but then they started to take their toll. In June 1986, I found a retirement center with multiple levels of care.

On June 22, 1986, Mom received a phone call that Grandpa Pete had been taken to the hospital for congestive heart failure. She called me at work and I made several calls to the hospital checking on his condition. He was stable, but the prognosis was poor. Mom asked if I would take her to see him that night. I asked her to hang on a minute and turned to my boss to ask if I could use a couple of hours vacation time again.

In a very understanding way, he nodded his head yes and motioned for me to go. "Mom, I'll see you in about half an hour."

Her beautiful thick, dark hair was mostly white now and getting thinner each day. Most of her clothes hung in the closet or stayed folded in the dresser drawers, because they didn't fit anymore. Her body appeared weaker and thinner each time I saw her.

Reaching the hospital, Mom and I made our way to the entrance. Once inside, I could see she was getting exhausted. Pointing to my mother, I asked a nurse if there was a wheelchair that I could borrow.

We were soon wheeling our way down hallways and up elevators to Grandpa Pete's room.

"There's the room, Mom, just ahead."

She held up her hand for me to stop just outside the room. It had been several weeks since they had seen each other, and I was praying that the visit would be good for both of them.

"I don't want him to see me in the wheelchair. How does my hair look, Linda?"

"You look great, Mom, as always."

"Do you think he will know that I have a wig on? He doesn't know about the cancer, does he? You didn't tell him, did you?" Her voice was fearful.

"No, Mom, I didn't tell him. He just thinks that you haven't been feeling well. That's all."

As I helped her out of the chair and watched her walk on her own into the room and over to Grandpa's bedside, a tear leapt to my eye. The inner strength that she had that afternoon came out of the love for her father. She just wanted to protect him from the truth.

He was lying in the bed by the window, peacefully resting with a sheet covering him to mid chest. The IV hanging beside the bed was a familiar sight. His eyes were partly closed, and his breathing was heavy. Mom and I stood beside him.

His gray-white hair needed a little trim around the edges. His callused hands were motionless beside his body. Mom reached out, placing her hand over his.

"Dad, wake up. It's Alice. Come on, Dad. It's time to wake up. Linda is here with me, too."

His eyes opened. He was so happy to see her; tears began to roll down his aged, wrinkled face. Mom sat on the side of the bed talking to him. Tears flowed from his eyes as they talked, holding tightly onto each other's hands.

I turned and walked over to the window, so they could be alone. The street was busy as usual; the traffic never seemed to let up for a minute in this city. I glanced back for a moment to see how they were doing, and I heard Mom say, "Oh, Dad. Now there is nothing to worry about. Everything is all right."

Just by looking at Grandpa, I knew he didn't have long to live. At his young age of ninety-nine-and-one-half years old, he still was full of pride, dignity, and honesty.

As Mom and I said good-bye, Mom's sister, Kitty, and her husband, Joe, came into the room. They had arrived a couple of days earlier from Florida. We talked for a minute, then I walked with Mom to the wheelchair outside the door.

A young doctor came down the hall toward us as I was adjusting the footrest on the wheelchair. He stopped beside us and asked if we were family of Mr. Peterson. We both said yes, and he started to explain Grandpa's condition.

I suggested that we go to the end of the hall where it wasn't so busy or noisy. Once there, the doctor continued to talk about Grandpa and what they wanted to do to help him. At one point, Mom interrupted the doctor.

"Please just keep him out of any pain. He is ninety-nine-and-a-half years old. There isn't much more to life than that. My daughter will handle everything when the time comes. As you can see, I'm not doing very well myself. Please talk with Linda. She knows my wishes concerning my dad."

The doctor agreed with Mom's wishes and took my name and phone number.

I went to say good-bye to Kitty and Joe then took Mom back to her apartment. Mom handed me an envelope of papers. I looked inside to find Grandpa's insurance policy and other important papers that I would need in order to take care of things.

Three days later, on June 25, 1986, Grandpa passed away in his sleep. Reunited with his beloved wife at last, he can now share all eternity with her.

Somehow, I always had the feeling he knew Mom was in serious condition. Although he never said so, I felt that he didn't want Mom to go before him. Knowing Grandpa, he just didn't think it would be right. I think he wanted to go first so he could be there in heaven to greet her. It just seemed right somehow.

In August of 1986, it became necessary to move Mom into my home. I couldn't place her in a nursing home, as my heart wouldn't hear of it. We had both seen too many of them, and I couldn't bear the thought of placing her in one.

I moved her bedroom furniture into my spare room and sold the furniture that she no longer needed. Everything else, I boxed up and stored in my garage. Mom loved her new room and enjoyed sitting by the big double window in her powered recliner just watching the birds in the back yard. A huge flower garden was just beyond her window, and I always made sure that it flourished with an array of colorful flowers.

Mom would sit for hours and watch me work in the yard, pulling weeds, trimming plants, and watering. Once in a while she would venture out onto the patio to sit.

By the middle of September, I had arranged with my supervisor to take a leave of absence from work for three months. He understood completely, offered any assistance that I needed, gave me his home phone number, and encouraged me to enjoy the time with my mother. I was looking forward to spending the remaining time with Mom. I remember coming home from work. I put my purse down on the counter, then walked in and sat on the end of Mom's bed. She was sitting by the window in the recliner watching television and gazing outside.

"Well, guess what, Mom."

She smiled and turned off the television looking both surprised and hopeful. "What's up?"

"I am going to be home with you for awhile. I have arranged with my supervisor to take a couple of months off. So you're stuck with me twenty-four hours a day now. Think you can handle that?"

The smile on her face and the happy laughter told me all I needed to know. That Friday night was the beginning of the best three months we ever shared together as mother and daughter.

Our days were filled with chit-chat, doctor's appointments, my filling out medical forms, which had become a breeze by now, and, "How do you cook that stuff again, Mom?"

Each week seemed to bring something new. Grandpa's wheelchair found a place in the house instead of the garage. Walking to the bathroom became more and more difficult. Certain medical supplies became necessary to keep in her room.

In the evening after dinner, we left little tire tracks in the carpet leading from her bedroom to the master bath. I bought a hand-held shower attachment and helped her bathe. It worked great except when she would forget I was behind her, fully dressed, washing her back, and she would rinse off before I moved. "Thanks, Mom, I needed that!" After a couple of times, I got smarter and changed into my swimsuit before shower time.

By the middle of October, Mom was spending most of the day sleeping in the recliner. Gary would send a dozen red roses every couple of weeks. We would call each other so he and Mom could talk and I could give him updates.

Her hair became thin from all the medications, but we would find a way to comb it so it looked pretty. The once beautiful, graceful lady whom I admired so much was now almost skin and bones.

One evening I was finishing cleaning up after Mom brushed her teeth and was about to help her to bed.

"It's not fair that you have had so much in your young life. I don't know how you handled it all. You just do somehow. I don't know what I would have done without you. As I said before, maybe this is the reason mothers have daughters."

I sat holding her frail, thin hand, trying to find some snappy words to make us laugh. Then slowly a smile began to emerge across her face. As I helped her lie down for the night, she looked up and whispered, "I love you."

"You spent many years taking care of me: changing my diapers, feeding me, and clothing me. I guess that's why daughters have mothers.

"Besides, turnabout is fair play, Mom. I wouldn't give up this time with you for anything. I love you."

I patted her hand and, straightening the covers, started to stand up. We talked as I crushed fresh ice and filled her pitcher with fresh water. I sat on the end of the bed while she gazed out the window.

"You had better start planning for your birthday. It's only three weeks away. So figure out what kind of a cake and presents you would like to have, OK?"

Within seconds, she fell asleep smiling as she thought of her birthday, like a little child. I changed into my swimsuit. After pouring a glass of wine and reaching for a cigarette, I headed for the back patio to relax for a while. "Please, dear God, let her have this last birthday party, please. She always looked forward to her birthday. Just let her have one more, please."

On November 15, 1986, Mom celebrated her sixty-ninth birthday. Gary sent a big bouquet of red roses. Her friends sent cards and flowers all during the day.

Aunt Kitty baked a cake, and she and Uncle Joe spent the day with us. I had decorated Mom's room with Happy Birthday balloons and streamers. She slept most of the day, but I still took pictures of Kitty holding the cake next to Mom's bedside.

The evening of November 16, 1986, Mom went home to be with the rest of the family. I was scheduled to return to work the next morning, three month had passed so quickly. I called my supervisor at his home and informed him that I wouldn't be at work the next morning. I was taking Mom back to Illinois where Gary and I would bury her beside our father.

At the funeral home in Illinois, it seemed as though hundreds of friends came by throughout the evening of her viewing—many that I hadn't seen since I was a child, some I couldn't even remember. They had seen Mom's name in the local paper. Flowers filled the room with a colorful bouquet of mixed fragrances. Gary and I bought a spray of red roses for her casket.

After services at the cemetery, Gary, his little boy, Jeff, who was about ten years old, and I approached the casket to say good-bye.

As I stood there looking at her, I remembered Chris and my first night in Phoenix, a little more than ten years ago. From deep within my soul, I cried out the same as the night Christopher had died, but this time it was in silence.

Gary put his arm around me and asked if I was OK. I turned to him nodding my head. "Yeah, I'm OK."

We turned, starting to walk outside toward the limo, when Jeff yelled, "Wait a minute, Dad." He went back to the casket and pulled two red roses from the flowers that lay across the casket.

As the limo driver pulled away from the building and started the drive through the cemetery, Gary turned to his son. "Jeff, you know if you put those between a couple of books, you can save them forever."

Jeff looked down at the roses, smiling, then turned to Gary. "I'm not going to keep them; that's not why I got them. I got one for you and one for Aunt Linda." Jeff, deciding which one was the prettier, handed me the big red rose and then handed Gary the other.

"Aunt Linda are you OK?" Jeff asked with a confused look. "Why are you crying? I didn't mean to make you feel bad."

I held the rose in my hand while wiping a couple of tears from my cheek. I smiled at Jeff, wanting to hold him in my arms.

"I'm OK, sweetheart. I was just remembering another special little boy that also gave me a special red rose once."

29

Epilogue—Full Circle

In 1992, at the Annul Make-A-Wish Convention, I returned and told the story of Chris firsthand, once again. Ever since, I was introduced as the founding mother of the Make-A-Wish Foundation.

Well, little alligator, my knees were shaking as my escort stood up beside the table in the banquet room along with everyone else. Gently he extended his hand to help me up from the security of my chair.

I had a lump in my throat and a tear of desperation fighting to force its way down my cheek while I stood beside the table. The applause overpowered the entire room for several minutes, almost to a point of deadening silence, but as I turned to walk towards the stage, the silence lifted. My escort spoke encouraging words as I stood by my chair looking at the speaker, Karla Blomberg, on stage waving me upward.

"You're going to do just fine. There isn't a person in this room that doesn't want to meet you." I simply smiled back at him, as I gently touched my cheeks to wipe away the one desperate tear that forced itself down my face.

As I started to walk towards the stage, I glanced back over my shoulder for encouragement and noticed several others starting to stand and clap as I walked by. The lump in my throat seemed like it was getting larger, and I just knew that I would not be able to say a word by the time I reached the podium.

A couple more of those determined tears started coming to my eye, but I quickly wiped them away and pulled up the reserve from within me once again, something I had learned to do quite well during the three years of your illness, Chris.

Once I was on stage, Karla callethe names of the founders with perfect timing and serenity. "Frank Shankwitz, Scott Stahl, Allan Schmidt, Kathy McMorris, and with special recognition to Ron Cox and Tom Austin, please join us on stage."

One by one, each person stood and began to walk toward the stage. The audience never stopped applauding as each name was announced, and one by one each took his or her place beside me on stage.

Then Karla raised her hands in the air and began clapping herself, which only encouraged the audience once more. For several minutes, we stood there before everyone, united once again. I looked out over the audience and started remembering the first day we got together and decided to form the Make-A-Wish foundation. I don't think any of us knew then what it would become or the impact our idea and $37.76 to start a checking account would have on other people and their families across this nation and around the world.

So much happened back then, the trials and tribulation we all went through, the many people that volunteered their services as well as their hearts in pure simplicity to just help another fellow human being in time of need.

Your story, Christopher, was the inspiration for the Make-A-Wish Foundation that has helped thousands of terminally ill children worldwide capture their lifetime dreams also.

But I pray that the organization is put out of business someday, because medical research will find a cure for not only leukemia but also all the catastrophic illnesses that claim our children's futures. I hope all children can mature to adulthood and fulfill their own lifetime dreams, on their own terms.

The speaker leaned over and whispered, "Do you want to say a few words to everyone?" I didn't know what I was going to say or even if I would be able to speak. I had rehearsed words over and over in my mind, but nothing seemed to find its way to my mouth.

I started to walk across the stage trying to reach for some words at the last minute so as not to make a fool out of myself. As I reached the podium, I glanced out over the audience for a second, then down at the podium. I cleared my throat, tearfully received the microphone from Karla, and from my heart thanked everyone for helping other children's dreams come true.

When I handed the microphone back to Karla, she resumed order while presenting us with a plaque, with our names engraved on it, which was to be hung in the national headquarters in Phoenix. Each of us was presented with a Wishbone award engraved with our name. While the cameras were flashing and people started to gather to shake our hands and tell us of their stories, I glanced off to the side of the stage for just a few seconds envisioning a young man standing there. He was about twenty years old, standing tall and handsome, a young man smiling from ear to ear and clapping his hands with more happiness and enthusiasm than anyone in the room was. A small smiling trickle of a tear came to my eye as my mind heard these words, "I never forget our time together either, but I have to go now. I just wanted to tell you, I love you and always will. See you later, crocodile."

Over the past years, I have relived your special day and our memories, over and over. I've never stopped celebrating your special day and what it meant to you as a child to have your wish come true. This October, National and International Convention 2000, in Phoenix, will be the twentieth birthday celebration of eighty thousand wishes for children around the world.

For the past five years, my wonderful husband Gene has been by my side, holding my chair and speaking encouraging words as I'm about to be introduced. He has been a never-ending source of understanding, laughter, encouragement, and love for everything I do.

See you later, Alligator.

Love, Mommie

Make-A-Wish National & International January, 2000

- The Make-A-Wish Foundation has come a long way since its humble grassroots beginning in 1980, with our first volunteer Kitty Derby and our first donation of $15 from a manager at a Smitty's supermarket. Our little group reached into our pockets and shortly opened a bank account with a total of $37.76.

- In 1981, we incorporated and granted our first wish, to the little fireman, "Bopsy." In 1982, a national television program did a special on our little group, and the response was hundreds of phone calls from people asking how they could start a new chapter in their state. January of that year we did the first ever Super Bowl wish for a twelve-year-old boy and his dad.

- On May 13, 1983, Make-A-Wish of America was incorporated, and the first national board meeting was held in Phoenix. Seventeen people attended. Make-A-Wish had grown to six chapters in the United States.

- In 1984, Make-A-Wish held its first convention with twenty-eight official chapters attending. The first corporate sponsor held a fund-raiser with all proceeds going to the foundation. Our first national newsletter was printed and distributed.

- In 1986, Make-A-Wish participated in the Tournament of Roses Parade, garnering nationwide publicity.

- Major donors came on board, and New Zealand was established as an international affiliate. The year ended with fifty Make-A-Wish chapters.

- During 1987, 1,487 wishes were granted and Make-A-Wish had fifty-seven chapters.

- In 1988, more major donors joined the foundation, which now had granted 2,239 wishes.

- In 1989, a total of 2,796 wishes were granted, eight NFL teams granted wishes and three Super Bowl wishes were granted. Hollywood celebrities joined in granting a wish to a special child. A total of sixty-two chapters were in place.

- In 1990, the foundation celebrated its tenth birthday and granted its ten thousandth wish. The first official Make-A-Wish song was released and a major corporation named the foundation as its official charity.

- In 1991, a total of 3,998 wishes were granted and Puerto Rico became a chapter. Make-A-Wish launched its first national training program.

- In 1992, a total of 4,713 wishes were granted. Guam was established as a chapter. Make-A-Wish for Christmas album was released by prominent artists.

- In 1993, more celebrities joined with support in granting wishes, with 5,078 wishes during the fiscal year.

- In 1994, Make-A-Wish granted 5,402 wishes.

- In 1995, a total of 5,807 wishes were granted and Make-A-Wish celebrated its fifteenth birthday.

- In 1996, the Foundation granted 6,490 wishes and the Make-A-Wish Foundation web site went public.

- In 1997, the Foundation granted wish 50,000 to a little boy that wanted to be a cowboy. The movie, *Annabelle's Wish*, was released, resulting in national recognition and support. The youngest chapter was established in the Rio Grande Valley.

- In 1998, Make-A-Wish granted 7,498 wishes.

- In 1999, the foundation's first national public service ad campaign was released and for the first time, the Foundation granted more than eight thousand wishes in one year (8,188).

- In the year 2000, we are approaching our twentieth birthday party in celebration of 85,000 wishes around the world.

- There are eighty chapters in the United States and internationally, twenty countries on five continents around the world. Each chapter and affiliate granted one wish between May 1 and May 15 celebrating the granting of more than eighty thousand wishes.

The Make-A-Wish Mission

We grant the wishes of children with life-threatening illnesses to enrich the human experience with hope, strength, and joy.

My personal feeling of what Make-A-Wish means: The foundation has become a worldwide extended family of over eighteen thousand volunteers granting wishes each day. That's the *Volunteer Spirit* this organization was built around, the love and compassion of volunteers not people who were famous, or rich, or influential— normal, everyday people like you and me.

The Make-A-Wish *Giving Spirit* is because of generous people, businesses, and corporate donors that give money and resources each year to pay for wishes: Plane tickets, theme park passes, computers, toys, furniture, video games, and everything and anything else that is needed to make a wish come true.

Celebrities have generously volunteered their time to meet with a wish child and make it as special as possible for them. Everyone works towards one goal, to let a child make a wish and then make it happen.

The Make-A-Wish *Family Spirit* is special because it has personality. It has character, and our family atmosphere is evidenced in the special connection there is between Make-A-Wish people around the world. Something that I consider very unique is called "Wish Assist." A volunteer can wave good-bye to a family at the airport in one city and be sure that another Make-A-Wish person will greet the child and family on the other end of the trip; no matter where in the world it may be.

Your support is important in making these dreams come true for children around the world. A single dollar is one more than we had before and does make a difference.

I would like to thank everyone who supports this foundation whether it is monetarily or in your prayers. By God's grace, the foundation will continue to grow and by his continued grace, every child who is in need of a wish will have his or her special dream come true.

If you would like to learn more about this wonderful organization, please contact your local Make-A-Wish chapter, visit the Make-A-Wish web site (www.wish.org), or call the Make-A-Wish National & International Offices at 800-722-WISH (9474).

Thank you,

Linda J. Bergendahl–Pauling

30

Inspired Memories

This chapter is devoted to the inspired memories of the people you have just read about and a couple of new faces. The writers have told their own stories in their own words, reflecting on their personal memories of Chris and what Make-A-Wish means to them, volunteers who worked their hearts out, giving their endless time-giving talents to help launch Make-A-Wish to the world.

Personally, revisiting with them and talking about Chris's wish after twenty years was most enjoyable. I learned new "behind the scenes" information that happened the day of Chris's wish.

You will enjoy their stories, their memories, and their love for these very precious and very special children.

Thank you.

Frank Shankwitz
Department of Public Safety
Arizona Highway Patrol #1091 (Retired)
Co-Founder & Volunteer
May 10, 1999

In 1980, I was with the Arizona Department of Public Safety, assigned to the Highway Patrol Bureau as a motorcycle officer. The motorcycle squad I was on was assigned to work special details throughout Arizona, assisting smaller cities, towns, and counties with special needs in traffic control. This included everything from DUI patrol to parade traffic.

During this time, there was a television show that was popular with the younger children that depicted two California Highway Patrol motorcycle officers. In the towns we worked, the younger children were no longer afraid to approach us and would call out to us. We would talk to the kids and let them get on the police motorcycles and play with the red lights and siren. When we were assigned to a town for a week or more, we would contact the local grade school and ask permission to meet the children and talk about bicycle safety. The kids loved getting on the motorcycles.

In April 1980, fellow DPS Officer Ron Cox called and told me about a special request he was setting up for a seven-year-old boy named Chris. Ron related he was working on a task force with a U.S. Customs Officer who told him about a little boy that had leukemia whose prognosis wasn't good. Chris had a dream of being a police officer, a highway patrol motorcycle officer like his television heroes.

Ron was working on a special day for Chris and had arranged for the Department of Public Safety's helicopter to pick Chris up at Scottsdale Memorial Hospital and fly him to the DPS headquarters compound near downtown Phoenix.

Ron was aware of my involvement with the school children throughout the state and asked if I would be there when the helicopters landed to meet Chris and show him my motorcycle. Ron had also arranged other events for Chris, a ride in a Highway Patrol car and a tour of the state police headquarters.

The helicopter landed, and I expected a very sick little boy to be helped out of the helicopter. Instead this seven-year-old bundle of energy came leaping out and ran up to me and said, "Hi, I'm Chris" and proceeded to tell me what a neat motorcycle I had. When asked if he wanted to get on the motorcycle, Chris was all grins, which got even bigger as he turned on the red lights and activated the siren.

Chris was fascinated with the motorcycle wings I wore on my uniform, and I explained how motorcycle officers go through special training and earn their wings.

I asked Chris if he wanted to go for a ride on the motorcycle, and he got a worried expression on his face and declined. I told Chris I was a little puzzled because he had just ridden in a helicopter. Chris explained that the helicopter had doors and the motorcycle didn't. Doors were very important to Chris. He told me all about the

officers on his favorite television show then thanked me
and went on to his other adventures, which included
riding in and helping drive a patrol car. While driving,
Chris was chewing bubble gum and blew a big bubble,
which earned him the nickname, "The Bubble Gum
Trooper."

Chris was later given a badge and trooper hat and
made the first and only honorary Highway Patrolman in
the history of the Arizona Highway Patrol.

The following day, Ron Cox called and told me he
had made arrangements with John's Uniforms, who made
the uniforms for the Highway Patrol, to custom make a
uniform for Chris. Officers had received permission to go
to Chris's home and present the uniform and visit with
Chris, whose illness had taken a turn for the worse. Ron
asked if I could join him, because Chris really liked
the motorcycle.

I asked fellow Motorcycle Officer Bill Hansen and
Officer Dave Schroder to join me, and on the appointed
day, we led several patrol cars to Chris's house, making
sure the motorcycles were making a lot of noise. Chris
was presented his uniform, which he put on right away
along with a toy gun-belt and toy gun. Chris was now a
policeman, complete with uniform, and was having a
grand day.

After awhile, Chris came over to me and said hello.
He asked if he could get on my motorcycle again, which
he did. I had made arrangements with the radio supervisor
to allow Chris to talk on the police radio, and when Chris
heard that, he really lit up. Chris keyed the microphone
and said, "Hi, Phoenix. This is Officer Chris." The radio

supervisor had programmed a series of radio repeaters that relayed Chris's transmission to almost every on-duty Highway Patrol unit throughout the state.

Chris touched my uniform motorcycle wings and asked how he could become a motorcycle officer. I explained he would have to take a special motorcycle skill test and started thinking I would have him ride a tricycle or bicycle to take a test. Chris was ahead of me. He jumped off the motorcycle, ran into the house, and came out riding a small battery-operated, three-wheel motorcycle marked Traffic Patrol. His mother explained that Chris would ride up and down the sidewalks with a notepad, issuing tickets to parked cars.

I set up a proficiency test for Chris to drive through, and he passed with flying colors. Chris now had his final wish come true—he was a Highway Patrol motorcycle officer. As we left Chris's house that day, he thanked me and as he said good-bye, touched my uniform motorcycle wings again.

That afternoon I ordered a set of wings from the jeweler who custom made the wings. He said he would have them ready in a day and there would be no charge for our special trooper. I also contacted the television studios in Burbank, California, and was able to tell the public relations department about Chris and his T.V. heroes. I requested autographed pictures be made out to Chris. The studio said it would comply.

On May 2, 1980, I received a call from Ron Cox who told me Chris was in the hospital and was not expected to live. About that same time, the uniform motorcycle wings were delivered and also a special delivery package from

the television studios with autographed pictures to Chris
from the two actors who played California Highway
Patrol officers on his favorite television show.

I called the hospital and received permission from
Chris's mom to come to his room. When I entered the
room, Chris was in a coma. His highway patrol uniform
was hanging from a window in his room, visible to Chris
when he was awake. As I pinned the motorcycle wings to
his uniform, Chris woke from the coma. He saw his
uniform with the wings attached, and his smile lit up the
room. He was an official motorcycle officer. I talked to
Chris for a short period and gave him his autographed
pictures and said good-bye, as he was growing weak.
Chris died the following day, and I know his "Wings"
helped take him to heaven.

I learned Chris was to be buried in Kewanee, Illinois,
and since the Highway Patrol had lost a fellow officer, it
was suggested that Chris be given a police burial. I was
told DPS could do nothing official, however, whatever I
could arrange on my own, the department would try
to assist.

I was acquainted with Jerry Foster, a local television
helicopter pilot and reporter who was a friend of then-
U.S. Senator Barry Goldwater. At the time, the Air Force
National Guard flew weekly training missions to the
Chicago area, landing at the National Guard base at
O'Hare Field. I asked Foster to contact Senator
Goldwater, tell him the story of Chris, and request
permission to load two Arizona Highway Patrol
motorcycles and officers on the Air Force tanker during

the training flight to Illinois. From there we could ride to Kewanee for the funeral.

Senator Goldwater did obtain permission and we were set to go. I asked fellow motorcycle Officer Scott Stahl, whose family lived in Joliet, Illinois, to assist me in the mission, and he agreed. Since I also had family who lived in the Chicago area, we had lodging during our trip.

The day before we were to leave for Illinois, Senator Goldwater's office notified me that another senator, who was in charge of the Ways and Means Committee, had learned of the use of the military aircraft and canceled the mission because it was not military related.

As word of the canceled trip spread through the Department of Public Safety, a collection was started to purchase airline tickets for Scott and myself for the trip to Illinois, minus two police motorcycle. Within hours, enough money was raised for one airline ticket, at the time $750 each. Jerry Foster called me and expressed Senator Goldwater's regrets and inquired about our plans. When told fellow officers had raised the money for one airline ticket, he said he would be right over with his personal check to cover the second airline ticket.

Scott and I left the following day for Chicago and were met at the airport by Chicago police. The FOP (Fraternal Order of Police) Lodge in Phoenix had alerted a Chicago FOP lodge, and the officers offered us transportation to wherever we needed to go in the Chicago area. We stayed at my stepbrother's house in Chicago, "stole" his vehicle for the drive to Kewanee, and stopped in Joliet to see Scott's parents.

There we changed into our Highway Patrol motorcycle uniforms and continued on to Kewanee. En route we were stopped by the Illinois State Police, not for speeding but because the troopers thought something was wrong with two people in some type of police uniforms driving a civilian car.

After identifying ourselves and explaining our mission to the troopers, they set up state police escorts for the rest of our trip. It's a small world, because I had just finished motorcycle training a good friend of one of the officers who used to live in the area and had moved to Arizona in hopes of becoming an Arizona Highway Patrol motorcycle officer. The trooper had just talked to his friend a few weeks prior and recalled my name.

Arriving in Kewanee, we were met by more state police and Kewanee City Police, who asked permission to join in the funeral procession for Chris. Also awaiting us were two matching fully dressed motorcycles, all shined and polished. The owners had heard of our attempt to bring our Highway Patrol motorcycles to Illinois and offered the use of their motorcycles for the funeral procession.

At the funeral home, we met Chris's mother, Linda, and paid our last respects to our "Bubble Gum Trooper." Chris was wearing his Highway Patrol uniform, complete with badge and motorcycle wings. Scott and I led the funeral procession on the borrowed motorcycles to the cemetery, where Chris was given a police funeral. His casket was covered with the Arizona State flag, which we folded and presented to his mother. At the end of the ceremony, all the officers responded to the "present arms" command and saluted Officer Chris. Chris's grave marker lists his name and "Arizona Trooper."

While in Kewanee, Scott and I were interviewed by local television stations, which also covered the funeral procession and graveside ceremony. The following day on our flight back to Arizona, a flight attendant approached us and asked if we were the officers from Arizona who had been at the little boy's funeral in Kewanee. When told we were, she informed us the captain of the aircraft had seen the T.V. coverage and requested we gather our belongings and move forward to the first-class cabin. There we were seated and treated like VIPs for the remainder of the flight.

Also during the flight, Scott and I started discussing how happy Chris was that his wish came true and how the wish seemed to take some of the hurt away, which was replaced by smiles and laughter. We talked about that, if we could grant a wish for one child, maybe we could do that for other children. It was at that moment the idea of the Make-A-Wish Foundation was born.

After returning to Phoenix, I talked to several people, including those who put together Chris's wish, about our idea of granting wishes for terminally ill children. Duty schedules prevented Ron Cox and Tom Austin from becoming involved, as well as other officers. Before continuing with our plan, I contacted Chris's mother, explained our idea, and asked for her endorsement, and she agreed.

My next step was, "How do you start a foundation?" Phoenix lawyer Patrick J. McGroder III was a friend and offered his help in establishing a charter and filing the legal papers. Pat donated his fee but did bill me for publishing costs. Another friend, Doug Bell, was an accountant, and he was tapped for obtaining our IRS tax-free status. He also donated his services and billed me for the filing cost. I never paid either bill.

The founding board of the Make-A-Wish Foundation was: me as president, Scott Stahl as vice-president, Kathy McMorris as secretary/treasurer, Linda Bergendahl (Chris's mother) as board member/liaison to find us the wish children, Allan Schmidt as board member/public relations.

Like most police officers, I worked off duty providing undercover security. The manager of a Smitty's grocery store where I worked learned what I was doing and asked how much money we had collected. When I told him we hadn't even opened a bank account, he dug into his wallet, pulled out $15, and suggested I open a bank account at the bank branch in his store. That was our first donation.

In late November 1980, we received our tax-exempt status and fund-raising began in earnest. Local newspapers and television stations interviewed me as the people of Arizona endorsed our idea, being generous with donations. Our office was whoever's kitchen was available for a meeting or the highway patrol offices after duty hours.

Kitty Derby was a Highway Patrol district secretary and had followed our progress with the foundation. For each donation received in the mail, I wanted a thank-you letter returned. As the volume of mail received became larger, I asked Kitty to help us in answering our mail. Kitty agreed and didn't realize what she was getting herself into. For several hours after work each day, she wrote letters, presenting a stack for me to sign the following day. Kitty also sat on our board, assisting in drafting policy for the new foundation. Kitty is recognized as the first volunteer for the foundation, and it became apparent to the board that several more volunteers would be needed in the future.

In March 1981, we had raised over two thousand dollars and were ready to take on our first wish. We learned of a seven-year-old Indian boy from Guadalupe, Arizona, named "Bopsy" who was dying of leukemia.

The philosophy of the Make-A-Wish Foundation at inception was to grant one wish for a child. Bopsy had three wishes, and he couldn't decide which he wanted to do. He talked about being a firefighter, riding in a hot air balloon, and going to a theme entertainment park in California. We knew his time was short, and I made the decision for him; he would get all three wishes.

Having Bopsy become a firefighter was easy. One call to Phoenix Fire Department, and things got under way. Bopsy was taken to a Phoenix fire station, dressed in a uniform and turnout coat, and given a helmet, all made special for him, and made an honorary firefighter. He also got to ride on a fire truck and work a hose line. Bopsy had a great day. I knew a local businessman who was a hot air balloon pilot and owned a balloon. Again, one call and Bopsy was flying.

The entertainment park in California was another story. The policy of Make-A-Wish is to include all family members in the wish and cover all expenses, including days missed from work. We realized the families of these children have tremendous financial burdens, and we wanted them to enjoy being with their child, not have to worry about the cost of a snack or meal. We didn't have the finances to fund the California trip.

I called the theme entertainment park and tried to explain about the new Make-A-Wish Foundation and tell them the story of Bopsy. The entertainment park people said sorry several times and hung up. I finally got someone to listen and asked for possible reduced or free admission to the park. They said they would plan a special day for Bopsy, complete with private tours, meals, snacks, and gifts.

Twenty years later, the theme entertainment park in California is one of the bigger supporters of the Make-A-Wish Foundation.

I called a local airline asking for help on airfare. They had seen the story on Bopsy on television and offered free round-trip airfare for Bopsy and his mother.

When we took Bopsy to the airport, the captain of the airplane gave Bopsy a tour of the cockpit, a uniform T-shirt, and his captain's hat. This was Bopsy's first trip in an airplane, and he was thrilled. Sheraton Hotels & Resorts called and offered a room and all meals during Bopsy's stay.

We had done it. We had put together Bopsy's wish, the first wish of the Make-A-Wish Foundation.

I had concern for Bopsy's medical welfare while he was in California. I called the local fire department, told them about our first Wish Child and that he was an honorary Phoenix fireman and would soon be in their city. I asked if they would assist Bopsy and his mother if he had any problems. They not only agreed to assist, but picked up Bopsy at the airport in a fire truck and drove him to the Sheraton Hotel & Resort near the theme entertainment park.

The following day, the fire department again picked up Bopsy at his hotel in a fire truck and drove him to the main gate at the theme entertainment park.

Bopsy and I bonded, and he thought it was funny that both our first names were Frank or "Poncho." When he left for the theme entertainment park for his special day, he asked me if he could bring me back a gift. I told him I would like an autograph from my favorite cartoon character. When Bopsy came back, he gave me a hug and a program autographed by that famous cartoon character.

A week after Bopsy came back from the theme park, I was notified he was in the hospital and the prognosis wasn't good. Phoenix Fire Department called and asked if they could go to Bopsy's room on a certain day and time, which they did. Bopsy was in bed asleep, with a look of pain on his face.

His hospital room was on the third floor with a window facing the street. All of a sudden there was a knock on the outside of the window and the window opened, with a firefighter calling out to Bopsy. Bopsy awoke and started laughing and laughing as five Phoenix firefighters came crawling through the window. With the permission of the hospital and Bopsy's doctor, they had parked a ladder truck under Bopsy's room and crawled up to the window. The firefighters talked to Bopsy for awhile and left. He fell asleep this time with a smile on his face. Bopsy died later that evening.

I knew the Make-A-Wish Foundation could not cure the life-threatening conditions being endured by the children, but from Chris and Bopsy, we learned the smiles and laughter do offset the pain, even for a short while.

Having completed our first wish, I made a bold prediction at a board meeting that some day the Make-A-Wish Foundation would have both national and international chapters. This was met with mild laughter from the board as our bank account was again near zero dollars.

Twenty years later, I get the last laugh, as there are eighty chapters in the United States and twenty countries internationally. Over eighty thousand children worldwide have had their wishes granted, all because of a seven year old by the name of Chris who wanted to be a Highway Patrol motorcycle officer.

Bill Hansen
Department of Public Safety
Arizona Highway Patrol #2055 (Retired)
June 20, 2000

It seems hard to believe that Chris has been away from us so many years now. It only seems a short time ago that my motor partner, Frank Shankwitz, and I were riding together on the Phoenix Freeway en route to St. Joseph's hospital, to see a sick little boy. In hindsight, this was not your ordinary lad . . .

This special boy was put on this earth to touch people's lives forever. Because all great things start out simple, sometimes we forget how they began. There are people living today that have heard of the Make-A-Wish Foundation, but don't know that it started out because of one little boy that was attracted to a tan motorcycle policeman's uniform.

Back in the era when a popular television show featuring two highway patrol motor officers caught the eye of a little boy, who would have thought that this alone would spark an organization that has brought joy granting wishes to so many "Chrises" all over the world.

The Make-A-Wish Foundation has exceeded everyone's greatest expectations and has been able to grant last wishes for terminally ill children all over the world. It makes me proud that I can say that I contributed to something that will last forever and that there are lots of boys and girls with Chris smiling because they left us with a "WISH" in their hearts.

R. Scott Stahl

Department of Public Safety
Arizona Highway Patrol (Retired)
Co-Founder & Volunteer
May 1997

Do you believe in fairy godmothers and fairy godfathers, too? Well, you should, you know, because they make wishes come true. How do I know, you ask with a grin? It's a wonderful story, so let me begin. A long time ago in a place not too far, a special little boy made a wish on a star.

His wish was a secret and not to be told. After all, this boy was just seven years old. His wish was not strange for a boy of his size, but something was special about his dream in the skies. A fairy was summoned to answer the call. This wish would be granted, he would go to the ball! No, no, no!! I'm sorry—that's another story. Let's see, where was I? Ah, yes . . .

The fairy was busy and engrossed in the task. The wish had to be granted that this boy had asked. A simple request and easy to see, this wish was for something he wanted to be! A friend was summoned, a policeman by trade. Through him this wish would be made. "Cops and Robbers" was the game of the day, and during the game, the boy was heard to say, "A motorcycle policeman is what I want to be. Is there any way you can do that for me?"

Now that it's known, the fairy could say, this little boy would soon have his day. The boy, Chris Greicius, that was his name. No one knew then, but he was destined for fame.

The friend and policeman spoke to a guy, another policeman, you wonder why? Was this conversation just for fun, or had Chris's wish just begun? A call was made to set the stage and it was about time to turn the page.

Motorcycle engines set the tone as the officers began to arrive at Chris's home. Chris heard the motors and cracked a smile, and the glare could be seen for over a mile. Chris was immediately filled with joy, and the officers fell in love with this little boy. As the officers left and went on their way, they knew they would be back another day.

The wish was in progress and gathering speed because the officers knew this little boy was in need. Chris loved policemen, and that was clear, so it wasn't difficult to hold him dear. A tour was planned on his behalf—anything at all to make him laugh. A Bell Ranger helicopter flew him to town, and rest of the day was about to go down. When he walked from the copter after finishing his flight, a smile lit his face that was wondrous and bright. He was given some tours and many special things. It looked as though he had grabbed several "Golden Rings."

Many words were spoken before Chris had to leave, but officers still had one surprise up their sleeve.

Chris was excited, that was easy to see, but here's the part that interests me. He was led to an office away from the crowd, and when he came out he walked on a cloud. Chris was walking on air with a smile so bright; he would go home to bed a "POLICEMAN" that night! Chris was taken as one of their own; he had been given the keys to another home.

Now he was an officer, but with no motorcycle wings. He couldn't get those until he did several things. His wish was not over, but almost complete. He had a small fear he had to defeat. Chris loved seeing motors and watching officers ride by, but when it came to riding motors he said "It's safer to fly." Doors were important to his little boy, so the motorcycle he rode was his little toy.

A course was established in his driveway at home. He felt very safe and of course free to roam. The course was established to test Chris's skills, and strict instructions were given to add to the thrill. He drove through the course and smiled the whole way, as this was the end of a wonderful day. A day full of pleasures and wonderful things and now it was official: Chris had motorcycle wings. He hugged all his buddies and said, "Thanks for the day," and they fired up their motors and rode away.

Chris, tired and sleepy, got ready for bed. Thoughts of the day ran all through his head. He laughed and giggled and smiled so bright, but his star wasn't in the sky that night. The star was so bright; it had left the rest to take its place on Chris's small chest. The fairy did smile as he looked at the boy. What a wonderful thing, this emotion of "joy." I'm glad I could share this. I'm glad I could see how wonderful, at times, a boy's life can be.

The story is told and I think it's easy to see, this little boy meant a great deal to me. The boy was a model, sent from above. His mission in life, "Caring and Love." His days were tough and filled with strife, but if you looked at his eyes, they were full of life. Chris left a message that he wanted done. "Help little kids, just have fun!" A foundation was formed with him in mind, its primary purpose to be warm and kind. Find all the children and find them fast. Grant their wishes, and make the memories last.

Ron Cox
Department of Public Safety
Arizona Highway Patrol (Retired)
July 22, 1999

As the years pass, parts of our ability to recall past experience goes with those years. I remember Tom Austin telling me about a young man dying of leukemia and that all this young man wanted in the world was to grow up and become a policeman. At that time, we decided that we would try to do something for him when his time came, but the full extent of what would eventually "snowball" had never entered our minds.

Some months later, Tom called me at work and said, "It's time." I sat and pondered for a few minutes and called our DPS Air Rescue unit based at Falcon Field in Mesa, Arizona. I briefly told them the situation with Chris and asked them if we could give him a "Show and Tell" of the ranger helicopter. Over the phone I got a resounding, "Hell no, we'll give him a ride in the damn thing." They in turn called their chain of command and got a resounding, "Yes, let's make it happen."

I made another call to our DPS public relations man, Allan Schmidt, and told him the story. From that point on, the "snowball" began rolling. Hurried calls were made to various people, and then those people made more calls.

Chris got his helicopter ride, a tour of the DPS compound, a Smokey Bear hat and hat badge, a certificate making him Arizona's first and only honorary Highway Patrolman, a ride in a patrol car, in which he sat on Sergeant Jim Eaves's lap and steered the car. He sat on a motorcycle, and sat down with Ralph Milstead, the director of DPS, and discussed a few matters and received a real honest-to-goodness Arizona Highway Patrol badge. The badge was pinned on him by Lieutenant Colonel Richard Shafer, and it was that badge that Lieutenant Colonel Shafer had been issued when he was first hired on. What a day.

These are just a few of the things that happened to Chris over a brief few days. The response from the entire police community was phenomenal. There was a memorial service in Phoenix, and a funeral service in Illinois, both of which were complete with all the respect and love due a fallen officer. I found out that tough cops do cry.

I haven't mentioned many names in this story, because I have forgotten who did what and who all became involved. I do want to thank Frank Shankwitz and Scott Stahl for calling us all together later and forming an organization that over the years has done so much for so many unfortunate children—children that realized that there was someone out there that cared and subsequently were able to see a dream come true that might otherwise never have been.

I want to thank Tom Austin for getting me involved, Chris's mom, Lynn, for allowing me the opportunity to meet her son and in some small way help make his final days easier, also Ralph Milstead, yet another victim of cancer, for allowing it all to happen. Tom Austin and I spoke with Ralph some years later and thanked him. He said, "I couldn't *not* let it happen. I lost a teenaged son to a horrible auto accident, and when Chris's situation came up, I wondered what my son's last wish might have been."

Lastly, my thanks to God, for bringing someone like Chris Greicius into our lives. As I said in the beginning, memories fade with time. But there are still times twenty years later, that when I get to feeling sorry for myself, I can recall a very strong young police officer and remember some of the misery he suffered, yet he never complained, and it makes my life somewhat easier.

Every time another one of our officers dies, in a private moment, I ask Chris to greet *them* and show *them* the ropes.

Thank you Chris Greicius, Arizona Trooper.

Lieutenant/Colonel
Richard E. Shafer
Department of Public Safety
Arizona Highway Patrol (Retired)
June 8, 2000

I consider it an honor and a privilege that I was a small part of making a young boy's dream come true. I shall never forget that special day when Chris stood on my desk and allowed me to swear him in to office and pin one of my badges on his chest. All of the personnel who met Chris were proud to call him one of *our* troopers. We all knew that he was seriously ill at the time, but one would have not known it by the smiles and excitement he displayed. There was no doubt that he was one happy young man.

We were all saddened with the news of his passing a few days later. We had really lost one of our own. I still have Christopher's picture displayed in my home, and I still get a lump in my throat when someone asks if he is one of my grandsons, and I tell them his story.

Sergeant Allan Schmidt
Department of Public Safety
Arizona Highway Patrol (Retired)
Public Relations Officer & Co-founder

It is my observation that most good or great things in this life start with an embryonic idea: a whim, a fancy, a notion, and a wish. Many are accidental discoveries while someone pursued a different idea, concept, or dream. Today it may appear that the Make-A-Wish Foundation began life from a great deal of thought and planning, but such is not the case. In truth it evolved, most appropriately, not unlike a child, and I have often referred to its beginnings as a "birth."

Tommy Austin asked Ron Cox to help give this little boy a tour of the DPS. Ron called me to ask who had a few ideas. I called some other guys, who had some ideas. Frank Shankwitz and Scott Stahl joined in. A helicopter ride. Sitting on a motorcycle, helmet and all. A ride in a patrol car to headquarters. A hat. A badge. A tour. A big day. Great stuff for a seven year old. Great stuff for the thirty- to forty-year-old crowd, too.

It got in the newspapers, and people called to say "what a nice thing to do." People called wanting to help. A uniform cut to fit. A hospital, a funeral, a marker that says "ARIZONA TROOPER."

There really was no reason for it to go any further. But some things are not really in our power. Just as with the beginnings of a great idea, or a child, something irrepressible began to grow. You can't see it. You can't feel it. You can't smell it, or taste it, or hear it. Or can you? Without knowing it, I think all our senses were filled with one of the beautiful things in this life—the reward of granting the gift of a wish to a deserving soul. In this case, it was for a boy named Chris.

Frank said we did a good thing. We all agreed. Someone said it would be neat to do it again. We all agreed. Someone said let's try. We all agreed. That's about it. There's no genius here. No rocket scientists, no Einstein, no Ferme, no Churchill. It wasn't brain surgery. Just a few folks moved by an almost accidental incident in our lives, touched by the event in a deep way, and inspired to try to do it again because it was a "good thing."

Did we know what we were doing? Sort of. Did we know where it was going? Not really. A few of us thought it might grow, but never imagined it would become what it is today. So then, how did it happen? I don't know. But I do know this: the Make-A-Wish Foundation is a living example of how people of different minds, different backgrounds, and different life experiences can be joined together in a common goal. And when that happens, the group is vested with enormous power. A boy named Chris got his wish. And while I don't recall wishing for it, we received a gift as well. We were granted a measure of wisdom—in my view, the greatest gift of all.

Now the wonder of all this is that despite the usual human frailties and failings of all the folks in the beginning and since, Make-A-Wish was born, it lived, and it grew. Don't ask why. Don't ask how. Just give thanks.

Tommy Austin
U.S. Customs Agent
June 26, 2000
Excerpts from 1992 story written by Tom Austin

In June 1977, in Scottsdale, Arizona, I came home from work one day and found my youngest daughter, who was about four at the time, with a little boy who was about the same age, lying on my living room couch. The boy had short hair, and it had been years since I had seen a child with short hair. I walked to the couch and rubbed his head and said, "What do we have here?" With a toy gun in his hand, he turned over, pointed the gun at me, and said in the fiercest voice, " Freeze. I'm a police officer."

I froze hands above my head. He got off the couch with the gun trained on me and carefully searched my pockets for weapons. He somehow missed the .357 magnum in the upside down shoulder holster on my left side. After Chris was satisfied that I was OK, he put his gun back into his holster, stuck out his hand to shake, and said, "Hi, my name is Chris."

From that point on, he had my heartstrings in his hand and in a downhill pull. We became fast friends. That day I found out that he loved cops, so I gave him a U.S. Customs patch.

The reason Chris was at my home on that fateful day was that his mother, Lynn, went to college with my wife, Kay, and they were studying for a test together. I found out that Chris had short hair as the result of his having chemotherapy for leukemia; his hair had fallen out. The prognosis was not good for Chris; in fact, it was rather bleak.

My friend Ron Cox and I had been up about forty-five hours straight on a stake-out in the desert, when I began to tell him of this little boy I knew who believed that if your home caught on fire, the first person you should call was a police officer. After telling him the story, we got out of the car and regained our composure. In our infinite wisdom that night, we decided to give Chris a helicopter ride and a "Smokey Bear" hat, but we were going to wait until he really needed it.

About a year and a half after we had been in the desert, his mother called and said that Chris was in the hospital, and the doctor was giving him platelets, and the end was growing near.

I called my good friend Ron Cox and told him, "It's time to get that old Smokey Bear hat. Chris is really sick." Ron had an old hat, but it was pretty well beat up from use. So Ron called Allan Schmidt, the public relations sergeant for the Department of Public Safety and explained our plan to him. Allan then spoke to the director, Ralph Milstead, who authorized giving a Smokey Bear Hat and a helicopter ride; however, he could not authorize a badge for Chris as a badge is an accountable item and must be issued. Colonel Richard Shafer, the deputy director, became involved and decided that we couldn't have a trooper running about without a badge.

The authorization came late Thursday afternoon, and Ron called me that night and advised that the helicopter crew had been cleared to give Chris a ride on April 29, 1980.

When I arrived at his house to pick him up, Chris was already in the driveway. When I pulled into the drive, a smile broke out on his face that could not be wiped off. He knew it was going to happen.

We arrived at the hospital; he paced nervously, anxiously awaiting the helicopter. I believe the best part of the day for him was when the helicopter arrived, blowing the garbage cans out into the street. Chris was ecstatic. He was screaming, "Look at that, Tommy. Look at that." As he got on the helicopter, his face was beaming, and he waved with all his might as they took off.

The pilots flew him all around Phoenix, and when they landed at DPS headquarters, there was a motorcycle and squad car waiting for him. The pilots let him shut off the helicopter, and the officers let him wear a motorcycle helmet and sit on the bike.

Then I saw Chris sitting in the lap of a friend of mine, Sergeant Jim Eaves, and driving the patrol car. He had a huge bubble blown as he drove past me, on his way to Colonel Shafer's office.

Colonel Shafer stood Chris on his desk and made him raise his right hand. Using the formal oath of office for the state, he swore Chris in as the very first honorary state trooper in the history of the state of Arizona. Then the colonel presented Chris with a graduation certificate from the academy and pinned a badge on him.

As we took Chris around the department, in a Pied Piper fashion, he had a following that grew and grew with more and more people. The employees of the department gave him pens, pencils, patches, and anything else they could think of as we went along the corridors.

Everyone involved was excited to be a part of such a historical event. The director, Ralph Milstead, came out of his office to see what all the noise and conversation was about and, finding Chris there, promptly asked his secretary to cancel all his appointments. He then took Chris into the conference room and spent prime time with him.

The event made the news at noon, the front page of the afternoon paper, and the news at 6:00 p.m. This was the first time in history that a civilian had ever been made an honorary state trooper.

Ron called John's Uniform Shop and since the women that worked there had seen the news at noon, they agreed to make Chris a uniform. The women stayed through the night to make the uniform. It was full regulation, complete with collar stays, military creases on the shirt and pants, offset belt loops, and watch pocket. John made a name plate for the right-hand shirt pocket, which was a miracle in itself, because it might be months before a nameplate could be had.

Arrangements had been made to give Chris the uniform the next day at his house—May 1, 1980.

On Friday, he was put into the hospital for the last time. The helicopter was at the hospital on a run and found that Chris was upstairs. The pilots went up to his room to see him. Chris woke up just long enough to say "oh, neato" and then lapsed into a coma. As the helicopter left the hospital, the crew flew around to the side where Chris was, hovered by his room, sounded the siren, rocked the helicopter in a good-bye salute, and flew away. It was like everyone knew this was the end.

I must make an observation and say this little boy who knew no one involved in the wish, except for me, before that day certainly changed a lot of lives in one week. He so profoundly touched lives that those who met him will never forget. Today, those that were involved still get misty eyes when talking about Chris.

In the twenty years it takes to reach retirement, an officer could never touch so many lives in such a positive way as Chris has. He lives even in death, for Chris is a part of every wish granted by the Make-A-Wish Foundation. I believe the bravery, grace, and dignity that he exhibited in facing his death on a daily basis carried over into the foundation.

I am amazed and astounded that a single act of kindness turned into the Make-A-Wish Foundation.

Bill Denny
Channel 12 News
May 18, 2000

I remember the first story of Make-A-Wish that I ever saw. It was, in fact, a story of a small boy who dreamed of someday becoming a Department of Public Safety officer. We aired the story on Channel 12, a story in which members of DPS asked Jerry Foster to become involved. He did and in a Big way. Since that first exposure, Make-A-Wish has grown to a national and international forum.

As for Jerry, I remember him coming back into the television station that afternoon. As we talked about the story, Jerry started tearing. That, of course, got all of us in a very tearful mood. I remember Jerry saying how hard it was to watch this happy little guy, knowing he wouldn't ever see his teens. He'd never be able to play ball, or go out on a date, or drive a car. Yet this single event motivated Jerry to do more for Make-A-Wish and its children. He did a number of stories on the foundation— not for publicity for him or the station, but because he knew he was helping these young people realize a dream. That in itself was satisfying to Jerry. But Make-A-Wish was just a launching pad for Jerry Foster.

Over the years, he assisted the sheriff's office, local police, and other agencies in rescue missions. During the floods, he flew his chopper inches above raging floodwaters to help those trapped on the roofs of cars and in the bed of pickups. He was involved in searches for people stranded in the hot desert and flew into remote areas to help extricate a climber who had fallen and was injured.

Jerry Foster can be described a thousand different ways by a thousand different people, but love him or hate him, he is a very special person who cared and felt deeply about others in need. And the Make-A-Wish foundation could, with clear conscience, credit Jerry with being the single biggest reason the foundation got off to such an auspicious beginning in 1980.

I worked alongside Foster for many years and never once questioned his dedication to those who needed help; he was always there. His helicopter, better known to viewers as "Sky 12," allowed him the luxury to be available to help those in a crisis situation. Channel 12 allowed him the vehicle to gain financial support for many in need and in particular the Make-A-Wish Foundation. DPS, Jerry Foster, and Channel 12 were there in the beginning, and because of all of those factors, you can bet we will all be there when the Make-A-Wish needs our help.

William F. "Bill" Denny
Former Sports Director
KPNX TV
Phoenix, Arizona

Dr. Paul V. Baranko
St. Joseph's Hospital and Medical Center
Presently Phoenix Children's Hospital
April 30, 1999

I remember Chris as a very cute little boy, always willing to do what was asked of him medically. He never complained. He would give a little whimper when we were ready to do sedation on a regular basis for procedures, but he was always willing to go through whatever had to be done as long as he had an explanation. Even though his mother was a single parent, it was a reflection of the security he had at the time of his illness that going through the therapy was more palatable for him. Never did he rebel, throw tantrums, scream, or holler. I don't ever remember him doing that. But what I do remember is Chris being uncomfortable on occasions, but only releasing a little whimper or being easily consoled.

As far as Make-A-Wish Foundation is concerned, I'm flabbergasted, because when Chris was in his terminal phase, they dressed him up in a state trooper uniform, and they had pictures of him, and then he died shortly afterwards. The next thing I knew, Bopsy was going for a ride in a fire engine, and he was dressed up in a firefighter's uniform. Then over at St. Joe's, the fire department brought a hook-and-ladder truck to the hospital, parking it in the front lawn. I sort of lost track of what was going on, and the next thing I know is I hear of this Make-A-Wish Foundation, and kids with very serious illnesses are being granted wishes. Then the word got back to me that it was because of Chris and your [Linda's] workings that all of this happened. I can honestly say that over the years it has been somewhat mind boggling to see how this thing grew from a grassroots effort on your [Linda's] part to an international organization. I think parents take the health of their children for granted. Society tends not to think about the children who are not healthy, especially those who have nowhere to turn for medical care.

Sometimes a knock between the eyes—like a family member with a very serious problem—changes the perspective that our society has of life. To have volunteers who may or may not have had kids with serious illness to spend the time they do to raise money for families for trips and wishes—it is just gut wrenching to me to see how people come together—and the benefit is only for the kids. It is just very satisfying to me to have known the inspiration for this idea and to be part of the inspiration, which are Chris and his mother.

Make-A-Wish not only gives a child a good time, but if they are, unfortunately, going to die, Make-A-Wish gives the parents good memories. Instead of being tied down to a hospital bed or being uncomfortable, they remember the good times, going on a trip, a new bedroom set, or a computer—whatever their wish was. I think the philosophy of Make-A-Wish is to help children forget the bad times and remember the good times. So it's making the best of a bad situation and helping those who can't help themselves, mainly the kids.

Sister Madonna Maria
June 22, 1999

I had been working in pediatrics since 1971, when I met Linda and Chris. I knew immediately that I was in for one great big "hurt," because I fell in love with them both immediately. Falling in love with my little patients and their families was a devastating habit that I had gotten into (no pun intended).

Working in a large medical center with several medical doctors with specialties in certain fields, often, I encountered many "little" patients who were terminally ill, and it was my job to prepare the families and the sweet innocent children for their final journey. Although I had many love affairs in the past, I knew that this one was to be exceptional.

One look and you could tell that Chris was "special." As our relationship developed in the short time we had together, it became apparent to me that Chris was too good for our troubled world. He belonged in the arms of his heavenly Father. I also knew that in the not-too-distant future this would be reality. This knowledge and the fact that Linda was alone in a strange city gave me a sense of urgency—urgency to help make the most of their time together, to be there for them in whatever way I could and for whatever time it would take.

My relationship grew not only with Chris but with Linda as well. I looked forward with mixed feelings to our visits. I was so happy to see my friends, but usually the visit meant that Chris was to receive a treatment, and that is what made me sad. I was so grateful to God for bringing Linda and Chris into my life. Linda was such a fun person to be with even in these difficult times. She had a wonderful attitude on life in spite of the hardships she had already experienced. Obviously, God loved her deeply and filled her with His Spirit.

I remember Linda in the little waiting room on the second floor outside pediatrics at St. Joe's, as Dr. Paul Baranko told her of her son's illness and life expectancy. She was scared—worried—yet this internal strength showed through. We sat and talked a short time, and then I remember asking her if she wanted to go see her Christopher. We both wiped our eyes, and we walked down the hall to his room.

Chris was such a good little boy, always with a smile and warm hugs for me—a cute little guy that never complained as long as he had an explanation for what was going on. When Chris and his mother Linda would come to the hospital for treatments, we explained to Chris that Mom and I were going to have some coffee and talk for a little while. Of course we would be gone for at least a half an hour or so, but we knew Chris would be "OK" because he knew his mom just needed to talk to someone.

It was hard for Linda, being a single parent, living in a strange new city, finding a job, and having her only son slowing dying of leukemia. She was starting all over, and I knew the good Lord wanted me there by her side. I knew that throughout the next three and a half years, the three of us would become very good friends. Chris was to become my little buddy, and Linda was to become a good friend.

Hanging on my wall is the eight-by-ten-inch picture of Chris in full uniform. Every time I look at it, I think back to those days we first met, and I say a little prayer for both Linda and Chris.

Although our time together was short, we "packed" that time with fun, laughter, tears, joy, and lots and lots of love. When Chris's time to leave us finally came, although sad, I was happy for him. He would no longer have to suffer, and every day would be filled with fun, laughter, joy, and lots and lots of love. As I held Linda in my arms, the tears flowed freely, for my heart was rejoicing in my little "Buddy." I knew Linda would be all right, for she was a fighter, and she was strong in the spirit, and I knew that God's love would sustain her.

Thank you, God, for allowing Linda and Chris to touch my life and for the privilege of being with them during this very special time of their life.

God bless.

"Thank You"
21 Years Later for A Special Red Rose

I wanted to say thanks to the man in the back room of the florist shop, which sold Chris a rose for three pennies that day in 1978, even if it took me twenty-one years. My neighbor, Bobby Greathouse, contacted the owner of the McCormick Ranch Flowers, Dan Grimes, and asked him for any information.

After several days of digging through old records, he called with three names and one phone number of someone who might know who the gentleman was and how to reach him. As Dan and I talked on the telephone, I explained the story of Make-A-Wish and how Chris was the inspiration for the founding of the organization.

I made the phone call and left a message to please call me back. A few days went by, and I decided to call the phone number again. This time a little girl answered, and I asked to speak to her mom or dad. Her father knew of the gentleman and said he would try to find his phone number. That evening, his wife called, and within a short time, I was dialing Maryland and leaving a message.

A few days later, I personally stopped in to McCormick Ranch Flowers to say "thanks" for Dan's time and assistance.

On July 10, 1999, I had the opportunity to express a very long overdue "thank you" to the nice gentleman in the back room that sold Chris the beautiful red rose for three pennies. His name is Dick, and he is now retired and living in Maryland with his wife. He, along with two other gentlemen, ran the Flower World of McCormick Ranch from 1972 through 1981. Dick and his wife have four children (two girls and two boys) that are grown now. And they volunteer their time with local charities in their area.

Dear Dick,

"Thank you" for being there that day so long ago and smiling down on a little blond-haired, blue-eyed boy who had only three little pennies of pure love. Our life was filled with love, happiness, and adventure as we shared seven short years together. The story of my red rose is one of my special memories of those years. I thank you for your kindness.

Sincerely,

Linda

Jean Rhodes
Volunteer, 1980-1983
February 15, 2000

When I think back on the time that I was fortunate enough to be on the Make-A-Wish board, I always feel a great satisfaction and pride in my heart with being associated with something so well worthwhile. The early days of MAW were sometimes difficult, because we were a new group that had a new concept for people to adjust to. We didn't have much money in the beginning, and we not only had to grant wishes, we also had to raise the money for the wishes on our own.

I shall always be thankful for the television magazine-format program. They came to Phoenix and televised one of our board meetings, and things really started to turn around for MAW. We had calls from all over the country wanting more information on how they could start a chapter in their state. I met many wonderful people from all over the United States, including Hawaii. It's been wonderful.

I have been asked by friends which wish that I participated in stood out the most in my memories. This is very difficult to answer, because to me each and every wish was important and very special. I came to the board just as the second wish had concluded. I will never forget the firefighters who helped make Bopsy's wish so very special. I also remember the precious little girl from Paradise Valley that wanted to go to a theme entertainment park in California. The love of her life was a yellow bird. How well I remember the morning that Lynn (Chris's mom) and I rented a bird costume and went into Sky Harbor Airport. Lynn was dressed as her favorite cartoon character . . . it was adorable. Make-A-Wish got a lot of attention that morning as the little girl was just overjoyed, and she sat in the bird's lap until it was time to board her flight.

Things like this have endeared Lynn to me so very much. She was always such an inspiration to me as we did many wishes together. I love her dearly. Her personal pain never showed as she did a wish for a child.

I remember the day we received a call from a church in Sedona asking for a board member to come and talk to one of their meetings about MAW. They were interested in perhaps getting something started in Sedona. Lynn and I arose early one morning and drove to the church nestled on the side of the mountain. The people were extremely nice and very interested in our message. Lynn and I decided not to use notes in our talks but just to speak from our hearts.

We had about fifty people present, and as we were concluding our presentation, the church presented us with a check for five hundred dollars. We were overjoyed, as this was a huge help in our next wish. I remember another wish, also to visit a theme entertainment park in California, for a beautiful teenage girl in a wheelchair. She was from a neighboring community and had the most beautiful red hair I have ever seen. She looked like a Dresden china doll. I remember her grateful father as he thanked MAW.

I shall never forget all the wonderful airline people we contacted. They never refused to fly any of our wishes at no cost to the foundation; they simply helped us any way they could. I also remember the Sheraton Hotels in California that came to our assistance with much-needed lodging for our families of the children.

I can't soon forget the day several of us went to the first-grade class of a little boy with a brain tumor. His entire class joined in with helping us present his wish to this precious little boy. He was so happy. He especially appreciated the toy aircraft, which was a replica of the one he would be flying in to the theme entertainment park in California. MAW members provided refreshments for the entire class. One incident during this wish gave everyone the scare of our lives. Our little honoree became lost from his mother and aunt at the park, and the whole staff, including the animal characters, joined in the search until he was found.

I have saved the story of the wish of Andy for the last. Andy was a Hispanic boy, twelve years old. He was so sweet and so very handsome. He was blessed with a lovely caring family. Andy was dying, and he knew it. As he lay in his hospital bed in Bellflower, California, his greatest wish was to die at home. The airlines could not fly him home as he was much too ill, and his illness had exhausted much of the family funds.

A relative of Andy's called the governor's office and asked for help in getting him home. The governor called state Senator Alfredo Gutierrez and asked if he could look into the situation. To my surprise, I received a call from the governor asking if we could arrange for the wish. Of

course, money was a big issue with young MAW. We did
not have the ready cash to send the Air Ambulances to
Andy's hospital so the governor called Air Evac Services
and asked if we could pay after the boy was home, as time
was of the essence. Senator Alfredo Gutierrez sent out
letters asking for donations. The money started rolling in;
it was almost like a miracle.

Air Evac Services was on its way and as MAW
needed some legal documents signed, the pilot said he
would see they were signed. The hospital had a notary
standing by, and all paperwork was properly taken care
of. We were lucky to have such a compassionate pilot. He
was truly great.

Air Evac Services informed us that Andy would arrive
at Sawyer Aviation at Sky Harbor Airport about one in the
morning. Four of the MAW board members, Lynn, Kathy,
Theresa, and I were there anxiously waiting. A ground
ambulance was also there waiting to take Andy to the
hospital.

At this time in history, Air Evac Services flew out of
Sawyer Aviation at Sky Harbor. The four of us waited by
the Sawyer Radio that had direct contact with Air Evac
Services, which was bringing Andy from California. Fifty
miles out, the pilot indicated things weren't going well
and perhaps we should line up a helicopter instead of land
transportation. The four of us joined hands and prayed.

Soon Air Evac Services landed, and we thought after
seeing Andy that it was too late—but a *miracle* did
happen! Suddenly Andy moved slightly, and his mother
came over and hugged each and every one of us, not only
for bringing Andy home but also just for our support in

being there that night. The helicopter took Andy to the hospital, and it seemed as though Andy rallied and became aware of those around him. The next day he expressed a desire to meet one of the Phoenix Suns players. The miracle continued, as the Suns were in practice at a nearby gym. MAW told the story of Andy to the Suns, and the response was overwhelming from them. They took him an autographed Suns basketball and spent several minutes with him in the hospital. A very happy young man of twelve years grinned from ear to ear.

At the end, Andy asked to be taken to his home in west Phoenix to spend his last days. He was moved to his home, where he passed away surrounded by his beloved family.

Thank you, Governor, Senator Alfredo Gutierrez, Air Evac Services, and the Phoenix Suns. After all was over and settled a bit, I received a warm, wonderful thank you letter from Andy's mother. I treasure this letter very much.

Soon after this wish, MAW was nominated for the Freedom Foundation Award for the wonderful work MAW was doing. I am happy to say MAW won this prestigious award. It is wonderful to see how the foundation has grown compared to our humble beginnings. I shall never forget our precious little Chris Greicius that started this entire thing, and I will always be thankful for those policemen who made his wish possible.

A woman in Ohio who heard about MAW on television immediately made a dozen of the most unusual rag dolls and mailed them to me to give to our wish children. The dolls were so beautiful and so original. The children cherished them. She was always so interested in our wish children, and I tried to keep her informed with newspaper clippings and articles.

An unusual conversation took place with one of our wish children, an adorable little girl, whose wish was to go to an entertainment park. As our little girl was enjoying all the beauty of the park, a Los Angeles television reporter stopped her. The story was being carried live in California and Arizona. The little girl talked of her illness and how much she was enjoying her trip when all of sudden she insisted on telling that her father was a deadbeat dad who wouldn't pay child support. The reporter desperately tried to change the subject, but our little girl was intent on getting out her story. As they say, "Kids say the darnedest things."

One of the greatest things that happened to young MAW was due to the employees of Mountain Bell Telephone Company, (now Qwest). The employees from all over the state decided to raise money for the foundation and did just about everything possible under the sun to accomplish their goal.

They presented us with a check for ten thousand dollars, and we were speechless. Some of the MAW people participated in some of the fund-raising projects. We toured several telephone offices over the entire state. The thing I remember most was in Tucson at a large gathering where we cooked hamburgers to sell. They were cooked on a grill out in the summer's heat. We all got a nice reddish tan that day.

Geoffrey Bruce
First Business Donor
May 3, 2000

I got involved in Make-A-Wish way back in the early days because of my contact with Jose Montilla. He was my client at the Sheraton Greenway Hotel & Resort, and he said, "Geoffrey, I have a project that I need you to help me on. There is this wonderful organization coming together, and they need a logo. They need corporate identity; they need imagery and brochures. Will you do it?" Of course, I didn't know what I was getting into, but once Jose told me the story of Chris, I couldn't say no.

As things progressed, it was a wonderful grassroots opportunity. It wasn't fancy. It wasn't corporate. Jose was just pulling every string he could pull to get people involved at that point. The Greicius Make-A-Wish had to have an image. At this time, nobody had any ideas of what that imagery should be. I enlisted the help of a dear friend of mine, Amy Myers, who was a wonderful character, an animated woman who was an artist, a painter, a writer, and an illustrator of children's books. She was housed in my office in those days.

Amy drew fifteen or twenty sketches with rainbows, angels with wands, wishbones, wands with stars on them, and lots of wonderful little images. At one of the meetings, everyone picked the image they liked the best, and the wishbone with multi-colored ribbons tied around it won, hands down. Upon our next meeting, Amy had hand sewn about ten wishbones and decorated them with rainbow-colored ribbons.

So now we had imagery and the logo. We now needed the layout of stationery and business cards, and that was my job. Barbara Lanterman was another graphic designer, and she had incredible handwriting. She wrote the original script for Greicius Make-A-Wish Memorial. Then it was a matter of pasting it all together, coming up with camera-ready artwork, and then going to a printer. The pitch I used to use with all my suppliers was, "Look, I need a favor. There is this non-profit organization called Greicius Make-A-Wish Memorial, and we really need support financially, because we are granting wishes to kids, and we really can't afford to pay very much, so here is what I'd like to do. You give it to me free the first time; I'll pay cost the second time, and the third I never want to pay list." I think they are still donating their printing costs to the foundation today.

Then we needed a brochure. My ex-wife wrote it—all the words. We had some pictures at that point to use in laying out the brochure. In printing circles, four-color printing is expensive. We got a printer, and if I'm not mistaken, they printed the first brochure—it was a six panel, four-by-nine brochure, five or six colors on the best possible paper—and again they did it for cost.

From that time on, we really had the best of marketing materials for a young organization.

Within two years, it became apparent, because of the publicity, that the organization had to split. There needed to be National Make-A-Wish Foundation. Jose Montilla actually invented the first fund-raiser, which became known as the Silent Auction—first held at the Sheraton Greenway Hotel & Resort around the poolside. He involved his staff and manager at that time. They dressed up as cowboys for the entertainment of guests and invited prominent people from all walks of life. The early Silent Auctions were just the volunteers and a few special followers. They in turn invited their friends and spent a lot of money. At later Silent Auctions, Jose invited the governor of the state, and what a night that was.

Later a manager at another resort invented a balloon race as a fund-raiser. At that time, we had twenty-five or thirty balloons. A friend of mine had a twin-engine plane, and we flew up and around all the balloons, taking pictures. What a magnificent sight.

As president, in 1985, of the local Make-A-Wish chapter in Arizona, I was given a huge framed collection of photos from those days. It is wonderful.

Author's note:

I called and talked with Amy Myers, June 2000, about the wishbone, along with good old times. She enlightened me that she would hand paint each ribbon in multiple colors of the rainbow and hand tie it on each hand-sewn wishbone. She loved every minute of it.

Amy, I wish to thank you for your dedication and creative talents.

Jose Montilla
Volunteer, Business Donor, Wish Granter
Combined memories of Linda Pauling, Geoffrey Bruce
May 3, 2000

There are many ways to describe Mr. Montilla, but I think the best is as follows: a warm-hearted man with a matching flamboyant personality that would do anything to get anything for a cause he believed in. Such a cause was the Make-A-Wish Foundation in the early years.

He was the manager of the Sheraton Greenway Hotel & Resort in Phoenix, Arizona, where I happened to work. He would arrange for conference rooms when our little group needed to meet or arrange for hotel rooms for the families when they needed to spend a night because they were out of town.

Several of the first wishes were to California, and Mr. Montilla called other Sheraton Hotels & Resorts managers and arranged "comp" rooms for them. He and an associate of his helped arrange the first Super Bowl wish for a twelve-year-old boy from Globe, Arizona, just a week and a half before the game. That young man is now the father of a twelve-year-old son and wishes to be a part of Make-A-Wish.

Geoffrey Bruce and Jose Montilla go hand in hand in their support of the foundation, not only for their financial and business support but also for their love for the kids.

Neither left it at just that. Mr. Montilla went on to help kick off our present-day National Make-A-Wish

Foundation as the first president, and his spirit is still there today.

In October 1994, Make-A-Wish held its international convention in Phoenix, Arizona. At this particular convention, we not only honored our donors but honored our past presidents and people who have helped make Make-A-Wish what it is today. Jose Montilla was one of those individuals that we honored. This particular evening was a surprise to me, because I hadn't seen Jose for many years, almost since the Sheraton Greenway days. When he was introduced on stage to the audience, he told the story of Chris and then extended his hand and invited me to join him. It was a tearful reunion as we gave each other a big hug.

Thank you, Jose Montilla, for your support, love for the kids, and your super personality. A grateful mother.

Linda

Code 1000
Sgt. Dave Cool, Fund raiser
May 15, 2000

Within the Maricopa County Sheriff's Office, CODE 1000 has a very important meaning. It is the call sign that signifies when an officer is in a possible life-threatening situation and needs immediate assistance. CODE 1000 means much more than that today. It is our call sign for the immediate assistance needed to grant wishes for the children of the Make-A-Wish Foundation with life threatening illnesses.

> "...our courage pales in comparison to the courage displayed by the children of Make-A-Wish."

"Dealing with society's worst of the worst and placing your life on the line for each other every day takes an extraordinary amount of courage. Our courage pales in comparison to the courage displayed by the children of Make-A-Wish." I spoke those words, fighting back the tears, with a lump the size of Maricopa County in my throat, before forty officers of the sheriff's office, seven years ago. Law enforcement personnel are supposed to be strong, to be stone-faced, to never show this type of emotion.

No, it's not a policy, just another one of those human effects that we tuck away, deep down inside. But, somewhere, deep inside my soul, I knew it was a safe place to cry. A voice from a blurred image of one of the officers nearby softly said, "It's OK, Sergeant; we're all cryin' too." I never knew what the impact that night would be on my family and me or the lives of my brothers and sisters in the badge. The foundation has touched so many lives, and I am honored to be able to tell of the blessing that it has been to me.

Working inside these jail walls, we have a good day when we get home at the end of the day safely. Please don't misunderstand. Street cops live in an amazingly unpredictable and dangerous arena and deserve our greatest respect and admiration. The difference is that after they arrest the molester or murderer, the perpetrators are turned over to detention officers. It is our job to control and contain these outcasts from society twenty-four hours a day, seven days a week.

Society forgets that they exist. You know, out of sight, out of mind. As for the officers that personally deal with these people, there are hundreds of thousands of these silent heroes watching the criminals of the world with the same goal as the cop on the beat: Keep our family and community safe from harm. We accepted this duty with the understanding that there are no accolades for the keepers of the keys. In truth, the only press we generate is when someone escapes or dies in custody. Every eight hours, a detention officer is involved in some kind of assault in Maricopa County jails.

Again, we knew the risks and accepted them gratefully. However, no one hears of the life-saving efforts or counseling that occurs when an inmate becomes

suicidal or homicidal when in custody. In our world, life
depends on courage, people skills, and teamwork, just like
street cops and fire fighters.

Police throughout the world, all a part of the thin blue
line, work toward what appears to be an unattainable goal:
safety and security for our friends, family, and
community. We strive for this goal, hoping that justice
will prevail and that we set the right example. But, what
do we do when we cannot control that safety and security
any longer? What if the one in danger is a young child and
no matter how you want to save them, you can't? This is a
very frustrating and haunting feeling for those of us that
live at the entrance to that door every day. No matter how
you try to conceal the emotion, the overwhelming wave
cannot be contained. What do you do? You get involved
and find a way to make that innocent child's life the most
magical imaginable, and there is no limit . . . Ever . . .

Frank Shankwitz and Scott Stahl, two motor officers,
lived the frustration and built a world of love, caring, and
proactive support for thousands of us who stopped to
smell the roses and found a child in need. Make-A-Wish
was founded on only one premise, "All of God's children
should have a fairy godmother or godfather." CODE 1000
is not just another fund-raiser. It is personal, it is
important, it is about children, maybe our children.

The People of Make-A-Wish

I was very concerned that the murder mysteries that I
was producing would not generate enough money to grant
a wish for the children of the foundation. Then I talked to
Linda, and she explained two facts to me. First, all wishes

brought to the foundation that could be granted would be granted. Second, she said, "Make-A-Wish is proud to have anyone, especially law enforcement, raise funds for the children." She continued, "I don't care if it's just ten dollars, we are still honored to have you help." I was stunned, because this was not what I expected to hear from the founder of an organization with such a prestigious reputation. From that moment on, the focus was not on the money we generated, but it was on the children. I have found that Make-A-Wish is not an "I" organization; it is based on "They," and it doesn't matter what I do or how I do it, only that I try. The children are the foundation, and all other priorities are diminished because of the children.

Logistically, producing a professional murder mystery, charging admittance, and entertaining your guest, one could easily understand how a nightmare could be created. My father, Gary Clarke, (original cast member of *The Virginian*) offered to cast the event. The response was incredible, and everyone we asked to become involved responded with, "Just tell me when and where." There were no conditions to be met, or schedules that couldn't be changed if it meant the success of the fund-raisers for the children. The cast was created of people from all areas and lifestyles. Scott Stahl, also a co-founder of Make-A-Wish, became a regular on the set with enormous enthusiasm and talent. Robin Ross is a nurse, actor, and proud mother of her first child and has always been there to take her place as the scorned woman. Alan Ripa and Frank Tonis are both Realtors with very busy schedules and lives to live. Jim Mapstead, owner of a successful engraving company, couldn't do enough to aid in any portion of the productions donating trophies and engraved goods as well as acting. Butch Brown, a mortgage broker, actor, and the King at the annual Phoenix Renaissance Festival, was spectacular in all his appointed roles. Bill Strauss, talk radio host, father, and friend, like the rest, echoed the sentiment.

Employees from all areas of the sheriff's office joined in the production. Deputy Ed Mays and his wife Bonnie, from the records and I.D. division, was a never-ending source of support virtually every year. Even our local union, Maricopa County Deputies Association, donated thousands of dollars in support of this event.

They all worked hundreds of hours because of their desire to help, and they did it for the children and they needed no other prompting. I am blessed to call these fine people friends and will never forget their selfless donations to the children of the Make-A-Wish Foundation.

Some of the actors came from the interior of the sheriff's office and some came from years of donations to the event—like Michael Monte, owner of the famous Monte's Steak Restaurants in Phoenix. He was the masterful murderer in the 1998 event and generous donor to most of our events.

Geordie and Jamie Hormel paid fees, for the second year in a row, to provide the facilities of the Wrigley Mansion Club for our annual event. Over the years, our annual event has been on billboards, radio, newsprint, and the lips of thousands of Phoenicians.

Wishes Do Come True

In 1998, Linda and her husband, Gene, invited Marie and I to join them at the international convention held in Phoenix. We were honored to attend such an event, and as the evening progressed, wish children presented the awards for their donations. As each child came to the stage, I found myself becoming increasingly anxious about the children.

Each child with its individual illness, which would eventually take him or her home, was so talented, so honest, so untainted, and most of all, happy. The children didn't let the pressure of their lives beat them. They lived each day as only children do, glad to be alive. Then she came to the stage, a little angel all of eight years old, commanding the stage like any professional movie star. The master of ceremonies asked her what her wish was. She looked at him with wide eyes and then glanced at the audience. Shyly, she said, "My wish was to see my grandma."

I lost it at that point. I have worked forty-two years to manage my life, and in one moment, this child showed me just how futile my efforts have been. With all of my technology and years of wisdom, I found family, friends, God, and myself humbled by the simple love of a child and the simple things in life.

Linda, as well as the local chapter executive director, noticed the stunning effect that this little girl had on me. Later that year, CODE 1000 was awarded a Make-A-Wish coloring page from a wish child, framed and ready for display. This time, she gave the detention officers the coloring page that the little girl from the convention had colored. As I explained to the audience the story of our fund-raiser, they were as moved as I was. At this particular event, we adopted the wish of a child of one of the officers at Madison Street Jail.

The Thin Blue Line

Some volunteers hold Make-A-Wish as an honorable place to donate their excess hours of free time. Still others, especially law enforcement circles, hold this vessel, founded in the badge, close to their hearts and protect its heritage and the memory of our youngest motor officer ever to earn his wings. This foundation was formed on the love of children—children that will not have the opportunity to earn their wings or protect and serve. Linda asked me to write this as a message to police officers all around the world. That message is, "We have been charged, as members of the thin blue line, to carry out the tradition that Chris Greicius, Frank Shankwitz, Scott Stahl, Linda Pauling, Kathy McMorris, and Allan Schmidt created on Mother's Day, 1980.

As for CODE 1000, I would close this chapter with the prayer with which I end each event: "I pray to God that there will be no need to make the CODE 1000 call next year. But if there is a need, I pray that there will be people like you to answer the call. God bless you." With your help and passion for the children of the Make-A-Wish Foundation, wishes will continue to come true.

James Dury
July 22, 2000

I had the privilege of talking to Mr. James Dury, the star of *The Virginian*, on the phone. He was a special guest star of the CODE 1000 in 1997. I would like to share with you the story he relayed to me about a special little nine- or ten-year-old-boy named Josh.

Josh's dream was to ride like the wind as a cowboy. But Josh had an inoperable brain tumor the size of a golf ball. A week's stay had been donated for Josh at a Dude Ranch near the Houston area, and Josh wanted to learn to ride before his vacation, so he could look like a pro.

The Make-A-Wish chapter contacted Mr. Dury and asked if he could help make Josh's wish come true. Jim contacted a friend who is a world champion horse trainer.

Jim said that when he first saw the boy he was as gray as the inside of a cereal box, thin and weak. Then they brought the horse over to him; he climbed into the saddle and held the reins in his hands. Josh came alive; all the colors in a rainbow surrounded Josh as he sat there in the saddle smiling from ear to ear and glowing brighter than the sun.

Within two days, the trainer had Josh riding like a real cowboy around the corral, reining the horse and backing him up upon command and spinning away from fences. As Jim said, "He's doing things that I do, and he 's only been riding for two days!"

A few weeks ago, Mr. Dury happened to be at a book signing and little Josh, who is not so little anymore but in fact about twenty two years old, heard that Mr. Dury would be there and showed up to say "hi."

Josh informed him that when he went back to he hospital for tests, the doctors couldn't find any traces of the tumor. One and a half years later, he did have an operation to remove a small mass, but it was a complete success and there have been no signs of any health problems since.

Today Josh is a professional cutting horse trainer and living a full and completely healthy, happy life as a cowboy.

As Jim said, "I feel that I was present for a miracle after those two days. I had a hard time believing my eyes, but there was Josh doing things that I do with horses. Josh is and will be a credit to the horseman industries and a credit to the human race."

I wish to thank Mr. James Dury for sharing Josh's wonderful, inspiring wish story with me

To Josh,
I wish the very best that life has to offer, and may God bless you for being a brave young man.

Linda

Tony Greicius Jr.
Chris's Daddy
June 19, 2000

Dear Christopher,

Your mother asked me to write whatever I wanted about my memories of you—but I couldn't do that even though I tried and tried. The only thing that I could do was to write a letter to you to express some of my memories. Since it is only a couple of days before Father's Day, you have been on my mind more than usual. Of course, I think of you every day in many ways, but lately those thoughts have been especially vivid.

Daddy Remembers

Chris, I remember the first time I saw you in the hospital—so red and wrinkled—only a few days shy of my twenty-fifth birthday. How proud I was! What a bundle of joy! A SON! We named you Christopher after my favorite saint and James after my cousin.

As you grew, you wanted to help Daddy and both grandfathers. We were always working and tinkering, so you wanted to help. Remember when I sat you on the back of the gentle cows and when I taught you to drive the tractor with me? We had good times on the farm in Kewanee with Grandma and Grandpa, and visits to Geneseo to see grandparents, and trips to the park and Lake Storey. Chris, remember sledding in Illinois and that special wooden sled I bought you the Christmas before you got sick? What fun we had. I thought the good times would go on forever.

Then your grandfather died. You and your mother moved to Phoenix, Arizona, to be with your grandmother. Things happened so quickly after that. Linda called to say you were sick. My head was in a spin. I planned to quit my job and move to Phoenix to be near you, but that was not to be. A lawyer friend said my insurance would not transfer to another job—right when we needed it the most. Chris, I made one of the most difficult decisions of my life—FOR YOU. I returned to work in Illinois and left you and your mother in Phoenix. Even in the midst of my disbelief that you had cancer, that it couldn't be that bad, I KNEW YOU WOULD LIVE—YOU WOULD BEAT THE ODDS.

On my first visit, you were fat and happy, like a little butterball. The medication really gave you an appetite. The calls, the letters, and the too-few and too-short visits are engraved on my heart, along with all the memories we shared.

Through it all, I never saw you complain. We got you a three-wheeled battery scooter for traveling in stores and other places. You even went to school when you could.

Your mother kept me posted on the treatments and the remissions. Once, during a remission, I was able to bring you back to Kewanee for a visit with Grandma and Grandpa Greicius. They knew it would be your last. I think you did, too, although no one said anything.

Chris, how you loved to trim Grandma's palm tree and dream about becoming an Arizona Highway Patrolman when you grew up. We took you to a theme entertainment park in California, to Flagstaff, to see the desert, anywhere you wanted to go. You even had a little girlfriend that you were so proud of. There was a popular T.V. show about California Highway Patrolmen, and you had seen every episode. It was your favorite. Then Mommy made some friends who were REAL highway patrolmen. What excitement!

When the doctors said the leukemia was terminal, some of Linda's friends decided to do something. They had a special uniform made for you—just like their own. We bought you a helmet and a pair of black boots. How happy you were with them.

Chris, the final days started with a nosebleed. The doctor said you were out of remission and would go downhill rapidly. I carried you from his office to St. Joseph's Hospital across the street, and you rested your head on my shoulder. In admitting, the nurse wanted to put you in a wheelchair, but I said I would carry you to your bed. It was the last time you were in my arms.

The doctor came to start an IV, and your veins were collapsed. As he poked you the second time, he apologized for the pain. You bravely said, "Everybody's got to do what they got to do." The doctor promised us that you would never suffer, and you were able to enjoy your Highway Patrol trophies until the end.

Chris, on May 3, 1980, you went to heaven. We flew your body back to Kewanee, Illinois, to be buried. The airline was on strike in St. Louis, so your mother and I were delayed, but your casket received special handling. Cavanaughs and Schueneman handled all the arrangements. I spoke with the priest about services.

There were several officers at your funeral, and they gave you the same tribute that is given to one of their own.

Chris, I just want to give your special thanks to the officers and everyone who made your wish come true. A special thanks to Linda for all she did for you and for Make-A-Wish.

All my love, Daddy

DADDY'S TRIBUTE

Christopher was full of laughter and smiles with a look in his eyes that made you feel great. Every day was special and every moment precious. Although his life was short, it was full, for he touched many hearts with love and compassion. Holding him was a warm feeling of love that is missed every day of my life.

Christopher wished to experience life at its fullest and in doing so earned a special place in the hearts of everyone he touched.

Christopher is gone, but his memory lives in my heart and in the special memories of Make-A-Wish. May God bless all the special people as Christopher now walks in the presence of angels.

Linda J. Bergendahl-Pauling
Co-Founder & Volunteer
May 3, 1992

Dear Christopher,

I can still remember our time together so clearly. Sometimes I wish I couldn't, but I don't know if I could handle that either. Thanks to your trusting little smile, boyish grin, and inspiring eyes that reached out to anyone who met you, your wish of becoming a police officer was the inspiration that has made other children's dreams come true also.

It's hard to put into words how proud I am of you and your legacy as a little boy of seven years old and how much you accomplished in such a short amount of time. I never realized how much I still miss you until I wrote this book. I started it ten years after your death.

Ten years later, your story is now finished. When I talk to groups, part of me is trying to remain professional, while the other half is remembering being your Mommie: The times when I was holding you in my arms watching you sleep, crying with you when your feelings were hurt as I wiped away your tears, and you wiped away mine because I hurt just as much as you.

I cherish all the wonderful times we shared laughing and singing as we went driving down the road in little Herbie to some new adventure or played in our apartment while we devoured our hamburgers and fries. I recall the birthday parties you loved so much and having all your little friends share in your special day. I can still see the glow on your face complemented by a different kind of innocent smile as you walked down the street with a present under your arm to see your little girlfriend, Dawn, and wish her a happy birthday.

I look with laughter upon the Christmases we shared sitting in church while you ached to go home to open the presents under the tree. I treasured every one of our colorful, construction-paper Christmas decorations. We went through our share of plastic tablecloths as they became covered with paste, paints, and crayons.

I recall the many evenings we cooked dinner together while you sat on the counter, stirring the pots and waiting patiently to shake the salt and pepper. And the times we made cookies and both of us ate more dough than we baked, at least until it was time for your favorite police show to come on television. You did have your priorities.

Thanks for the times back on the farm when you were two or three years old and you would crawl into the laundry basket because the clothes were so warm and cuddly. I especially remember you playing with your toys in the living room and the time you were watching a television program that was teaching children where baby chickens came from. After the program was over, you went to the kitchen to get a wooden spoon from the drawer and opened the refrigerator. You decided to see if our eggs had baby chickens in them like the ones on television.

I found your scientific experiment about an hour later with all twelve eggs smashed and still dripping all over the bottom of the refrigerator. When I asked you if you knew anything about it, you replied with a grin, "Mommie, the television had baby chickens in their eggs, but we don't have any in ours."

Each and every memory has a home in my heart, but most of all, our Friday night dinner dates will forever be special to me. You would dress up in your little suit, and I would wear a nice dress. Then I would put money in your wallet so you could be the little gentleman and pay for the dinner. Off we would go in little Herbie down Camelback Road to our favorite restaurant.

I wish I could tell you "Thank you, Christopher, for the memory of that special red rose." Many times my heart has returned to that day when I woke up on the sofa in our little studio apartment to find you sitting on the floor, smiling from ear to ear with your hands behind your back holding a beautiful red rose purchased with three little pennies of pure love. To this day, every time I see a single red rose, I think of that afternoon, your smile, your happiness but most of all, your love.

I thank the man in the flower shop who sold you the rose that remarkable afternoon. He will probably never know how much love and happiness three innocent little pennies purchased that day.

See you later Alligator,
Love Mommie

A Special Thank You To Daddy
May 20, 2000

A special "thank you" to Tony, Anton S. Greicius, for his tender and supportive role as a father to our son, a special little boy that loved *you,* very much.

We each have had our trials and tribulations in life, but we each have overcome. There has always been a simple "trust" between us of honesty, truth, and dignity. Although we divorced, we have remained friends through the years and only want the best for each other.

Our lives twenty-three years ago were filled with desperate hope for a medical miracle for Chris's life. The illness claimed his life, but it could not claim the love for life he had, or the inspiring love for him by those whom he touched through his dream.

God has a way of working things out for the best and by thousands of children around the world having their dreams fulfilled, just like Chris. To me the miracle lives on, as each child is an inspiration for another wish at another time

Linda

May 1, 1980

Thank You

DPS, Air Rescue
DPS, Arizona Department of Public Safety
DPS, Director Ralph "Tom" Milstead
DPS, Officer Allan S. Schmidt
DPS, Officer Bill Hansen
DPS, Officer Lt. Colonel Richard E. Shafer
DPS, Officer Dave A. Schroder
DPS, Officer David Mann
DPS, Officer Frank E. Shankwitz
DPS, Officer Gerald R. "Doc" Holloway
DPS, Officer Major Thomas Milldebrandt
DPS, Officer Ronald B. Cox
DPS, Officer R. Scott Stahl
DPS, Officer Sergeant James Eaves
DPS, Officer Sergeant Joseph A. "Fred" Lizarraga
DPS, Officer Steve Lump
DPS, Officer Windsor W. "Duke" Moore
DPS, Photographer, Paul M.
DPS, Radio Room Supervisor & Crew

*To all the officers and DPS personnel who rose
above and beyond the call of duty on
April 29 and May 1, 1980 to make
a little boy's dream come true.
"Thank you"*

Thank You

Air Evac Services, Inc.
Amy Myers
Anton "Tony" S. Greicius Jr.
Barbara Lanterman-Ritz
Channel 12 News, Bill Denny
Channel 12 News, Jerry Foster & Sky 12
Chet Lyle, Kewanee, Illinois
Chicago Police, FOP Lodge
CODE 1000, Alan Ripa
CODE 1000, Bill Straus
CODE 1000, Eugene Peak "Butch" Brown II
CODE 1000, Ed & Bonnie Mays
CODE 1000, Frank S. Tonis
CODE 1000, Gary Clark
CODE 1000, George A. Hormel II
CODE 1000, Jamie Hormel
CODE 1000, Madison Street Jail
CODE 1000, Maricopa County Deputies Association
CODE 1000, Michael Monti, Monti's Restaurants
CODE 1000, Robin Ross
CODE 1000, Wrigley Mansion
CODE 1000, Sergeant Dave Cool
Douglas Bell, CPA PC
Dr. Paul Baranko MD & Nursing Staff
Falcon Field, Mesa, Arizona
Gary Bergendahl
Gary M. Combs, Kewanee, Illinois

Thank You

Grandma Agnes Greicius
Grandma Alice R. Bergendahl
Grandma Nora "Pete" Peterson
Grandma Violet "Vie" Bergendahl
Grandpa Anton "Tony" Greicius Sr.
Grandpa Clearance "Pete" Peterson
Grandpa Wallace E. Bergendahl
Graphisphere, Scottsdale, AZ, Heidi & Bob Whitney
Geoffrey H. Bruce,
Hansen Mortuary, Phoenix, Arizona
Illinois State Police
James Dury
Jeff Bergendahl
Joseph & Kitty Kunes
John's Uniform Company, and the two seamstresses
Jose Montilla
Katherine "Kathy" McMorris
Karla Blomberg,
Kay Austin
Keven Pauling, Keven's Landscaping
Kewanee Police Department
Kitty Derby-Shankwitz
Leukemia Foundation of Arizona
Make-A-Wish Foundation of America & International
Marie Cool
Martha E. "Jean" Rhodes
McCormick Ranch Flowers, Dan Grimes

Thank You

McCormick Ranch-Stillman Park
National Guard
O'Hare International Airport
Octaviana Vennia Trujillo, Ph.D. Bopsy's Mother
Old Tucson Movie Studios
Patrick J. McGroder III, Attorney
Paula Van Ness
Phoenix Fire Department
Phoenix Renaissance Festival
Phoenix Suns
Rev. George F. Remm
Rev. Walter McCarthy JS
Robert Greathouse, Volunteer
Sawyer Aviation, Darrell A. Sawyer
Schueneman & Tumbleson Funeral Home, Kewanee, IL
Formerly Cavanaughs & Schueneman Funeral Home
Scottsdale Memorial Hospital / Scottsdale Healthcare
Senator Alfredo Gutierrez, Arizona
Senator Barry Goldwater, Arizona
Sheraton Hotels & Resorts
Sister Madonna Maria Bolton R.S.N.
Sky Harbor International Airport, Phoenix, Arizona
St. Joseph Hospital and Medical Center, & Nursing staff
Star-Courier Newspaper, Kewanee, Illinois
Theresa Dotson
Qwest *formerly* Mountain Bell Telephone
Tommy Austin, U.S. Customs Agent
Wallace & Ladmo Show

**Order your copy today! Tell a friend and
Share The Power of a Wish.**

Little Bubble Gum Trooper
Co-founder and Author, Linda J Bergendahl-Pauling

A mother's true story of how the Make-A-Wish Foundation® began.

<u>**First hardbound Edition**</u>   <u>**Please allow 4-6 weeks for delivery**</u>

☐ 1 to 5 copies $29.95 ea. $4.95 S&H   ☐ 6-to 10 copies: 10% off plus S&H

☐ Case lot (28 per carton) 25 % off (Plus USPS shipping rate)

Name (please print clearly): _____

Address: _____

Home Phone: (____)_____ Work Ph: (____)_____

Signature: _____ Date: _____

Number of book (s) ordered: _____	Shipment available for overseas orders. Billing will have appropriate shipping charges added.
1 to 10 books S&H only $4.95. $_____	
1 to 5 books $29.95 ea. $_____	
6 to 10 books $26.95 ea. $_____	
Case lots of 28 $22.46 ea. $_____	
Az residents add 7.1% sales tax. $_____	
Total. $_____	

(Optional) For conformation, please include your E-mail, fax number

☐ ✓ use address above

E-Mail: _____ Fax Number: (____)_____

✂--------✂---------**Mail above portion to:**-------✂-----------✂

Check payable & ✒ *to:* **Red Rose Press LLC**
P.O. Box 520
Scottsdale, Arizona 85252
—OR —

☎ **1-888-443-6593 —— http://www.mawchris.com** 💻

Visa   Mastercard   Amex   Discover   Check
AZ residents add 7.1% sales tax.